Marcus Heidmann

# The Role of Management Accounting Systems in Strategic Sensemaking

# GABLER EDITION WISSENSCHAFT

## Research in Management Accounting & Control

Herausgegeben von Professor Dr. Utz Schäffer
WHU – Otto Beisheim School of Management, Vallendar

Die Schriftenreihe präsentiert Ergebnisse betriebswirtschaftlicher Forschung im Bereich Controlling. Sie basiert auf einer akteursorientierten Sicht des Controlling, in der die Rationalitätssicherung der Führung einen für die Theorie und Praxis zentralen Stellenwert einnimmt.

The series presents research results in the field of management accounting and control. It is based on a behavioral view of management accounting where the assurance of management rationality is of central importance for both theory and practice.

Marcus Heidmann

# The Role of Management Accounting Systems in Strategic Sensemaking

With a foreword by Prof. Dr. Utz Schäffer

Deutscher Universitäts-Verlag

Bibliographic information published by Die Deutsche Nationalbibliothek
Die Deutsche Nationalbibliothek lists this publication in the Deutsche Nationalbibliografie; detailed bibliographic data is available in the Internet at <http://dnb.d-nb.de>.

Dissertation European Business School, Oestrich-Winkel, 2006

D 1540

1st Edition 2008



Readers: Frauke Schindler / Anita Wilke

Deutscher Universitäts-Verlag is a company of Springer Science+Business Media.
www.duv.de



Cover design: Regine Zimmer, Dipl.-Designerin, Frankfurt/Main
Printed on acid-free paper
Printed in Germany

ISBN 978-3-8350-0633-1

## Foreword

The starting point of Marcus Heidmann's dissertation thesis is the insight that managers need to identify and understand strategic issues in order for their companies to successfully cope with strategic change. Information from management accounting systems (MAS) can be helpful in this process – as long as MAS are defined as formal systems that provide information from the internal as well as the external environment. Consequently, the desire to better understand the role of these systems in the process of strategic sensemaking comes to mind. It is even intensified when considering the impression from management accounting practice that the tool box of controlling – especially the traditional one, used in day-to-day management – rather impedes strategic sensemaking.

Due to the explorative nature of the research questions, and the objective of studying strategic sensemaking in its natural setting, the empirical approach of this dissertation is based on a multiple-case study design und generates an array of interesting findings.

Heidmann shows, for example, that managers do not primarily use MAS to identify strategic topics – a fact that is explicitly or implicitly assumed in most studies on strategic sensemaking: instead, they use management accounting systems to search for additional information that help them to make sense of these issues. In addition, the study at hand underlines the relevance of communication several times. This is true for the communication processes in the context of adaptation and preparation of management accounting systems as well as for their actual use.

Ekkehard Kappler's plea for an intensified consideration of communication processes is thus impressively confirmed in the work of Heidmann. Furthermore, Gidden's idea of the interaction between structure and agency is nicely illustrated when Heidmann hints at the link between interactive use and system design which facilitates and enables the former.

In summary, Heidmann proposes three guiding principles for the design of management accounting systems:

- The use of systems as a platform for communication,
- the regular system adaptation and

- the provision of an adequate interaction between managers.

Moreover, this dissertation thesis is a rich source of interesting results that encourage further thought and hopefully stimulate future scientific work.

Utz Schäffer

## Preface

In order to be successful in the long-term, companies have to react to changing customer demand, increasing competition, and new technologies. Top and middle managers need to make sense of strategic issues in order to prepare strategic decisions. However, strategic sensemaking is a complex cognitive process that occurs permanently and, therefore, is difficult to control. Companies cannot institutionalize strategic sensemaking through a dedicated process. Instead they invest large amounts of resources in management accounting systems that help managers to control the existing business. Unfortunately, not much is known about the role of management accounting systems in strategic sensemaking. This is the starting point of this research which aims to provide academics and practitioners with a better understanding of how the design of management accounting systems affects their use for strategic sensemaking. This research was accepted in November 2006 as a dissertation at the European Business School in Oestrich-Winkel.

This work would not have been possible without the help of several people. In particular I would like to thank:

- Prof. Dr. Utz Schäffer for his dedication and support throughout all phases of this research. I am grateful for intensive discussions that helped to shape my thoughts and encouraged me to consider different perspectives.
- Prof. Dr. Susanne Strahringer as my second assessor for challenging my findings from an information systems research perspective.
- Dr. Herbert Pohl for providing advice and financial support that helped me during this research. I would also like to thank McKinsey & Company, Inc. for allowing me to complete this dissertation during a leave of absence.
- Dr. Tanja Prinzessin zu Waldeck, Dr. Manuela Stoll, and Dr. Daniel Kauer for intensive discussions within our research team.
- My colleagues from the Chair of Management Accounting & Control for helpful advice during our monthly office days in Oestrich-Winkel.

- Special thanks go to my 34 interview partners for their time and interest in this research project. Given their seniority in their firms, it is not easy to carve a minimum of two hours from their busy schedules for a project with an unknown outcome. I hope that findings from my research help them to improve strategic sensemaking within their companies.

Most importantly I would like to thank my family and Anita Wiest. Their continuous support not only throughout this research helped me to develop and to strive for the best possible results. This work is dedicated to them.

Marcus Heidmann

# Contents

## Tables

# Figures

# A Introduction

*"They [the companies] did not listen. They did not see. They did not react. These organizations failed to acquire accurate information about environmental events, or they did not interpret it correctly. They did not learn."*
*Richard L. Daft and George P. Huber* [1]

## 1. Research Topic and Objectives

Constant shifts in consumer demand, severe dislocations in factors of production, sudden changes of the social environment – organizations face an uncertain, changing world. In a recent survey of 16,476 business executives from 148 countries, 84% of the respondents claim that competition in their industry has increased over the past 5 years and 80% of the executives expect that it will continue to intensify.[2] Price erosion, the entry of new competitors and faster development of new products are examples for current competitive pressures.[3]

Survival in a competitive environment requires managers to identify and make sense of strategic issues as a prerequisite for strategic change. Strategic issues are "... major environmental trends and possible events that may have a major and discontinuous impact on the firm".[4] They are usually poorly structured, poorly documented, and open to multiple interpretations.[5]

To deal with strategic issues, organizations acquire, interpret, and control flows of environmental information in order not to be blindsided by threats, or even unprepared for opportunities.[6] In order to make sense of strategic issues, managers must relate the firm's strengths and weaknesses to specific opportunities and threats embedded in these issues. This requires information from the internal as well as the external environment.[7]

---

1 Daft and Huber (1987), p. 2.
2 McKinsey (2005), p. 61.
3 Ibid., p. 62.
4 Ansoff (1975), p. 25.
5 Thomas et al. (1994), p. 1253.
6 Sutcliffe (2001), p. 197.
7 Garg et al. (2003), p. 741.

Management accounting systems (MAS) are formal systems that provide such information to managers.[8] They include reports, performance measurement systems, computerized information systems, such as executive information systems or management information systems, and also planning, budgeting and forecasting processes required to prepare and review management accounting information. Management accounting systems provide information that is required for strategic sensemaking and therefore it is important to understand their contribution. The objective of this research is to explore the role of management accounting systems in strategic sensemaking. In order to achieve this research objective it is helpful to draw on the *interpretive* and the *systems-structural or logistical perspective* of organizational information processing.

Researchers following *the interpretive perspective of information processing* define strategic sensemaking as a learning process where individuals learn about the relationships between the organization and its environment.[9] More generally, management accounting researchers like BURCHELL ET AL. claim that management accounting systems can serve as "learning machines",[10] which raises the question how management accounting systems contribute to learning through strategic sensemaking. Several typologies of management accounting information use have been developed, but most do not provide references between information use and learning. A notable exception is SIMONS's differentiation between interactive and diagnostic use: He suggests that the interactive use of management accounting systems can guide organizational learning and influence the process of strategic sensemaking, while the diagnostic use of management accounting systems helps to implement past and present strategies.[11] A line of management accounting research has focused on the interactive use of management accounting systems and suggests some ways for how this type of use can contribute to strategic sensemaking. ABERNETHY AND BROWNELL show that the interactive use of management accounting systems contributes positively to performance during strategic change.[12] They speculate that management accounting systems used interactively can serve as integrative liaison devices. This would enable the interchange of information concerning strategic issues, by breaking down functional and hierarchical barriers in-

---

[8] Bouwens and Abernethy (2000), p. 223.
[9] Daft and Weick (1984), p. 286.
[10] Burchell et al. (1980), pp. 14-15.
[11] Simons (1991), p. 61.
[12] Abernethy and Brownell (1999), p. 198.

hibiting information flows.[13] Furthermore, the interactive use of management accounting systems seems to moderate the impact of innovation on performance. BISBE AND OTLEY suggest that interactive management accounting systems provide direction, integration and fine-tuning to translate innovation into performance.[14] Directions signal preferences for search and provide the basis for a selection of initiatives. Integration provides a forum and an agenda for an organization's members to engage in face-to-face dialogue and debate about different interpretations of strategic issues, while fine-tuning assists in altering strategies, because of changing conditions of innovative contexts. VANDENBOSCH finds that the interactive use of management accounting systems is associated with perceived improvements in competitiveness, while the use of management accounting systems for score keeping, as a diagnostic use, is even perceived to reduce competitiveness.[15] She recommends conducting further research in order to understand ways of encouraging some types of information use and discouraging others.[16]

The *systems-structural, or logistical, perspective of information processing* focuses on the acquisition and distribution of information.[17] Management accounting systems are perceived as passive tools providing information to assist managers.[18] Contingency-based research following this conventional view has studied the impact of uncertainty, strategy and organizational factors on the relationship between management accounting information dimensions and information use for decision making,[19] perceived usefulness of information,[20] and ultimately managerial performance.[21] This line of research does not focus explicitly on the relationship between management accounting system design and strategic sensemaking. However, it suggests management accounting system dimensions that could be relevant in trying to understand the role of management accounting systems in strategic sensemaking.

Overall, the interpretive or systems-structural perspectives of information processing alone are not sufficient to explain the role of management accounting systems in stra-

---

13 Ibid., p. 192.
14 Bisbe and Otley (2004), p. 727.
15 Vandenbosch (1999), p. 88.
16 Ibid., p. 89.
17 Sutcliffe (2001), p. 204.
18 Chenhall (2003), p. 129.
19 See Bouwens and Abernethy (2000).
20 See Chenhall and Morris (1986).
21 See Gul and Chia (1994), Mia and Chenhall (1994), Chia (1995), Chong (1996).

tegic sensemaking. On the one hand, research from the interpretive perspective of information processing suggests some ways for how the use of management accounting systems might contribute to strategic sensemaking, although it neglects the relationship between management accounting system use and management accounting system dimensions. On the other hand, research from the systems-structural perspective suggests some potentially important management accounting system dimensions, but it does not explain how these dimensions contribute to strategic sensemaking.

Therefore, two research questions help to explore the role of management accounting systems in strategic sensemaking: (1) How do managers use management accounting systems for strategic sensemaking? (2) How do management accounting system dimensions shape the role and use of management accounting systems in strategic sensemaking?

## 2. Plan of the Study

The presentation of this exploratory study on the role of management accounting systems in strategic sensemaking follows the three main phases of the research process: the theoretical foundation and review of previous research, the design of the research and the development of propositions from the research results, and finally the discussion of the findings (see Figure 1).

*Figure 1: Plan of the study*

Part B provides the theoretical foundation for this research. Based on organizational learning theory this study describes strategic sensemaking as a learning process with observation, interpretation and communication as the relevant process steps at the individual level. The interpretive and systems-structural perspectives of organizational information processing seem particularly suitable to explain the role of management accounting systems in strategic sensemaking. Part C reviews previous research on the impact of management accounting systems on observation, interpretation and communication of strategic issues. A transfer of results from information systems research helps to develop a comprehensive set of management accounting system dimensions. Tentative theoretical relationships between these dimensions and strategic sensemaking conclude the literature review.

Part D describes reasons for choosing a multiple case-study design. It explains the process for selecting thirty top and middle managers from seven large corporations. Furthermore, it provides a brief introduction to each company, an overview of available information sources for strategic sensemaking, and descriptions of management accounting systems used by the interviewees. Several quality measures during research design, data collection and data analysis help to ensure construct, internal and external validity as well as reliability. Part E presents quantitative and qualitative research results from the case studies. These results provide the basis for new propositions on the roles of management accounting systems in strategic sensemaking and their relationships with management accounting system dimensions.

Finally, part F discusses the theoretical and managerial implications of the findings. It presents the limitations of this study and suggests further research.

# B Theoretical Foundation

*"The essence of management is coping with change."*
*Balaji S. Chakravarthy* [22]

## 1. Adaptation to Change

Strategic management is the process of continuously adapting to changes in a firm's external and internal environment in order to ensure its long-term survival and growth.[23] To better understand their environment and to derive the strategic relevance of changes for their organization, middle and top executives have to make sense of "weak signals".[24] They have to understand how relevant the indicated changes are for their organization, whether they could become "strategic issues",[25] and finally have to decide on a response strategy.

"Explaining how and why organizations change has been a central and enduring quest of scholars in management and many other disciplines".[26] There are numerous theories and approaches relating to how organizations adapt to change.[27] VAN DE VEN AND POOLE propose a frequently cited typology of theories that explain how and why an organizational entity changes and develops.[28] Based on an extensive, interdisciplinary literature review, they developed four basic ideal types[29] of process theories that ex-

---

[22] Chakravarthy (1982), p. 35.

[23] Ibid., p. 35.

[24] Ansoff (1990), p. 385 introduced the concept of weak signals. Weak signals precede environmental changes and can be described as "... not enough information to make reliable estimates of the impact and of the effectiveness of response to permit a commitment to an irreversible unambiguous response". Konrad (1991), pp. 184 describes weak signals more explicitly as information without broad diffusion, having a qualitative and strategic character, without causal connections and with attributes like unclear, vague, imperfect, inaccurate, utopian, muddled or abstruse.

[25] In a complex and variable environment there are "... development[s] and events which have the potential to influence the organization's current or future strategy ...", see Dutton and Duncan (1987), p. 280. Ansoff describes "strategic issues" as "... major environmental trends and possible events that may have a major and discontinuous impact on the firm." Ansoff (1975), p. 25.

[26] Van De Ven and Poole (1995), p. 510.

[27] A short overview can be found at Pawlowsky (2001), p. 62.

[28] According to the Social Science Citation Index, the typology of Van De Ven and Poole (1995) has been cited 167 times (as of April 6, 2006).

[29] Ibid., pp. 525-533 note that most specific theories of organizational change are more complicated than the ideal types, but can be described as combinations of several ideal type theories that operate at different times.

plain how and why change unfolds in social entities: life-cycle, dialectical, evolutionary, and teleological theories.[30]

According to *life-cycle theory*, the development of an organization follows a prefigured logic, program, or code, which regulates the process of change.[31] External environmental events can influence the development process, but cannot change the unitary sequence of prescribed stages of change as the process progresses towards the final end state. Life-cycle theories are based on the metaphor of organic growth and often reference stages in the development of individual careers, groups and organizations as startup births, adolescent growth, maturity, and decline or death.[32]

*Dialectical theory* assumes that the organizational entity exists in a pluralistic world of colliding events, forces, or contradictory values that compete with each other for domination and control. Organizational change is generated by conflict and confrontation between contradictory values or events. Dialectic theory requires at least two distinct entities that embody these oppositions to confront and engage each other in conflict.[33]

*Evolutionary theory* describes change as a recurrent, cumulative and probabilistic sequence of variation, selection and retention events. According to specified population dynamics, evolutionary models can predict how the overall population of organizational entities evolves through time, but cannot forecast which entity will survive or fail.[34]

*Teleological theory* explains the purposeful and adaptive development of an organizational entity toward a goal or an end state.[35] The entity constructs an envisioned end state, takes action to reach it, and monitors the progress. The change process is a recurrent, discontinuous sequence of goal setting, implementation, and adaptation of means to reach the desired end state.[36] Unlike life-cycle theory, teleology does not prescribe a necessary sequence of events. However, the purposeful actions of organizational entities are constrained by the organization's environment and resources. Individuals make

---

[30] Ibid., p. 511.
[31] Ibid., p. 515.
[32] Ibid., p. 513.
[33] Ibid., p. 517.
[34] Ibid., pp. 517-518.
[35] Ibid., p. 516.
[36] Ibid., p. 514.

use of these constraints to accomplish their purposes. Since goals are socially constructed and enacted based on past actions, changes in the external or internal environment can push the organization to a new development path.[37]

The teleological school of thought is of particular interest for this research. Unlike dialectic and evolutionary theory, teleological theory focuses on single entities as the units of change.[38] Strategic sensemaking is a purposeful activity of individuals within an organization. Management accounting systems provide information about the internal and external context and are a formal element of control to evaluate progression towards a defined goal. Therefore, the mode of change is constructive, rather then prescribed as in life-cycle theory.

Organizational learning as part of the teleological school of thought[39] seems particularly helpful in understanding the relationship between strategic sensemaking and management accounting systems. The next section will present an assessment of the suitability of organizational learning as the theoretical foundation for this research.

## 2. Organizational Learning

*"Learning without thinking is in vain; to think without learning is dangerous."*
*Confucius*[40]

Organizational learning is an area of research that integrates numerous contributions from different academic perspectives.[41] This makes it difficult to reach consensus on a definition or typology of organizational learning: "Although there exists widespread acceptance of the notion of organizational learning and its importance to strategic performance, no theory or model of organizational learning is widely accepted."[42]

---

[37] Ibid., pp. 516-517.
[38] Ibid., p. 520.
[39] Ibid., p. 516 mentions the pioneering work of March and Simon (1958) on decision making and March and Olsen (1975) on adaptive learning, as examples for the teleological school of thought.
[40] Cited in Gambino (1993), p. 191.
[41] Easterby-Smith (1997), p. 1087 mentions psychology, management science, sociology/organization theory, strategy, production management, and cultural anthropology. See also Dodgson (1993), p. 375: "Organization theory, industrial economics, economic history, and business, management and innovation studies all approach the question of how organizations learn. A number of branches of psychology are also revealing on the issue."
[42] Fiol and Lyles (1985), p. 803.

This may still hold true, as more recent reviews and attempts to categorize the field show.[43] One possible way to categorize existing research is using the debates that have influenced research in the field of organizational learning:[44]

- What is the unit or level of analysis in organizational learning? (Level)
- When does learning occur? (Focus)
- How do organizational entities learn? (Type)
- What influences organizational learning? (Context)

## 2.1 Level of Organizational Learning

The debate about the unit or level of analysis focuses around the question of whether organizational learning is simply the sum of individual learning, or whether there are other influencing factors.[45] There seems to be general acceptance that organizational learning occurs at the individual, group, organizational, or even inter-organizational level.[46]

Researchers studying learning at the individual level assume that organizations learn "(a) by the learning of its members, or (b) by ingesting new members who have knowledge the organization didn't previously have."[47] Researchers following the individual perspective criticize the attribution of human characteristics to inanimate objects such as organizations.[48]

Learning at the group level is often seen as an extension to individual learning and emphasizes the importance of information sharing and development of a common meaning.[49] SIMON, as a proponent of individual learning, notes that the transmission of information between organizational members is especially important, which makes individual learning a social phenomenon rather then a solitary one.[50]

---

43 See Bapuji and Crossan (2004), Bell et al. (2002), Easterby-Smith et al. (2000), Easterby-Smith (1997), Crossan et al. (1995), Huber (1991), Levitt and March (1988).
44 Based on Easterby-Smith et al. (2000), pp. 784-790 and Crossan et al. (1995), pp. 338-355.
45 Easterby-Smith et al. (2000), p. 785.
46 Ibid., p. 785, Crossan et al. (1995), p. 338.
47 Simon (1991), p. 125.
48 Easterby-Smith et al. (2000), p. 785.
49 Crossan et al. (1995), p. 344.
50 Simon (1991), p. 125. See also Weick and Ashford (2001), pp 720-727.

Several researchers stress the role of organizations in organizational learning. According to CROSSAN ET AL. researchers easily accept the view that organizational components, such as systems, structures, and procedures, affect learning.[51] Other theorists propose that learning is stored in organizational components.[52] "Although organizational learning occurs through individuals, it would be a mistake to conclude that organizational learning is nothing but the cumulative results of their members' learning. Organizations do not have brains, but they have cognitive systems and memories. ... Members come and go, and leadership changes, but organizations' memories preserve certain behaviors, mental maps, norms, and values over time."[53]

Furthermore, models that integrate the individual, group and organizational level have been developed.[54] According to EASTERBY-SMITH ET AL., there appears to be a broad acceptance of various levels of analysis. However, they emphasize that research on organizational-level artifacts such as systems, data, and information should especially consider the individual perspective of organizational learning.[55]

## 2.2 Focus of Organizational Learning

The question of when learning has occurred originates in the field of psychology, and differences of opinion exist between behavioral and cognitive theorists.[56] According to behavioral theorists, learning occurs if there has been an actual change in behavior or action. For cognitive theorists learning occurs when there has been an adjustment or change in the way information is processed, shared meaning is developed, and events are interpreted.[57]

*Behavioral learning* theories approach the question of how entities learn by relating input stimuli to output behavioral responses. They assume that input stimuli cause a certain behavior and learning occurs when certain stimuli result in a changed behavior. Success of this behavior can change the strength of the relationship between stimulus

---

51 Crossan et al. (1995), p. 345.
52 Ibid., p. 345 and Easterby-Smith et al. (2000), p. 785.
53 Hedberg (1981), p. 6.
54 Corner et al. (1994), Crossan et al. (1999), Crossan and Berdrow (2003), Bontis et al. (2002), Holmqvist (2004).
55 Easterby-Smith et al. (2000), pp. 785-786.
56 Fiol and Lyles (1985), pp. 805-806.
57 Crossan et al. (1995), p. 348. See also Akgün et al. (2003), p. 842.

and response.[58] Based on a review of behavioral theories for understanding change within companies, HUFF ET AL. note that individuals are not at the center of behavioral theories, as there is more emphasis on organizational forces as the source of change within a firm.[59] Behavioral theories describe processes within the firm, but the individual that transforms the input into an output remains a black box.[60]

*Cognitive learning* theories make an effort to understand what happens between stimulus and response, as they consider behavior to be purposeful rather than just reflex.[61] They try to get into the black box of individuals, because "... understanding managerial cognition is critical for gaining insights into organizational actions ... strategic change ... organizational learning ... and ultimately, firm performance ..."[62] According to cognitive theorists, individuals use "mental models to make sense of what happens around them".[63] Mental models are units of knowledge that consist of the knowledge itself as well as information about how to use the knowledge.[64] "A core premise of the cognitive school is that humans come to any task with mental models created out of their prior experience and understanding. These mental models determine how environmental stimuli will be interpreted and incorporated or synthesized, and even whether or not cues will be noticed and used."[65] This makes information processing more efficient, because it is not necessary to construct meaning from scratch when similar stimuli are received.[66] By imposing a structure on environmental stimuli, mental models al-

---

58 Cyert and March (1963) transferred results from the general learning literature to the organizational context. See Birnberg and Shields (1989) for a review on behavioral accounting research. See also Schäffer (2001), pp. 27-28 for influential behavioral learning experiments.

59 Huff et al. (2000), p.13.

60 See Birnberg and Shields (1989), 45; Huff et al. (2000), p. 13; Schäffer (2001), p. 27.

61 Schneider and Angelmar (1993), p. 347. For an overview see also Schäffer (2001), pp. 29-32.

62 Thomas et al. (1994), p.1252.

63 The terms "cognitive map" or "schema" are coequally used in psychology to explain the processes of human memory, see Vandenbosch and Higgins (1996), p. 200. Kiesler and Sproull (1982), p. 556 present the underlying assumption of mental models, that "... a person operates on representations of the world that exists in the mind. ... In information-processing structures [mental models], knowledge of prior behavior and expectations about behavior are organized in abstract structures called schemas, scripts, or stereotypes ...".

64 Huff et al. (2000), p. 42. For Kim (2001) mental models "... represent a person's view of the world, including both explicit and implicit understandings. They also provide the context in which to view and interpret new material, and they determine how stored information will be applied to a given situation." Kim (2001), p. 21.

65 Vandenbosch and Higgins (1996), p. 200.

66 Ibid., p. 200.

low individuals to function effectively in an otherwise vast and confusing environment.[67]

Therefore, mental models of individuals play an important role in the analysis of how managers recognize and give meaning to data about environmental changes. In this process their mental models can help them to quickly distinguish important from unimportant information, and provide evaluative schemes to determine how environmental changes may effect their organizations, and how they have to react to them. Learning occurs when mental models are changed. Behavioral change can be a result of mental model change, but it is not a requirement for learning to occur.[68] EASTERBY-SMITH ET AL. observe that the debate between behavioral and cognitive learning has gone silent, as a broad definition of organizational learning has been accepted.[69] Organizational learning includes a behavioral and a cognitive perspective, which is exemplified by the definition of HUBER: "An entity learns if, through its processing of information, the range of its potential behaviors is changed".[70]

## 2.3 Type of Organizational Learning

In principle, organizational learning researchers distinguish two types of learning: more routine learning versus more radical learning.[71] They differentiate between these types of learning by the amount of change they cause. In hindsight, it is relatively easy to differentiate between routine and radical learning. More difficult is to examine the process as it unfolds in order to understand how changes in cognition relate to changes in behavior at individual and organizational levels of analysis.[72] Table 1 below provides some examples of important typologies to distinguish between these two types of learning.

---

[67] Huff et al. (2000), p. 42. See also Simon (1955) and Weber et al. (2000), pp. 241-242.
[68] Fiol (1994), p. 404. See also Crossan et al. (1995), p. 354.
[69] Easterby-Smith et al. (2000), p. 786.
[70] Huber (1991), p. 89. For other definitions see Bontis et al. (2002), p. 439.
[71] Easterby-Smith et al. (2000), p. 786.
[72] Crossan et al. (1995), p. 355.

| Author | Routine learning | Radical learning |
|---|---|---|
| MAIER (1945) | Reproductive thought | Productive thought |
| PIAGET (1954) | Assimilation | Accommodation |
| BATESON (1972) | Learning I | Learning II |
| ARGYRIS AND SCHÖN (1978) | Single-loop learning | Double-loop learning |
| NORMAN (1982) | Accretion | Structuring |
| FIOL AND LYLES (1985) | Lower level learning | Higher level learning |
| MARCH (1991) | Exploitative learning | Explorative learning |
| LANT AND MEZIAS (1992) | First order learning | Second order learning |
| KIM (1993) | Operational learning | Conceptual learning |
| CROSSAN ET AL. (1995) | Incremental learning | Transformational learning |
| VANDENBOSCH AND HIGGINS (1996) | Mental model maintenance | Mental model building |
| MINER AND MEZIAS (1996) | Incremental learning | Radical learning |

*Table 1: Examples for routine and radical learning typologies*

A frequently cited typology for organizational learning is ARGYRIS AND SCHÖN's distinction between single-loop and double-loop learning. They define learning as single-loop learning whenever an error is detected and corrected without questioning or altering the underlying values of the system. Double-loop learning occurs when an "... error is detected and corrected in ways that involve the modification of an organization's underlying norms, policies and objectives."[73] The learning typology from ARGYRIS AND SCHÖN suggests that learning takes place only when new knowledge is translated into behavior that is replicable.[74] As already shown in section B2.2, the relationship between changes in cognition and changes in behavior is complex. What seems as incremental change at one level (individual) may appear as transformational change at another level (organizational).[75]

Cognitive researchers like KIM or VANDENBOSCH AND HIGGINS relate different types of learning to mental model changes that do not necessarily lead to changes in behavior. VANDENBOSCH AND HIGGINS use the term mental model maintenance when managers believe that existing mental models are appropriate and new information fits into

[73] Argyris (1976), p. 367, Argyris and Schön (1978), pp. 2-3 and Argyris (1992), p. 8.
[74] See also Kim (1993), p. 38.
[75] Crossan et al. (1995), p. 354.

them.[76] Contrarily, when frameworks and criteria for the evaluation of new ideas, markets or products are missing, mental model building is required.[77] The challenging of existing conditions, procedures, or conceptions leads to new frameworks in the mental model that "can open up opportunities for discontinuous steps of improvement by reframing a problem in radically different ways."[78]

All radical learning typologies are based on changes of mental models. However, they do not distinguish between mental model changes where the objectives of organizations are adapted while interpretations of the environment remain unchanged or mental model changes that go along with a new interpretation of the environment.[79]

## 2.4 Context Factors of Organizational Learning

Researchers have identified several context factors that influence organizational learning. In their literature review, BAPUJI AND CROSSAN describe internal and external context factors as organizational learning facilitators.[80] Internal context factors include culture, strategy, structure, organizational stage and resource position, while external context factors relate to the environment.[81] According to ELSBACH ET AL., there is evidence that the organizational context influences organizational learning, but the role it plays remains unclear.[82] Although there is some progress in empirical research on the role of contextual factors,[83] more empirical testing is required.[84]

Theoretical conceptualizations of how context factors relate to organizational learning provide a starting point. OCASIO's "attention-based view of the firm" provides a model

---

[76] Vandenbosch and Higgins (1996), p. 202. According to Kim (1993), p. 40, mental models consist of frameworks and routines. Operational learning, which is similar to mental model maintenance, is captured as routines.

[77] Vandenbosch and Higgins (1996), p. 202. Kim (1993), p. 40 defines this type of learning as conceptual learning.

[78] Kim (1993), p. 40.

[79] See also Schäffer (2001), p. 47.

[80] Bapuji and Crossan (2004), pp. 405-406. See also Fiol and Lyles (1985), pp. 804-805. Elsbach et al. (2005), p. 425 distinguish organizational contexts into institutional/cultural, artifact, physical, and socio-dynamic context.

[81] Bapuji and Crossan (2004), pp. 406-408. For a more detailed discussion of the organizational environment see section B2.5.1 Organizational Environments.

[82] Elsbach et al. (2005), p. 423. Simon (1991), p. 125 acknowledges that the organizational context influences individual learning. He mentions two influencing factors in individual learning: knowledge and beliefs of other organizational members and the kind of information that is present in the organizational environment.

[83] Bapuji and Crossan (2004), pp. 409-410.

[84] Templeton et al. (2004), p. 273.

that links structure and cognition to explain firm behavior and adaptation.[85] By explicitly linking individual information processing and behavior to the organizational structure through the concepts of procedural and communication channels and attention structures, OCASIO treats attentional processing as a multilevel process shaped by individuals, organizations, and the environment.[86] Attention, as a metaphor for organizational learning, is defined broadly to include organizational decision-makers noticing, encoding, interpreting, and focusing of time and effort on both issues[87] and answers[88]. OCASIO's model of the "attention-based view of the firm" is based on three interrelated principles of attention, which can be used as a framework to structure the relationship between context factors and organizational learning.

The first principle of attention is the *focus of attention*: "What decision-makers do depends on what issues and answers they focus their attention on."[89] At the level of individual cognition attentional processes focus the energy, effort, and mindfulness of organizational decision-makers on a limited set of elements that enter into consciousness at any given time.[90] The principle "focus of attention" links attentional processing to individual cognition and behavior.[91]

The second principle of attention is the *situated attention*: "What issues and answers decision-makers focus on, and what they do, depends on the particular context or situation they find themselves in".[92] Drawing on research from social cognition, and building on the perspective of Lewinian social psychology,[93] the principle highlights

---

85 See Ocasio (1997), pp. 187-188.

86 Ibid., p. 188.

87 "... the available repertoire of categories for making sense of the environment: problems, opportunities, and threats." Ibid., p. 189.

88 "... the available repertoire of action alternatives: proposals, routines, projects, programs, and procedures." Ibid., p. 189.

89 Ibid., p. 188.

90 Ibid., p. 190.

91 Ibid. draws on research from Shiffrin and Schneider (1977), who distinguish between controlled and automatic attentional processing. Action is dependent on the processing mode, and therefore the distinction between controlled and automatic attentional processing aids the understanding of the linkage between action and focus of attention. Ocasio (1997), p. 190.

92 Ocasio (1997), p. 188. Elsbach et al. (2005), p. 424 refer to situated cognition "as temporally bounded interactions of individuals or collectives engaged in specific cognitive processes, and specific organizational contexts at particular points in time."

93 Lewin was a humanitarian who believed that the human condition could only be improved by resolving social conflict. He stated that the key to resolving social conflict was to facilitate learning and thereby enable individuals to understand and restructure their perceptions of the world around them. Lewin's field theory is an approach to understanding group behavior. According to Lewin group behavior is an intricate set of symbolic interactions and forces that not only affect group

the effects of the organizational and environmental context in shaping individuals' focus of attention and action.[94] The principle implies that characteristics of the situation, rather than characteristics of the individual, are better suited to explain consistency (or variance) in attention.[95] The attention of decision-makers is situated in the firm's procedural and communication channels. OCASIO defines procedural and communication channels as the formal and informal concrete activities, interactions, and communications set up by the firm to induce organizational decision-makers to act on a selected set of issues. They include formal and informal meetings, reports and administrative protocols.[96]

The third principle of attention is the *structural distribution of attention*: "What particular context or situation decision-makers find themselves in, and how they attend to it, depends on how the firm's rules, resources, and social relationships regulate and control the distribution and allocation of issues, answers, and decision-makers into specific activities, communications, and procedures".[97] The principle "structural distribution of attention" builds on research and theory from organizational decision-making, strategy formulation, and cognitive anthropology.[98] The attention structures generate a set of values that order the importance of issues and answers, channel and distribute decision-making into a concrete set of communications and procedures, and provide decision-makers with a structured set of interests and identities that shape their understanding of the situation and motivate their actions.[99] Organizational actions and decisions result from complex interactions among discrete attentional processes, which are created through the firm's economic and social structures.[100]

An attention-based view of the firm implies that the ability of the firm to adapt successfully to a changing environment is conditional on whether the firm's procedural

---

structures, but also modify individual behavior. Individual behavior depends on the "field", which he defines as "a totality of coexisting facts which are conceived of as mutually interdependent". Lewin (1946), p. 240 and Lewin (1947) cited in Burnes (2004), p. 981. Lewin's field theory was rediscovered with the work of Argyris (1990) and Hirschhorn (1988) on understanding and overcoming resistance to change, and is still of interest to researchers studying organizational change. Burnes (2004), p. 982 and p. 997.

94 Ocasio (1997), pp. 189-191.

95 Ibid., p. 190.

96 Ibid., p. 194.

97 Ibid., p. 188. See also Gioia and Thomas (1996), pp. 371-372 how information processing structures and the strategies in use can guide interpretation.

98 Ocasio (1997), p. 189.

99 Ibid., p. 192.

100 Ibid., p. 191.

and communication channels focus the attention of organizational decision-makers on an appropriate set of issues and answers.[101] Management accounting systems are a major constituent of the procedural and communication channels. Therefore it is important to analyze how management accounting systems focus attentional processing of decision-makers.

## 2.5 Organizational Information Processing

*"Scientists tend not to follow in the trails of others if blazing their own trail leads to ownership of part of the landscape."*[102]

BELL ET AL. suggest that the most fundamental reason for the limited convergence of research in organizational learning is that organizational learning is embedded in different schools of thought.[103] On the basis of a comprehensive literature review, they suggest four schools of thought in organizational learning research: an economic view, a developmental view, a managerial view, and a process view.[104]

The *economic school* focuses on routine learning through the repetition of workflows and processes that accrue with continuous production. Learning is largely behavioral, focused on the individual production worker, and leads to incremental improvement in work processes through correction of past mistakes.[105]

The *developmental school* describes the evolution of the firm towards an organization that is capable of more radical forms of learning. Path-dependencies restrict the set of strategic options available to the firm.[106]

The *managerial school* provides normative prescriptions regarding how managers can create an environment or culture conductive to radical learning. The goal of achieving more radical learning requires the implementation of organization-wide values, sys-

---

[101] Ibid., p. 202.
[102] Huber (1991), p. 108.
[103] Bell et al. (2002), p. 70.
[104] Ibid., p. 71.
[105] Ibid., pp. 75-76.
[106] Ibid., pp. 76-77. This is similar to life-cycle theory as described by Van De Ven and Poole (1995), p. 515. See also B1 Adaptation to Change, pp. 5.

tems, and norms to meet a specific set of criteria.[107] The managerial school does not account sufficiently for environmental context factors.[108]

According to the *process school*, learning is grounded in the cognitive and behavioral capabilities of individuals and is socially constructed. It shifts the focus to information processing constructs, such as knowledge acquisition, information distribution, information interpretation, and organizational memory, that are common to all organizations.[109] The information processing perspective focuses on individual interpretation but relates it to an organizational level.[110] Organizational learning is contingent to organizational and environmental factors.[111] According to EGELHOFF, descriptions of organizations as communication systems, decision making systems, or systems that have to cope with uncertainty can all be subsumed under the broader notion of information processing.[112]

Table 2 below summarizes the characteristics of these four schools of thought in organizational learning. The process school, with its emphasis on information processing constructs at the individual, as well as the organizational level, and its consideration of internal and external contingencies seems most suited to serve as a theoretical foundation for this research on the role of management accounting systems in strategic sensemaking. The next sections will present different perspectives on the organizational environment and information processing.

| **School** | **Level** | **Focus** | **Type** | **Context** |
|---|---|---|---|---|
| Economic | Individual | Behavioral | Routine learning | Fixed |
| Developmental | Organizational | Behavioral/ later cognitive | Routine/radical learning | Path-dependencies |
| Managerial | Organizational | Normative | Radical learning | Certain conditions required |
| Process | Individual/ organizational | Behavioral/ cognitive | Routine/radical learning | Contingent |

*Table 2: Characteristics of organizational learning schools of thought*

[107] Senge (1990) describes five disciplines to establish organizational learning: personal mastery, mental models, shared vision, team learning, and systems thinking.
[108] Bell et al. (2002), pp. 77-78.
[109] Ibid., p. 78. See also Huber (1991), p. 90.
[110] Huber (1991), p.89 and Bell et al. (2002), p. 78.
[111] Bell et al. (2002), pp. 78-79 and Weick and Ashford (2001), p. 715.
[112] Egelhoff (1991), p. 342.

### 2.5.1 Organizational Environments and Strategic Issues

Organization information processing focuses on the environment as an important context factor.[113] According to SUTCLIFFE, processing information about the external environment is a key organizational and managerial activity.[114] "Organizations acquire, interpret and control flows of environmental information in order not be blindsided by threats, [and] unprepared for opportunities ..."[115] SUTCLIFFE suggests that existing research on the environment can be organized in three key perspectives: the objectivist perspective, the perceptual/interpretivist perspective, and the enactment perspective.[116]

The *objectivist perspective* describes the environment as a source of resources or as a source of information. Researchers following this perspective focus on characteristics or dimensions of the environment and pay little attention to the processes required to obtain or communicate information.[117] Organizational environments can be characterized as a set of components, stakeholders, or attributes.[118] The objectivist perspective assumes that there is a real environment.

The *perceptual and interpretivist perspectives* describe the environment "as a source of data that serves as the raw material from which organizational members fabricate information and subsequent organizational responses".[119] These perspectives view the environment as a flow of data and highlight the importance of perceptions and interpretations.[120] Critical variables are environmental uncertainty and the equivocality of information available to decision makers. Environmental uncertainty is "the difference between the amount of information required to perform the task and the amount of information already possessed by the organization".[121] Organizations can reduce uncertainty by acquiring new data. This is contrasted by the concept of equivocality.

---

[113] See section B2.4 Context Factors of Organizational Learning, pp. 5.

[114] Sutcliffe (2001), p. 198.

[115] Ibid., p. 197.

[116] Ibid., pp. 199-201.

[117] Ibid., p. 199.

[118] Ibid., pp. 199-200 provides as examples for components: economic, regulatory, technical, social, and for stakeholders: customers, competitors, suppliers. The dimensions stability, munificence and complexity for attributes of the environment are generally accepted.

[119] Ibid., p. 200. "For the interpretative or constructionist view, what is inside the human mind is not a reproduction of the external world. All that information flowing in through those filters, supposedly to be decoded by those cognitive maps, in fact interacts with cognition and is shaped by it. The mind, in other words, imposes some interpretation on the environment - it constructs its world" Mintzberg et al. (1998), p. 165.

[120] Sutcliffe (2001), p. 200.

[121] Galbraith (1977), cited in Daft and Lengel (1986), p. 556.

"Equivocality means ambiguity, the existence of multiple and conflicting interpretations about an organizational situation".[122] It is unclear what information might be missing, which makes it difficult to define questions. Additional data might not help to reduce equivocality. Instead, managers have to develop interpretations and share them with other organizational members in order to reduce equivocality.[123] Similar to the objectivist perspective, the perceptual and interpretivist perspectives also assume that there is a real, material, external environment. However, they differ in the extent to which decision makers are able to accurately assess this environment.[124]

The *enactment perspective* does not follow the conceptualizations of a "real" environment as in the previous perspectives, as "the environment is not an objective given; it is not even perceived. Rather it is made or enacted."[125] Decision makers focus on certain aspects of their environment, give meaning to the observed data and act on their interpretations. These in turn are informational inputs for other entities in the environment, which interpret these acts and subsequently react.[126] The product of enactment is an orderly, material, and social construction that is subject to multiple interpretations.[127]

In a complex and variable environment there are "... development[s] and events which have the potential to influence the organization's current or future strategy".[128] ANSOFF describes this events as "strategic issues" which are "... major environmental trends and possible events that may have a major and discontinuous impact on the firm."[129] DUTTON AND OTTENSMEYER describe strategic issues further as "... developments or events that emerge from an organization's internal or external environments; they are perceived to have the potential to affect an organization's performance".[130] According to ANSOFF, weak signals precede strategic issues and can be characterized by: " ... not enough information to make reliable estimates of the impact and of the effectiveness of response to permit a commitment to an irreversible unambiguous response".[131]

---

[122] Daft and Lengel (1986), p. 556.
[123] Ibid., p. 555-556.
[124] Sutcliffe (2001), p. 200.
[125] Weick (1979), cited in Sutcliffe (2001), p. 201.
[126] Sutcliffe (2001), p. 201.
[127] Weick (1988), p. 307.
[128] See Dutton and Duncan (1987), p. 280.
[129] Ansoff (1975), p. 25.
[130] See Dutton and Ottensmeyer (1987), p. 355.
[131] Ansoff (1990), p. 385. See also Ansoff (1975).

KONRAD describes weak signals more explicitly as information without broad diffusion, having a qualitative and strategic character, without causal connections and with attributes like unclear, vague, imperfect, inaccurate, utopian, muddled or abstruse.[132] These characteristics of weak signals make it hard or impossible to identify possibly resulting chances or risks at the moment of perception.

The identification and interpretation of weak signals helps companies to prepare for strategic issues so that they lose their "suddenness, urgency and unfamiliarity".[133] But due to their complexity and range of possible outcomes, strategic issues are still "... ill-structured ... poorly documented ... and open to multiple interpretations ... As such, strategic issues are not 'prepackaged' ..."[134] Strategic issues are characterized by the equivocality of the situation, which has to be interpreted by the involved managers. Increasing the amount of data alone will not help to define and solve the situation. Managers will also have to develop shared meanings, and the communication involved in this process can influence interpretation of others.[135] This conceptualization of strategic issues mostly reflects the perceptual and interpretivist perspectives of the environment.

Even when different people face identical stimuli they can, and very probably will, interpret the same situation in different ways. Interpretations differ, because managers possess different mental models formed by prior experiences and learning.[136] The development of shared meanings about strategic issues requires changes to the mental models of some or all involved managers. One could argue that without changes to the mental models, organizational members would not be able to develop different interpretations of the same situation and therefore would be unable to achieve a joint understanding of strategic issues. With regard to the type of learning involved, THOMAS ET AL. suggest that radical learning is required, because it "allows the organization to be more flexible in the face of future changes by suggesting alternative causal theories and by augmenting the repertoire of actions that an organization possesses."[137] As discussed in section B2.3, radical learning does not distinguish whether the environment is interpreted differently or not. However, making sense of strategic issues does not necessarily require a change in the interpretation of the environment as long as it in-

[132] See Konrad (1991), p. 184.
[133] See Ansoff (1975), p. 22.
[134] Thomas et al. (1994), p. 1253.
[135] Thomas and McDaniel (1990), p. 287.
[136] Ibid., p. 288.
[137] Thomas et al. (1997), p. 309.

volves the questioning of the organization's goals. Constant changes in interpretations of the environment would even prevent the rationalization of processes and development of organizational routines that are required to succeed in the short-term.[138] Nevertheless, THOMAS ET AL. argue that initial sensemaking efforts will be most valuable to developing understanding, because they set parameters and define assumptions, while later routine learning is required to fill in gaps in understanding.[139] In a similar manner ARGYRIS notes that "Double-loop learning is more relevant for the complex, non-programmable issues – it assures that there will be another day in the future of the organization."[140] Therefore, it seems that radical learning is more relevant to strategic sensemaking than routine learning.

### 2.5.2 Information Processing Perspectives

According to DAFT AND HUBER organizations must solve two problems in order to learn about strategic issues: the logistics problem and the interpretation problem.[141] The logistics problem deals with the uncertainty associated with strategic issues. In order to decrease uncertainty, organizations need to acquire and distribute data about their internal and external environments.[142] Uncertainty leads to the acquisition of objective information about the world to answer specific questions.[143] This creates information processing requirements, which effective organizations match with the information processing capacity of their structure and processes.[144]

KELLER observes that "the problem organizations face is a lack of clarity (equivocality) rather than a lack of data."[145] The interpretation problem deals with the equivocality associated with strategic issues. Equivocality requires managers to exchange existing views in order to define problems and resolve conflict through the enactment of a shared interpretation.[146] ELLIS AND SHPIELBERG found that increased information gathering without a higher capacity for information processing increased equivocality.[147]

---

[138] See also Ibid., p. 309.
[139] Ibid., p. 310.
[140] Argyris (1992), p. 9.
[141] Daft and Huber (1987), p. 10.
[142] Huber and Daft (1987), pp. 142-150.
[143] Daft and Lengel (1986), p. 558.
[144] Tushman and Nadler (1978), p. 619.
[145] Keller (1994), p. 168.
[146] Daft and Lengel (1986), p. 557.
[147] Ellis and Shpielberg (2003), p. 1245.

This underlines the importance for information processing mechanisms to give meaning to data through interpretive processes: "Organizational members, through the sharing of information, and through interpretive processes, socially construct information filters through which information is selected and interpreted, and subsequently enacted through communication."[148]

The logistics problem, with its focus on information acquisition and distribution, is reflected in the systems-structural perspective of information processing. The interpretation problem, with its focus on information interpretation and sharing, is part of the interpretative perspective of information processing.[149] Both perspectives are required to understand organizational information processing and learning.[150] Figure 2 below characterizes strategic issues along the interpretation and logistics problems.

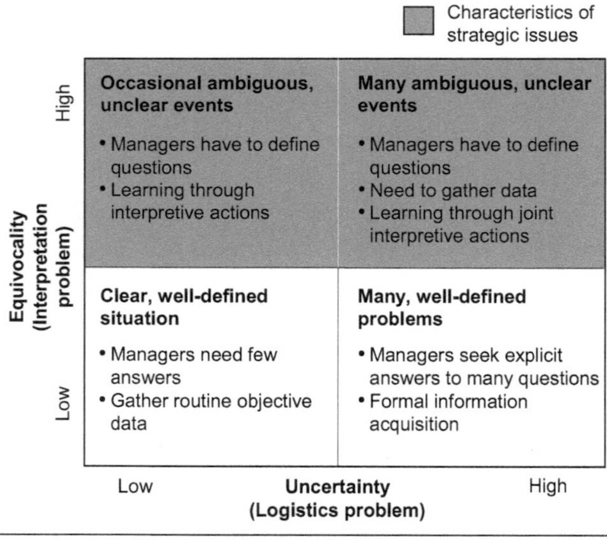


*Figure 2: Characteristics of strategic issues*[151]

#### 2.5.2.1 Systems-Structural Perspective of Information Processing

The systems-structural perspective, sometimes also known as the logistical perspective, examines how organizational design characteristics enhance or impede informa-

[148] Heath (1994), cited in Ellis and Shpielberg (2003), p. 1245.
[149] Daft and Huber (1987), pp. 10-11.
[150] Sutcliffe (2001), p. 204.
[151] Adapted from Daft and Huber (1987), p. 11.

tion processing.[152] It focuses on the question how an organization can acquire data about its environment and how it can ensure effective distribution within the company. "The learning implied is often of a low order – a readily interpretable fact is observed, such as the market availability of ... a new computer disk drive, and communicated to those organization departments best positioned to use this information".[153]

Following DAFT AND HUBER, information acquisition primarily occurs in two forms: *scanning* and *focused search*.[154] Organizations scan their environments for information about changes. Scanning is every activity pursued by the organization that "refers to the relatively wide-ranging sensing of the organization's external environment."[155] It can vary in intensity from high vigilance, active scanning to routine scanning or even passive search, as a state of alertness for non-routine, but relevant information.[156] Scanning is the behavior managers exhibit, when they browse through information without a particular problem to solve or question to answer.[157] It can provide useful information for strategic decision-making[158] and contributes to performance.[159]

Focused search occurs "when organizational members or units actively search in a narrow segment of the organization's internal or external environment, often in response to actual or suspected problems and opportunities".[160] HUBER suggests that two necessary and sufficient conditions for focused search to occur are: (1) a problem is recognized, and (2) a heuristic assessment of cost, benefits, and probabilities justifies the

---

[152] Sutcliffe (2001), p. 204.

[153] Daft and Huber (1987), p. 5.

[154] Ibid., p. 6 refer to focused search as probing. They define probing as actively initiated focused inquiries into the environment when more information is desired. In a later review, Huber (1991), pp. 98-99 refers to this kind of search as focused search. He relates the question whether focused search is largely reactive or proactive to the issue of determinism versus voluntarism in organizational change. He speculates that at lower organizational levels search is largely reactive to problems, but at higher organizational levels a significant proportion of search is a consequence of proactive managerial initiatives. Huber (1991), pp. 91-97 compiled a comprehensive list of ways for an organization to acquire data. In addition to focused search and scanning he distinguishes between the knowledge that already exists in the organization at the very beginning (congenital learning), knowledge that is acquired intentionally or unintentionally through direct experience with the environment (experimental learning), knowledge that is learned from other organizations (vicarious learning), and knowledge brought in from new members (grafting).

[155] Huber (1991), p. 97.

[156] Ibid., p. 97 and Daft and Huber (1987), p. 6.

[157] Vandenbosch and Higgins (1996), p. 202.

[158] See Aguilar (1967), p. 7.

[159] Daft et al. (1988), p. 136.

[160] Huber (1991), p. 97.

search.[161] In addition to focused search, HUBER describes performance monitoring as a formal and systematic process that includes both "focused and wide-ranging sensing of the organization's effectiveness in fulfilling its own pre-established goals or the requirements of stakeholders."[162] This suggests that performance monitoring is a process to recognize a problem that creates the precondition for focused search to occur. Therefore, monitoring is an antecedent to focused search and it is not necessary to consider monitoring separately.

For further sensemaking, organizations distribute the acquired information. This requires the processing of a large number of information-conveying messages, which can cause an overload on the cognitive or logistical capabilities of the involved entities. Organizations use two processes to solve this problem: *message routing* and *message summarizing*.[163] Both are attempts to reduce the information load that the involved parties have to process, by selective distribution (message routing) or condensation of information (summarizing). One major problem occurring when distributing information is the fact that information is often only valuable as "synergistic information", i.e. when organizational entities create new information by combining this information with existing knowledge or other bits of information. "Organizational units with potentially synergistic information are often not aware of where such information could serve, and do not route it to these destinations. Also, units that might be able to use information synergistically often do not know of its existence or whereabouts."[164] HUBER concludes that, "how those who possess non-routine information and those who need this information find each other is relatively unstudied ..."[165]

Hence the systems-structural perspective analyzes ways for the organization to obtain information, and defines systems and processes for the acquisition, as well as the distribution, of data. It implicitly assumes that entities know how to use the data and only need "the facts" in order to take action.[166]

---

[161] Ibid., p. 98.
[162] Ibid., p 97.
[163] Daft and Huber (1987), p. 7. Furthermore, Galbraith (1974), pp. 30-35 suggests four organization design strategies to reduce the need for information processing by the creation of slack resources and the creation of self-contained tasks, or to increase the capacity to process information by investing in vertical information systems and the creation of lateral relations.
[164] Huber (1991), p. 101
[165] Ibid., p. 101
[166] Daft and Huber (1987), p. 8.

2.5.2.2 Interpretive Perspective of Information Processing

The interpretive perspective of information processing, sometimes also known as the enactment perspective, focuses on the question of how an organization can make sense of, and give meaning to, equivocal information. It accounts for the idea that information has no inherent meaning and that it is given meaning through interpretive processes.[167] "From the interpretive perspective, data mean nothing until they are used by organization participants."[168]

The company's decision-makers are flooded by a continuous stream of qualitative, ill-defined incidents.[169] "Before organizations can use information they have collected, they must classify, sort, and simplify it into coherent patterns."[170] The focus of the interpretive perspective is primarily on how organizational structures, organizational processes, and the psychological and social-psychological characteristics of organizational members influence the interpretation of information.[171] Its ideas are rooted in symbolic interactions that conceptualize the organization as a dynamic web of human interpretations.[172] "Over time and through communication among organizational members, symbols evolve and take on meaning. Symbols provide meaning that can be used to interpret situations and adjust behavior."[173] Organizations learn through joint discussions and interpretations of events, and through gradual changes in the assumptions, symbols, and values of participants.[174]

The importance of communication for the development of a shared interpretation requires considering the way channels or media are used for communication. Communication channel research indicates that channels are not equal in their capacity for facilitating understanding.[175] DAFT AND HUBER define media richness "as the medium's capacity to change mental representations within a specific time interval".[176] They relate differences in the media richness capacity of channels to a blend of four characteris-

---

[167] Sutcliffe (2001), p. 204. See also Heath (1994).
[168] Daft and Huber (1987), p. 8.
[169] See Dutton and Jackson (1987), p. 76.
[170] Day (2002), p. 247. See also Dutton et al. (1989), p. 379.
[171] Sutcliffe (2001), p. 204.
[172] Huber and Daft (1987), p. 151 and Daft and Huber (1987), p. 8.
[173] Huber and Daft (1987), p. 151.
[174] Daft and Huber (1987), p. 10.
[175] Ibid., p. 13.
[176] Ibid., p. 14. Daft and Lengel (1984), p. 196 use information richness to describe the potential information-carrying capacity of data. Information richness is determined by the channel used to process this information, which leads to the presented definition of media richness.

tics: the opportunity for timely feedback, the ability to convey multiple cues, the tailoring of messages to personal circumstances, and language variety.[177] Face-to face communication is considered the richest medium, because it allows immediate feedback to correct and exchange interpretations. Furthermore, the simultaneous communication of multiple cues and the possibility to tailor the message to the receiver and the situation enhances the understanding of the message beyond its information content.[178] Formal, unaddressed documents are lowest in richness, because they are not adapted to the receiver and do not allow fast feedback.[179]

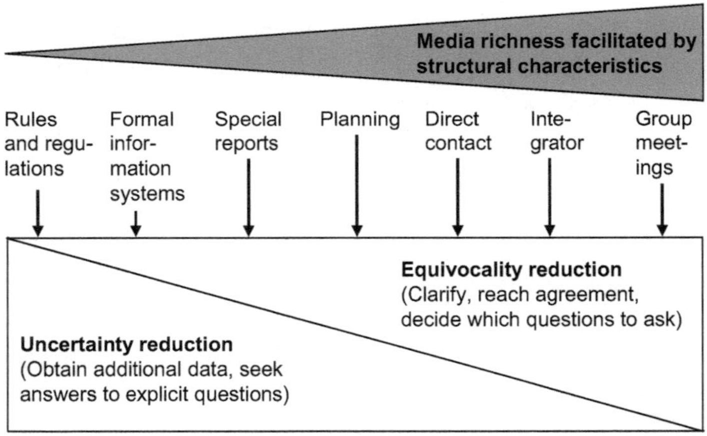


*Figure 3: Information role of structural characteristics*[180]

According to DAFT AND LENGEL, the communication channel has to be adapted to the underlying problem: Channels with high media richness, e.g. group meetings, are best suited to reduce the equivocality of new information. Channels with a large amount of information, like formal information systems, serve best to reduce uncertainty occurring with new information.[181] Based on previous research, DAFT AND LENGEL place

[177] Daft and Huber (1987), p. 14 and Huber and Daft (1987), p. 152.
[178] Huber and Daft (1987), pp. 152-153.
[179] Daft and Huber (1987), p. 15.
[180] Adapted from Daft and Lengel (1986), p. 561.
[181] Ibid., p. 559.

structural characteristics along a media richness continuum to reflect their capacity to reduce uncertainty and equivocality (see Figure 3 above).[182]

Empirical tests of media richness theory provide mixed results. DAFT AND HUBER's review of work on media selection provides evidence that rich media are the preferred mode of information processing when equivocality increases. "Face-to-face communication is a powerful means of resolving equivocality and changing mental representations, which is one important aspect of organizational learning."[183] However, MARKUS shows that media richness theory cannot explain the choice of electronic mail as the primary medium for internal work-related communication, especially in situations involving time pressure.[184] He finds that also less rich media like electronic mail can convey equivocal content.[185] In particular new information technologies have challenged the media richness scale. According to BÜCHEL AND RAUB, electronic media have introduced five new features that go beyond the original richness concept: increased speed of communication, reduced cost of communication, increased connection between people, increased communication bandwidth, with more information moving simultaneously to different people, and improved computing technologies that allow organizational members to retrieve information from a collective database.[186] Overall, a meta-analysis of empirical research on media choice shows twice as many supportive as non-supportive studies for the proposition that rich media are used for equivocal tasks.[187]

The conflicting empirical evidence on media richness theory has led the search for broader collective variables.[188] MARKUS observes that the choice of electronic mail was a "collective behavioral response to a socially constructed definition of the medium's appropriateness".[189] CARLSON AND ZMUD suggest, with their channel expansion theory,

---

[182] Ibid., p. 562 emphasize that the continuum is tentative and hypothetical. The relationship between structure and the reduction of equivocality and uncertainty has not been empirically tested, but the pattern is consistent with previous research.

[183] Daft and Huber (1987), p. 16.

[184] Markus (1994), pp. 518-519.

[185] Ibid., p. 516.

[186] Büchel and Raub (2001), p. 521.

[187] Straub and Karahanna (1998), p. 161.

[188] Whitfield et al. (1996), p. 224 find that the use of rich information channels by CEOs depends on at least two organizational design parameters: divisionalization and centralization.

[189] Markus (1994), pp. 522-523. According to the social influence model of technology use, perceptions of media attributes are socially constructed through information exchange and not based on objective, rational characteristics. See also Fulk and Boyd (1991), pp. 411-412, Fulk (1993), p. 942 and Büchel and Raub (2001), p. 523.

a model that considers not only the perceived media richness, but also prior experiences and intentions of communication participants.[190] This extension of media richness theory helps to resolve the conflicting evidence concerning the use of electronic media.[191]

Overall, the interpretive perspective, with its emphasis on the construction of meaning through interactions between organizational entities, helps to explain how managers can reduce equivocality associated with strategic issues.

## 2.6 Organizational Learning as Theoretical Foundation

Major assumptions of the information processing perspectives of organizational learning can be summarized along (1) perspectives on the environment, (2) perspectives on the individual, and (3) perspectives on the organizational context.

*(1) Perspectives on the environment:* Strategic issues emerge from an organization's internal or external environment and have the potential to affect the organization's performance. They can be characterized through the concepts of uncertainty and equivocality. Uncertainty defines a lack of data, and can be reduced by the acquisition and distribution of additional data. Equivocality means ambiguity and managers have to develop interpretations and share them with other organizational members in order to reach a common understanding as a basis for further decision making.

*(2) Perspectives on the individual:* Individuals have only limited data processing capabilities, and these limited capabilities must be used to process vast amounts of ambiguous stimuli provided by the environment. Mental models help to impose a structure on environmental stimuli and determine how they will be interpreted or whether they will be noticed at all. Differences in mental models and ambiguous stimuli contribute to the equivocality of strategic issues, which can be reduced through the sharing of different interpretations. This can result in learning through changes in the underlying mental models. Mental model changes that lead to a questioning of the organization's goals and eventually involve a new interpretation of the environment are defined as radical learning. Radical learning is especially relevant for strategic sensemaking.

---

[190] Carlson and Zmud (1994), pp. 281-282.
[191] Carlson and Zmud (1999), p. 164.

*(3) Perspectives on the organizational context:* Organizational learning is primarily about individuals learning within their organizations, but the transmission of information between organizational members makes individual learning a social rather then a solitary phenomenon. Management accounting systems as major constituents of the procedural and communication channels focus the attention of individuals on specific issues and answers and thereby influence organizational learning. Especially communication channels with high media richness contribute to learning and help to reduce equivocality associated with strategic issues. This suggests that two perspectives are necessary to understand sensemaking of strategic issues: The systems-structural perspective on information processing focuses on processes and systems for the acquisition and distribution of environmental data, while the interpretive perspective is concerned with the development of a shared interpretation of the acquired data.

## 3. Strategic Sensemaking as a Learning Process

Managers have to make sense of what is happening in their environments, in order to develop a shared interpretation that can serve as a guide to action.[192] "Noticing, interpreting, and incorporating stimuli are necessary and prior conditions for problem solving to occur."[193] Along with the interpretive perspective of organizational information processing, DAY suggests that advances in information technology shifted the interest from data acquisition to making sense of this data: "Recent developments in information technology can deliver more timely and detailed data, but the ensuing avalanche of numbers often smothers the collective ability to make sense out of that data. Since more data is not an answer, firms are looking to the underlying processes used to learn about their markets".[194] SCHREYÖGG AND STEINMANN emphasize the selective nature of sensemaking: "Creating clarity ('eliminating' equivocality) is a complex process of gathering information, interpreting it, and transforming it. However, since only a limited set of information can be handled, most of what is potentially available must be ignored. Basically, the whole process filters information, sets assumptions, and reduces complexity; by its very nature it is selective."[195] Strategic sensemaking helps managers to deal with uncertainty and equivocality of strategic issues because it cre-

---

192 Choo (1998), p. 5 and Schreyögg and Steinmann (1987), p. 93.
193 Kiesler and Sproull (1982), p. 550.
194 Day (1994), p. 9.
195 Schreyögg and Steinmann (1987), pp. 93-94.

ates "clear questions and clear answers"[196] as a prerequisite for strategic decision-making.[197] But sensemaking can also follow decision-making as "decision making often stimulates the surprises and confusion that create occasions for sensemaking."[198]

Researchers have developed a number of models to describe how managers make sense of issues and events in their environment.[199] MARCH AND OLSEN see sensemaking from a behavioral perspective as part of experiential learning in which "individuals and organizations make sense of their experience and modify behavior in terms of their interpretations."[200] STARBUCK AND MILLIKEN take a cognitive perspective and observe that, "sensemaking has many distinct aspects – comprehending, understanding, explaining, attributing, extrapolating, and predicting, at least. ... What is common to these processes is that they involve placing stimuli into framework (or schemata) that make sense of the stimuli."[201] THOMAS ET AL. note that sensemaking "involves the reciprocal interaction of information seeking, meaning ascription, and action" and that "each element of this sense making process is presumed to have some relationship to performance."[202] In order to define strategic sensemaking, it is helpful to focus on (1) the processes in strategic sensemaking, and (2) the level of analysis.

*(1) Processes in strategic sensemaking*: According to researchers studying information processing, it is helpful to separate the process of observing environmental stimuli

---

196 Weick (1995), p. 636.
197 Choo (1998), p. 3.
198 Maitlis (2005), p. 21.
199 Milliken (1990), p. 43 refer to this problem by noting: "Researchers have developed a number of models to describe the process by which decision makers notice and interpret issues and events in their environment .... Although there are many underlying similarities in these models, they tend to use different labels for the processes they describe, including environmental interpretation, problem formulation, problem sensing, issue management, and strategic issue diagnosis". Daft and Weick (1984), p. 286 also refer to this problem: "There are many interpretation images in the literature, including scanning, monitoring, sense making, interpretation, understanding, and learning ..." Some researchers refer to this as strategic issue management in order to stress a systematic approach with dedicated processes and personnel: "A strategic issue management system ... is a systematic procedure for early identification and fast response to important trends and events both inside and outside an enterprise." Ansoff (1980), p. 134. Dutton and Ottensmeyer (1987), p. 355 describe issue management as "organizational procedures, routines, personnel, and processes devoted to perceiving, analyzing, and responding to strategic issues ... [This implies to] collect, disseminate, and interpret information and by doing so, identify issues that require managerial interpretation."
200 March and Olsen (1975), p. 157.
201 Starbuck and Milliken (1988), p. 51.
202 Thomas et al. (1993), p. 240.

from the process of interpreting them.[203] DAFT AND WEICK distinguish three processes of strategic sensemaking: observation,[204] interpretation[205] of environmental changes, and action to respond to these changes.[206] Managers use formal systems or personal contacts to observe the environment in order to collect new stimuli. In the next step, they give meaning to this data through interpretive processes, and finally they act based on their interpretations. Feedback from actions provides new stimuli for observation and interpretation (see Figure 4 below). DAFT AND WEICK refer to this as a learning process "by which knowledge about action outcome relationships between the organization and the environment is developed."[207]

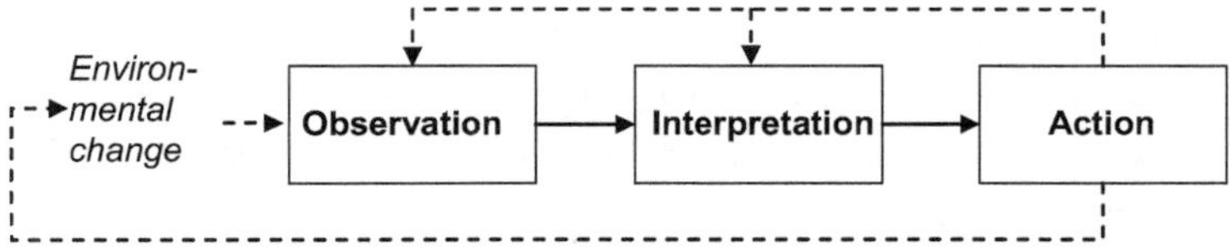


*Figure 4: Process of strategic sensemaking*[208]

The separation of strategic sensemaking into three process steps is helpful to focus attention on specific aspects in this process. In practice, these clear boundaries between the process steps do not exist: "Thus, the practice of segmenting the processes into stages with clear labels is essentially an analytic convenience. Because 'cognition' often begins with action ... and because performance outcomes tend to structure subsequent scanning and interpretation, the theoretically convenient boundaries among these

---

[203] "Disentangling the process of noticing environmental stimuli form the process of interpreting environmental stimuli is useful for better understanding organizational adaptation and responsiveness and isolating the communication dynamics related to each of the processes" Sutcliffe (2001), p. 205.

[204] Kim (2001), p. 20 and Daft and Weick (1984), p. 286 use "scanning" as a general term and "data collection" as an explanation in their model. Thomas et al. (1997), p. 300 note that "scanning has been investigated under the rubrics of information search, surveillance, sensing, attention, and acquisition ..." This research will use the more general term "observation", because scanning is also a specific term for the unguided search for new information (see B2.5.2.1 Systems-Structural Perspective, pp. 5).

[205] Thomas et al. (1997), p. 300 note "that interpretation has been studied under such notions as problem structuring, labeling, formulation, identification, and meaning ascription, among many others."

[206] Daft and Weick (1984), p. 286. See also Kim (2001), p. 20. Many authors build on this model of organizations as interpretation systems. See for example Dutton and Jackson (1987), Isabella (1990), Thomas and McDaniel (1990), Schneider and De Meyer (1991), Thomas et al. (1993), and Corner et al. (1994).

[207] Daft and Weick (1984), p. 286.

[208] Adapted from Ibid., p. 286, and Kim (2001), p.20.

concepts ... become rather blurred ..."[209] Especially observation and interpretation are difficult to separate as they happen at the same time and each of these activities depends on each other.[210] Furthermore, the process of strategic sensemaking is not linear but iterative. As soon as managers observe more about the related environmental changes, or observe a reaction to previous actions, they will start to rethink previous interpretations, learn further about them and act again. Therefore, the three stages of strategic sensemaking are interconnected through feedback loops.[211]

*(2) Level of analysis*: Sensemaking happens on the individual level as an organization can only learn through the individuals involved.[212] "A basic assumption is that insight and innovative ideas occur to individuals – not organizations."[213] With the focus on individual sensemaking, it is important to "study the processes by which information is moved around within the organization and 'reality' or 'learnings' are created."[214] This combines the interpretive perspective with the systems-structural perspective on information processing[215] and accounts for the assumption of DAFT AND WEICK that the organizational interpretation process is something more than that occurring in individuals.[216]

Although the original model for strategic sensemaking from DAFT AND WEICK describes learning at the organizational level it has been shown that the steps are equally valid at the individual level.[217] The following sections will describe the observation, interpretation and action steps of the individual process of strategic sensemaking in more detail.

## 3.1 Observation in Strategic Sensemaking

Individuals become aware of weak signals about strategic issues through observation. Because of their limited capacity to deal with all the stimuli in their environment,

---

[209] Thomas et al. (1997), p. 311.
[210] Starbuck and Milliken (1988), p. 45.
[211] Daft and Weick (1984), p. 286.
[212] Simon (1991), p. 125. According to Weick and Ashford (2001), p. 727 "Organizational learning is primarily about individuals learning within their organizations." Akgün et al. (2003), p. 856 defines sensemaking as an individual activity. See also B2.1 Level of Organizational Learning, pp. 5.
[213] Crossan et al. (1999), p. 524.
[214] Weick and Ashford (2001), p. 727.
[215] See B2.5.2 Information Processing Perspectives, p. 5.
[216] Daft and Weick (1984), p. 285.
[217] Kim (2001), p.20. Other examples include Kim (1993), p. 42 and Corner et al. (1994), p. 296.

managers cannot observe every aspect of the organization and its environment.[218] They direct their attention to certain areas and, even in those, they observe only some stimuli.[219] Managers may overlook important environmental features as observation is a limiting process in that the noticing of one thing can eliminate the simultaneous noticing of something else.[220] This filtering makes less data available for further interpretation.[221]

STARBUCK AND MILLIKEN explain the filtering of stimuli by referring to HELSON's studies[222] on the relative effects of foreground and background events on observation.[223] HELSON found that people do not notice stimuli that resemble adaptation levels, which are standards produced by experience for distinguishing or evaluating stimuli.[224] The adaptation level associated with a sequence of alternating stimuli shows that non-simultaneity helps people to concentrate on foreground events and to deemphasize background events in cognition.[225] Otherwise, simultaneity in background events exerts much more influence on not noticing than foreground events do. This means that "people tend to notice subtle changes in foreground stimuli while overlooking substantial changes in background stimuli, and so background stimuli may have to change dramatically to attract notice."[226] STARBUCK AND MILLIKEN suggest that "familiarity enables people to develop programs and habits for noticing foreground stimuli, whereas they attend less systematically and consistently to background stimuli."[227] These programs and habits may have negative effects on the observation of weak signals because foreground events are converted into background events that are noticed less reflectively.[228]

An underlying factor influencing the selective attention[229] of individuals is the processing mode: automatic or controlled. The automatic mode is the default mode that allows

---

218 Kiesler and Sproull (1982), p. 550.
219 Hambrick and Mason (1984), p. 195.
220 Sutcliffe (2001), p. 209.
221 Corner et al. (1994), p. 296.
222 See Helson (1964).
223 Starbuck and Milliken (1988), p. 47.
224 Helson (1964), cited in Starbuck and Milliken (1988).
225 Starbuck and Milliken (1988), pp. 47-48.
226 Ibid., p. 48.
227 Ibid., p. 48.
228 Tuchman (1973), cited in Starbuck and Milliken (1988), p. 48.
229 "Selective attention is the focus of consciousness at any point of time and is limited to approximately 7 items of information" Corner et al. (1994), p. 296.

individuals to direct attention to multiple stimuli simultaneously.[230] Executives in this mode are more likely to make generalized interpretations of environmental stimuli. However, they are unlikely to distinguish a strategic issue from its background unless it is sharply different from that background.[231] In the case of automatic processing, individuals do not exercise active control and cannot easily alter or suppress the highly routine and habitual processing.[232] DUTTON suggests in her research on strategic issue diagnosis that, "an automatic diagnosis involves the activation of ready-made issue categories in the minds of decision-makers that have been built from encounters with issues in the past."[233] Automatic processing is dependent on extensive long-term learning.[234]

Learning theorists use the term routines to describe cognitive regularities or cognitive patterns that serve the individual in an automatic processing mode.[235] At the individual level, routines are part of mental models that are activated dependent on information about uncertainties.[236] Individuals routinize their patterns of making causal attributions, which leads to less extensive information processing in recurring situations. At the organizational level routines, such as standard operating procedures, economize on the limited information processing and decision-making capacity of individual managers by allocating attention selectively.[237] According to ZOLLO AND WINTER "routines are stable patterns of behavior that characterize organizational reactions to variegated, internal or external stimuli."[238] In the case of semi-conscious processing of repetitive events, routines guide search by experience and reduce the space of behavioral options that individual managers should scan.[239]

Controlled processing represents a contrast to the automatic processing mode. Controlled processing is highly demanding of attentional capacity and is largely under the

---

230 Ibid., p. 296. According to Dutton (1993), p. 342, psychologists have given the modes different labels (e.g., automatic vs. controlled processing, mindless vs. mindful behavior, automatic vs. active strategic issue diagnosis).

231 Corner et al. (1994), p. 297.

232 Ocasio (1997), p. 190.

233 Dutton (1993), p. 341.

234 Ocasio (1997), p. 190.

235 According to Becker (2004), p. 645 routines can also be understood as behavioral regularities describing patterns of interaction. At the individual level, researchers often associate the term "habit" with recurrent activity patterns.

236 Kim (1993), p. 40 and Cohen (1991), p. 135.

237 Kim (1993), p. 41 and Becker (2004), p. 657.

238 Zollo and Winter (2002), p. 340.

239 Becker (2004), p. 657.

individual's control.[240] "It completely absorbs cognitive resources and facilitates the differentiation of strategic information from its environmental background."[241] Because of its high requirements on cognitive resources, controlled processing is strongly dependent on activity load.[242] The controlled processing mode involves a much greater degree of information search and analysis, and decision-makers are more likely to identify important strategic issues embedded within environmental information.[243]

Related to the automatic and controlled processing mode is research on information acquisition and mental models by VANDENBOSCH AND HIGGINS.[244] Based on cognitive learning theories they distinguish two types of learning: "mental model maintenance," in which new information fits into existing mental models and confirms them, and "mental model building," in which mental models are changed to accommodate new information.[245] "Mental model maintenance"[246] implies that basic routines remain appropriate and is the more likely behavior.[247] "Its returns are positive, proximate, and predictable."[248] Therefore, "mental model maintenance" is likely to occur during an automatic processing mode. In comparison, "mental model building"[249] is much riskier and its benefits are remote. It requires the formation of new models and is a purposeful activity requiring much cognitive effort.[250] Therefore, "mental model building" requires the individual to be in a controlled processing mode.

Finally, it is possible to link learning and observation in strategic sensemaking. According to the systems-structural perspective of information processing, information acquisition can be distinguished in two characteristic modes: scanning and focused search.[251] Scanning is the behavior of executives when they browse through information in order to understand trends or improve their understanding of the business. Fo-

---

240 Ocasio (1997), p. 190.
241 Corner et al. (1994), p. 297.
242 Ocasio (1997), p. 190. Dutton (1993), pp. 346-347 postulates that high time pressure and information load make the occurrence of automatic issue diagnosis more likely.
243 Dutton (1993), p. 342 and Corner et al. (1994), p. 297.
244 See Vandenbosch and Higgins (1996).
245 Ibid., p. 198.
246 "Mental model maintenance" belongs to the routine learning types. See B2.3 Type of Organizational Learning, pp. 5.
247 Vandenbosch and Higgins (1996), p. 202.
248 March (1991), p. 85.
249 "Mental model building" belongs to the radical learning types. See B2.3 Type of Organizational Learning, pp. 5.
250 Vandenbosch and Higgins (1996), p. 202 and Zollo and Winter (2002), p. 344.
251 See B2.5.2.1 Systems-Structural Perspective, pp. 5.

cused search occurs when executives verify performance results or look up specific information. VANDENBOSCH AND HIGGINS found, in their study of 327 users of executive support systems, that focused search is clearly linked to "mental model maintenance". Scanning, while being less frequent than focused search, is more likely to lead to "mental model building".[252] "Mental model building" is more relevant to strategic sensemaking than "mental model maintenance" which makes scanning the more suitable information acquisition mode.[253]

Overall, individuals are more likely to observe new strategic issues through scanning than through focused search. The identification of strategic issues requires a controlled processing mode, which creates the precondition for radical learning.

### 3.2 Interpretation in Strategic Sensemaking

Interpretation is the second process step in strategic sensemaking and describes how managers construct meaning for, or assign meaning to data that has passed through the observation step.[254] GIBBINS AND JAMAL synthesize research on interpretation in three steps:[255]

- Initial data from the task environment elicit an internal representation (problem space or frame) for the task.
- The initial representation then activates a cognitive process or strategy for acquiring and interpreting new data from the task environment.
- The initial representation is modified as new data are processed until an end state (solution) is reached.

As a first step in interpretation, data is transformed into an abstract internal representation, which is then infused with meaning.[256] Meaning infusion is achieved through a

---

[252] Vandenbosch and Higgins (1996), p. 209.
[253] See also B2.5.1 Organizational Environments and Strategic Issues, pp. 5.
[254] Kiesler and Sproull (1982), p. 550.
[255] Gibbins and Jamal (1993), pp. 454-455 use the term cognitive problem solving for interpretation. See also Thomas et al. (1997), p. 300.
[256] Corner et al. (1994), p. 297 define this step as encoding. Encoding is important for two reasons: (1) it determines which information is readily retrievable from memory for decision-making, and (2) it is an important point of entry for strategic choice biases identified in the literature. Mental models are a source of cognitive biases, as "they can also restrict our understanding to that which makes sense within the mental model." See Kim (1993), p. 39. For an overview of cognitive biases see

feature matching process that is governed by structures known as categories.[257] A critical assumption of categorization theory is that "cognitive categories are comprised of objects [issues] with similar perceived attributes and reflect the structure of the objects [issues] in the environment".[258] Categories encompass prototypes or idealized examples of category members, which can be described through shared features or attributes.[259] Other researchers use the term schemata to define "cognitive representations of attributes and the relationship between them."[260] Schemata are active cognitive structures that frame problems.

Cues in a problem-solving setting evoke a schema or category that is used to compare characteristics of the issue against features of the category prototype. Only data that passed this test for relevance is included in the final encoded representation that is suitable for storage in memory.[261] Data that does not match category prototype features is excluded from the final encoded representation. However, this process can falsely include prototypical features that are not part of the original data, because data is processed as an example of a category. In addition, individuals make inferences during encoding and store the results, along with information retained from the feature matching process, in information bundles. It is important to note that, "the information stored in memory is not accurate and that it is biased toward the category prototype."[262]

The initial representation then activates a cognitive process or strategy for acquiring and interpreting new data from the task environment. This individual cognitive process can be captured by two process characteristics: recursiveness and retroductivity.[263] Recursiveness describes the successive revision of judgment at the individual level as new data emerges. Data interpretation is not a systematic, sequential and unidirectional

---

Hogarth and Makridakis (1981), pp. 117-120, Schwenk (1988), p. 44, Tversky and Kahnemann (1974), and also Das and Teng (1999), Hodgkinson et al. (1999), and McFadden (1999).

257 Corner et al. (1994), p. 297. Categorization theory was developed by Rosch (e.g., Rosch (1978)) as an explanation of the cognitive processes underlying concept formation for natural objects. Dutton (1987), p. 77 proposes, that this general theory can be applied to categorizing strategic issues by decision makers.

258 Dutton (1987), p. 77. See also Kiesler and Sproull (1982), p. 556.

259 See Corner et al. (1994), p. 298 and Dutton (1987), p. 78.

260 Schwenk (1988), p. 46.

261 Kiesler and Sproull (1982), p. 557 and Corner et al. (1994), p. 298.

262 Corner et al. (1994), p. 298. Dutton and Jackson (1987), p. 78 mention three cognitive phenomena that can be explained through categorization theory: (a) that memory for category-consistent information is generally better than memory for inconsistent information, (b) that constructive errors of memory (gap-filling) occur; and (c) that information distortion follows predictable patterns.

263 Dutton et al. (1983), p. 312.

process, where observation precedes interpretation, because interpretations can also influence further search activities. As different data becomes available, new interpretations can supersede older ones and can cause the reinterpretation of old data. The new interpretations can alter perceptions about the issue, raise new questions and trigger search for new data. Also, data which emerges early in the interpretation process can bias individuals in their perception of the issue and influence the direction of their search process.[264]

Retroductivity describes the coexistence and interplay of deductive and inductive modes of thinking.[265] A deductive mode of thinking translates an individual's initial assumptions through logical conclusions into specific judgments or predictions about an issue. However, the choice of assumptions is, to some extent, arbitrary, and cannot be resolved within a deductive mode of thinking. Individuals operating in the inductive mode of thinking can draw inferences and conclusions beyond existing data. Past experience and learning helps individuals to built assumptions that enable them to deal with the conflicting, ambiguous and incomplete nature of strategic issues. The derivation of cause-effect relationships from conceptual categories further requires reasoning by analogy.[266] Individuals can infer relationships by approximating data to the closest similar situation they have experienced. Analogies can be effective in generating creative solutions. However, when strategic issues involve a great deal of uncertainty and complexity, "the use of simple analogies may mislead the decision-makers into an over-simplistic view of the situation."[267] It seems that variations in interpretations of strategic issues can be related in part to differences in mental models[268] and not only to differences in data available to individuals. HUFF ET AL. highlight that "individuals also frequently act on 'automatic pilot' without reconsidering the appropriateness of the patterns they follow."[269] Therefore, awareness or vigilance in problem solving can be

---

[264] Ibid., p. 312.
[265] See Ibid., p. 313 also for the following paragraph.
[266] See also Kiesler and Sproull (1982), p. 554 for the confidence enhancing effect of reasoning by analogy.
[267] Schwenk (1988), p. 48.
[268] Ibid., p. 45-46 use the term cognitive map. Cognitive maps consist of concepts about aspects of the decision environment and beliefs about cause-and-effect relationships between them. Cognitive maps are sometimes used in connection with the term schema and can be defined as a particular type of schema or a part of a broader schema. However, the distinction between cognitive maps and schemata in the literature is not completely clear.
[269] Huff et al. (2000), p. 15.

related to the amount of recursiveness and the degree to which the underlying assumptions and analogies are questioned.

Problem solving continues until an end state is reached. The goal or end state is part of the internal representation of a problem and can be changed if new interpretations become available.[270] However, the end state guides problem solving and can bias interpretations. The systems-structural perspective discusses two processes that are related to the interpretation step in strategic sensemaking: message delay and message modification. Message delay occurs in order to reduce information load and involves the prioritization of strategic issues.[271] In the extreme, an individual may have prioritized correctly, and may also thoroughly understand the impact of an issue on the organization, but still decide not to communicate his findings. Withholding information can be useful to achieve one's goals in a competitive environment or to avoid harm that the receiver of the information can cause to the sender.[272] Message modification is the distortion of the message's meaning. "Modifications may be conscious or unconscious, well-intended or malicious."[273] The ambiguity of strategic issues and biased perceptions of individuals make unconscious modifications likely, but especially harmful is the conscious and malicious modification of messages to achieve personal goals.[274]

Overall, the categorization of strategic issues, awareness during interpretation and intention to modify or delay messages affect the interpretation step in strategic sensemaking.

### 3.3 Action in Strategic Sensemaking

Action is the last process step of strategic sensemaking. One action can be an individual decision on a response strategy without further interaction with other managers. To do this requires sufficient personal power and means, but this research assumes that the top management team will make decisions concerning a change of strategy and therefore will not consider an individual decision on a response strategy.

A second action is to store information that does not require immediate attention for later use. Storage is the preservation of interpreted information for later retrieval when

---

270 Gibbins and Jamal (1993), pp. 454-455.
271 Huber and Daft (1987), p. 147.
272 Ibid., p. 148.
273 Ibid., p. 146.
274 Ibid., pp. 149-150.

a strategic decision is required.[275] At the individual level, strategic information is stored in an associative network of nodes. Connections between nodes reflect relationships between items that become stronger with repeated use and learning. Information is recalled with the help of a "spreading activation" mechanism that tends to activate nodes with help of their connections and retrieves related events and ideas.[276] As interpretations of strategic issues can change when new information becomes available, storage is only an intermediary step and this research will not consider it separately.

The most important action step in individual strategic sensemaking is communication. Communication is an essential part of strategic sensemaking, as the reduction of ambiguity from strategic issues requires different points of view and interpretations from different organizational members.[277] Individuals have to communicate with other managers to resolve the equivocality of information about strategic issues, but also have to communicate their interpretations to the top management team, as a basis for further decision making. Therefore, this research will focus on communication as the relevant action of individual managers.

Overall, strategic sensemaking is the process of observing, interpreting, and communicating strategic issues.

# 4. Management Accounting Systems and Learning

## 4.1 Definition of Key Terms

### 4.1.1 Definition of Management Accounting Systems

Management accounting systems (MAS) are formal systems that provide information from the internal and external environment to managers.[278] HORNGREN ET AL. define management accounting systems as "formal mechanisms for gathering, organizing, and communicating information about an organization's activities."[279] Management accounting systems do not only include reports, performance measurement systems and computerized information systems such as executive information systems or manage-

---

[275] Corner et al. (1994), p. 300.
[276] Ibid., p. 300.
[277] Sutcliffe (2001), pp. 211-212 and Weick et al. (2005), p. 413.
[278] Bouwens and Abernethy (2000), p. 223.
[279] Horngren et al. (2002), p. 6.

ment information systems; they also encompass the planning, budgeting and forecasting processes required to prepare and review management accounting information.

Because management accounting researchers do not agree yet on a single definition for management accounting systems, it is helpful to distinguish management accounting systems from the broader notion of management control systems.[280] ANTHONY defines management control as "the process by which managers ensure that resources are obtained and used effectively and efficiently in the accomplishment of the organization's objectives."[281] MARGINSON clusters management control systems into three groups.

The first group comprises procedures to prescribe and proscribe the firm's overall strategic purpose through belief and boundary systems.[282] A belief system is "the explicit set of organizational definitions that senior managers communicate formally and reinforce systematically to provide basic values, purpose, and direction for the organization."[283] Boundary systems "delineate the acceptable domain of activity for organizational participants. Unlike beliefs systems, boundary systems do not specify positive ideals. Instead, they establish limits, based on defined business risks, to opportunity-seeking."[284]

A second group consists of administrative controls that "enable managers to establish specific role expectations of the subordinate and to monitor and evaluate the subordinate's performance against these expectations."[285] This includes personal and clan controls that help to prevent performance problems when cause-effect knowledge is incomplete and standards of desirable performance are ambiguous.[286]

The third group of management control systems focuses on the provision of information that enables top management to monitor organizational performance against im-

---

[280] Chenhall (2003), p. 129 observes that, "The terms management accounting (MA), management accounting systems (MAS), management control systems (MCS), and organizational controls (OC) are sometimes used interchangeably. MA refers to a collection of practices such as budgeting or product costing, while MAS refers to the systematic use of MA to achieve some goal. MCS is a broader term that encompasses MAS and also includes other controls such as personal or clan controls. OC is sometimes used to refer to controls built into activities and processes such as statistical quality control, just-in-time management."

[281] Anthony (1965) cited in Langfield-Smith (1997), p. 208.

[282] Marginson (2002), p. 1021.

[283] Simons (1995), p. 34.

[284] Ibid., p. 39.

[285] Marginson (2002), p. 1021.

[286] Ouchi (1979), p. 837 and Snell (1992), p. 297.

portant dimensions of a given strategy.[287] SIMONS describes these systems as "formalized routines and procedures that use information to maintain or alter patterns in organizational activity".[288] Along with CHENHALL this research will refer to these systems as management accounting systems in order to distinguish them from the other two groups that are not explicitly concerned with information.

Therefore, management accounting systems are the formal systems to prepare and provide information from the internal and external environment that helps managers to monitor organizational performance.

### 4.1.2 Definition of Management Accounting Information

Management accounting systems provide management accounting information. DAVENPORT notes that "it is difficult to arrive at a precise definition of what constitutes management information, or information for that matter."[289] In order to define management accounting information more precisely, it is instructive to focus on the distinction between stimuli, data and information (see Figure 5 below).

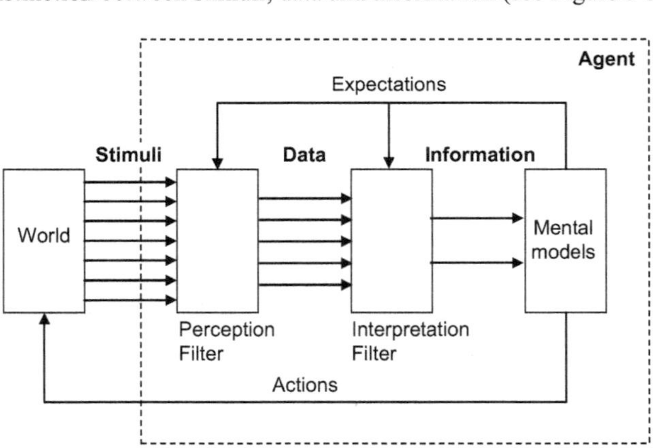


*Figure 5: Relationship between stimuli, data and information*[290]

According to BOISOT AND CANALS, agents are constantly "bombarded" by stimuli from the environment and much neural processing is required between the reception of

[287] Marginson (2002), p. 1021.
[288] Simons (1991), p. 49. See also Simons (1987a), p. 358.
[289] Davenport (1993) cited in Vandenbosch (1999), p. 78.
[290] Adapted from Boisot and Canals (2004), p. 48.

a stimulus and its availability as data.[291] The limited attentional capacity of individuals sets up perceptual filters and only stimuli that pass this initial filter get registered as data.[292] Interpretation then transforms data into information by extracting significant regularities residing in the data. However, these significant regularities depend on the receiving agent, and therefore information sets up a relation between incoming data and a given agent.[293] DAVIS defines information as "data that have been processed into a form that is meaningful to the recipient and is of real or perceived value in current or prospective decisions."[294] Conceptually, data has to pass an interpretation filter that is shaped by the individual's mental model.[295]

BOISOT AND CANALS' distinction between stimuli, data and information for agents is also valid for management accounting systems. Management accounting systems reduce complexity through selection and standardization. They focus on important areas of the environment and contain assumptions about what data is relevant.[296] Management accounting systems process data and provide the result as management accounting information to managers.

Traditionally, management accounting systems provided only internal, historical, and financial information. Over time, they evolved to include a broader scope of information, including external, future-oriented, qualitative and non-financial information.[297]

---

[291] Ibid., p. 46.

[292] Ibid., p. 47 and Corner et al. (1994), p. 296. See also B3.1 Observation in Strategic Sensemaking, pp. 5.

[293] Boisot and Canals (2004), p. 47. Schiemenz (1993) defines information as a relationship between data, a problem and the problem solver. This definition from information management emphasizes the goal-oriented interpretation of data in order to solve a specific problem. An interpretation of data in different contexts or by different problem-solvers can yield diverse information.

[294] Davis (1974), p. 32.

[295] Boisot and Canals (2004), p. 47. See also B3.2 Interpretation in Strategic Sensemaking, pp. 5.

[296] "Accounting systems, and information systems more generally, inevitably offer highly stylized views of the world. Any representation is partial, an interpretation through a particular framing of reality, rendering some aspects of events important and others unimportant ...."Dent (1991), p. 709. See also Hedberg and Jönsson (1978), p. 48.

[297] According to Chenhall (2003), p. 129 "The definition of MCS has evolved over the years from one focusing on the provision of more formal, financially quantifiable information to assist managerial decision making to one that embraces a much broader scope of information. This includes external information related to markets, customers, competitors, non-financial information related to production processes, predictive information and a broad array of decision support mechanisms ...". Atkinson et al. (2001), p. 5 observe that, "Traditionally, management accounting information has been financial; that is, its been denominated in a currency .... Recently, however, management accounting information has expanded to encompass operational or physical (nonfinancial) information, such as quality and process times, as well as more subjective measurements, such as customer satisfaction, employee capabilities, and new product performance."

Therefore, management accounting information includes internal/external, financial/non-financial, quantitative/qualitative, and historical/future-oriented information that passed the perception and interpretation filter of management accounting systems.

## 4.2 Use of Management Accounting Information and Systems

### 4.2.1 Information Use and Learning

As a starting point for understanding the role of management accounting systems and information in strategic sensemaking, it is helpful to review existing research on information use. However, ANSARI AND EUSKE note that "there is no single theory of information use in organizations from which hypotheses can be derived and empirically tested. The only feasible option is to group the many roles into a small number of finite categories."[298] This research conceptualizes strategic sensemaking as a learning process, where radical learning is particularly important.[299] Therefore, the following review of important information use typologies focuses on the relationship between information use and routine or radical learning (see Table 3 below).

BURCHELL ET AL. distinguish between uncertainty of cause and effect and uncertainty of objectives in order to describe the role of management accounting systems in decision-making. In situations with low uncertainty in both areas, management accounting systems can serve as *'answer machines'* to provide clear answers to specific questions. With clear objectives but uncertain causation, managers "need to explore problems, ask questions, explicate presumptions, analyse the analysable and finally resort to judgement."[300] BURCHELL ET AL. refer to this use as *"learning machines"*, but they do not explain how managers learn and the type of learning involved. Given uncertainty over objectives but relative certainty over cause and effect relationships, political processes become important and managers use accounting as *"ammunition machines"* to promote their own positions. Lastly, with high uncertainty in both areas accounting systems can serve as *"rationalization machines"* to legitimize actions that have already been decided upon.[301] This suggests that only the role of management accounting systems as "learning machines" is partially related to organizational learning.

---

[298] Ansari and Euske (1987), p. 551.
[299] See B2.6 Organizational Learning as Theoretical Foundation, pp. 5.
[300] Burchell et al. (1980), pp. 14-15.
[301] Ibid., p. 15.

| | | Reference to ... | |
|---|---|---|---|
| **Author** | **Usage Type** | **Routine Learning** | **Radical Learning** |
| BURCHELL ET AL. (1980) | Answer machine | – | – |
| | Learning machine | Partial | Partial |
| | Ammunition machine | – | – |
| | Rationalization machine | – | – |
| ANSARI AND EUSKE (1987) | Technical-Rational | Full | – |
| | Socio-Political | – | – |
| | Institutional | – | – |
| MENON AND VARADARAJAN (1992) | Action-Oriented | Partial | – |
| | Knowledge Enhancing | Partial | Partial |
| | Affective | – | – |
| HIRST AND BAXTER (1993) | Instrumental | Partial | Partial |
| | Strategic | – | – |
| | Symbolic | – | – |
| SIMONS (1995) | Diagnostic | Full | – |
| | Interactive | – | Full |
| VANDENBOSCH (1999) | Score Keeping | Full | – |
| | Problem Solving | – | – |
| | Focusing Attention | – | Partial |
| | Legitimizing Decisions | – | – |

*Table 3: References between information use and learning*

ANSARI AND EUSKE suggest three alternative theoretical perspectives on the use of accounting data in organizations: technical-rational, socio-political and institutional. Firstly, the *technical-rational* perspective on use of information is driven by considerations of efficiency. It emphasizes the need to coordinate and control the activities within the technical core of an organization. Accounting information is a critical element in measuring the internal efficiency, which provides the basis for resource allocation decisions.[302] The use of accounting information to increase efficiency is congruent with routine learning. Secondly, the *socio-political* role of information focuses "on the way in which accounting systems are used to rationalize and justify organizational actions to members, and to influence the attitudes and beliefs of participants to gain negotiating advantages."[303] This view is similar to the "ammunition machine" role of ac-

[302] Ansari and Euske (1987), p. 552.
[303] Ibid., p. 552.

counting systems from BURCHELL ET AL. and does not relate to learning. Thirdly, the *institutional* perspective serves legitimization purposes, "which stems from the need to put on an appropriate facade for the world to see."[304] It is similar to the socio-political role but with an external focus, and therefore is also not related to learning.

Building on prior research in public policy, sociology, marketing, and other administrative disciplines, MENON AND VARADARAJAN propose a conceptual model to describe marketing knowledge utilization in firms. They distinguish between action-oriented use, knowledge-enhancing use, and affective use.[305] *Action-oriented* use "is demonstrated by changes in the user's activities, practices or policies" by using information to solve a clearly defined problem.[306] Changes in behavior indicate a learning process. The application of information to an identified problem suggests more a routine learning. Furthermore, MENON AND VARADARAJAN also subsume symbolic use under action-oriented use. Symbolic use does not lead to learning. Therefore, action-oriented use is only partially related to routine learning. *Knowledge-enhancing* use "results in changes in the user's knowledge and understanding of the issues." Knowledge enhancement can be due to the final product (i.e. results) or because of the research process (i.e. conduct of the research study). Furthermore, product-based knowledge enhancement can occur directly when managers make conscious efforts to learn when they process the information, or more unconsciously through low-involvement learning.[307] The reference to a controlled processing of research results provides some evidence for radical learning, while the low-involvement learning is more likely to lead to knowledge accretion or routine learning. The combination of both learning types, and the similarity with the "learning machine" from BURCHELL ET AL. provides only partial references to routine and radical learning. Finally, *affective use* occurs to increase the general confidence in decision-making and to lower any cognitive dissonance.[308] Affective use is related to general levels of satisfaction or dissatisfaction and contains no references to learning.

In order to study choices in organizational settings, HIRST AND BAXTER suggest three roles of information: instrumental, strategic and symbolic. Within the *instrumental* perspective they further distinguish between four ways of using information. First, in-

---

[304] Burchell et al. (1980), p. 553.
[305] Menon and Varadarajan (1992), p. 61.
[306] Ibid., p. 62.
[307] Ibid., p. 62.
[308] Ibid., p. 63.

formation may be used to provide answers about the consequences of adopting a particular course of action. Second, it may help to learn about a problem and its potential solutions. Third, information can promote dialog when there is conflict over decision objects. Finally, managers can use information to trigger creativity or promote ideas in ambiguous choice settings.[309] The instrumental perspective is similar to "answer machines" and the action-oriented perspective, but also provides references to learning in ambiguous settings. Therefore, it presents implicit evidence for both routine and radical learning. In contrast, the *strategic* perspective refers to information use "in a political fashion – as ammunition – to promote and perpetuate the preference of powerful choice participants."[310] In the *symbolic* perspective, "information is valued for its evocative qualities, for sustaining an image of rationality and neutrality."[311] Both perspectives do not reference to learning.

SIMONS distinguishes between the diagnostic and interactive use of management accounting systems.[312] He assumes that organizations face unlimited opportunities, but that they are limited by scarce management attention. A fundamental problem in creating value is to focus attention appropriately.[313] *Diagnostic* control systems are used to motivate, monitor, and reward achievement of specified goals.[314] The diagnostic use helps to conserve management attention.[315] In contrast, *interactive* control systems are used to direct organizational attention in order to stimulate organizational learning and the emergence of new ideas and strategies.[316] SIMONS explicitly relates diagnostic and interactive use to learning. Interactive control systems guide the allocation of attention to areas with strategic uncertainties, where learning needs are high. They facilitate double-loop or radical learning by questioning the basis upon which strategies have been created.[317] Diagnostic control systems constrain innovation and opportunity seeking to ensure the predictable goal achievement needed for intended strategies. They facilitate single-loop or routine learning to keep the process within desired bounds.[318]

---

309 Hirst and Baxter (1993), p. 191.
310 Ibid., p. 192. See also Feldman and March (1981), pp. 176-177.
311 Hirst and Baxter (1993), p. 192. See also Feldman and March (1981), pp. 177-178.
312 Simons (1995), p. 7. This book summarizes his prior research on control, e.g. Simons (1987a), Simons (1987b), Simons (1990), Simons (1991), and Simons (1994).
313 Simons (1995), p. 17.
314 Ibid., p. 7.
315 Ibid., p. 70.
316 Ibid., p. 91.
317 Ibid., pp. 105-106.
318 Ibid., p. 91.

VANDENBOSCH suggests a typology of information use consisting of: score keeping, problem solving, focusing attention and legitimizing decisions.[319] *Score keeping* involves the comparison of operating results to expectations and often can inhibit substantive change. Score keeping can result in nothing more than single-loop or routine learning.[320] Managers perceive a negative impact of score keeping on the enablement of competitiveness.[321] During *problem solving*, managers use information to quantify the impact of decision alternatives, in order to derive a recommendation for action. VANDENBOSCH does not provide reference for this type of information use to learning. *Focusing attention* is related to SIMONS' interactive use.[322] However, VANDENBOSCH does not focus on its relationship with radical learning; instead she relates focusing attention to the purpose of exercising power and along with BURCHELL ET AL.'s "ammunition machine", to promoting a particular point of view. Managers perceive focusing attention as the kind of use with the highest impact on enablement of competitiveness.[323] This suggests, that focusing attention is partially related to radical learning. Finally, *legitimizing decisions* is related to BURCHELL ET AL.'s "rationalization machine" and is used to justify the decisions that have already been made.[324] This type of use is not related to learning.

Overall, the review shows that only SIMONS' typology of interactive and diagnostic use of management accounting systems provides direct and full references to routine and radical learning. Radical learning is particularly important for strategic sensemaking, and therefore the next section will focus in more detail on the relationship between interactive use and strategic sensemaking.

### 4.2.2 Interactive Use and Strategic Sensemaking

The following provides an overview of conceptual and empirical research on the interactive use of management accounting systems. As both interactive use of management accounting systems and strategic sensemaking are related to learning, this section will describe the relationship between interactive use and strategic sensemaking. According to SIMONS "interactive control systems are formal information systems managers use

[319] Vandenbosch (1999), p. 79.
[320] Ibid., p. 81.
[321] Ibid., p. 88.
[322] Ibid., p. 79.
[323] Ibid., p. 88.
[324] Ibid., p. 79.

to involve themselves regularly and personally in the decision activities of subordinates. Based on the unique strategic uncertainties they perceive, managers use these systems to activate search. ... Interactive control systems focus attention and force dialogue throughout the organization. They provide frameworks, or agendas, for debate, and motivate information gathering outside of routine channels."[325] Interactive management accounting systems have four defining characteristics:[326]

- Management accounting information of interactive systems is an important and recurring agenda addressed by the top-management.
- Interactive management accounting systems demand frequent and regular attention from managers at all levels of the organization.
- Superiors, subordinates, and peers interpret and discuss management accounting information in face-to-face meetings.
- The interactive system fosters the continual challenge and debate of underlying data, assumptions, and action plans.

Interactive management accounting systems can create competitive pressures within the organization to innovate and adapt.[327] These competitive pressures help managers to break out of limited search routines and provide guidance on where to look for strategic issues.[328] Learning occurs throughout the organization as attention is focused on information contained in the interactive control system.[329] However, attention is limited and therefore only a subset of the available management accounting systems can have the attention of managers. Managers have to identify which strategic uncertainties are critical to their chosen business strategy.[330] Based on this, top managers have to decide which aspects of management accounting systems they want to use interactively in order to signal to the organization important strategic uncertainties for monitoring.[331] The

[325] Simons (1995), pp. 95-96.
[326] Ibid., p. 97.
[327] Ibid., p. 92.
[328] Simons (1990), p. 137.
[329] Simons (1995), p. 101.
[330] The identification of strategic uncertainties might be guided by senior management's strategic vision for the future of the business, as uncertainty and equivocality of the environment can make it difficult to comprehend the changes required to realize the business strategy. Ibid., p. 102.
[331] Simons (1990), p. 136. Managers in normal competitive conditions use only one system interactively for three reasons: economic, cognitive, and strategic. (1) Interactive control systems demand managers' frequent attention and therefore incur opportunity costs by diverting attention from other

debate and exchange of information related to these strategic uncertainties helps managers to question the assumptions underlying their business strategy, and thereby to learn. Finally, learning can result in an adaptation of business strategies as a response to identified strategic issues (see Figure 6 below). The interactive use of management accounting systems can make the organization responsive to the opportunities and threats embedded in the firm's strategic uncertainties.[332]

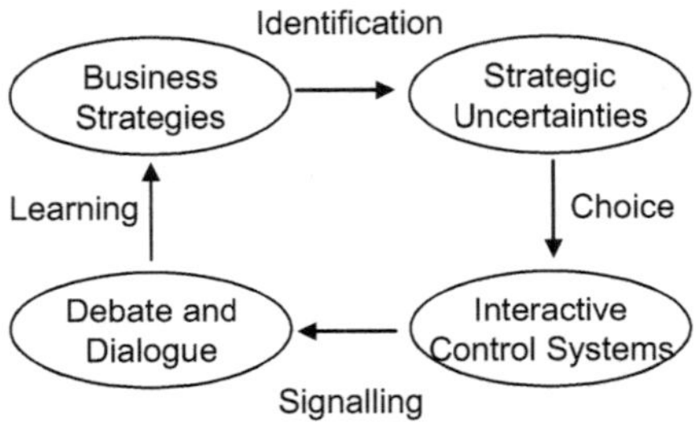


*Figure 6: Relationship between interactive control systems and learning*[333]

There is some empirical evidence to support the described relationship between the interactive use of management accounting systems and learning. In an exploratory study SIMONS conducted interviews with ten newly appointed top managers in order to understand how they used formal control systems as levers of strategic change and renewal. He found that, after putting the fundamentals of the business in place, nine managers began to use one control system interactively in order to focus organizational attention on the strategic uncertainties associated with their vision for the future.[334] The interactive use helped to generate organizational learning and, over time, new strategies would emerge from the process.[335] However, his research needs to be

tasks. (2) The interactive use of several management accounting systems can cause information overload on decision makers, which prevents them from processing all data. (3) The purpose of using management accounting systems interactively is to activate learning and experimentation. Focus on too many systems can risk superficial analysis, a lack of perspective, and potential paralysis. Only firms in crisis situations use several systems interactively, in order to figure out how to change and survive. Simons (1995), pp. 115-117.

332 Simons (1990), p. 137.

333 Adapted from Simons (1995), p. 102.

334 Simons (1994), p. 149 and p. 184.

335 Ibid., p. 184.

treated with caution as it relies on top managements' description of actions they took and the espoused reasons for taking these actions.[336]

Direct evidence for a relationship between the interactive use of performance measurement systems and organizational learning is provided by HENRI's survey of 383 mid-sized Canadian manufacturing firms. He finds strong support for a direct positive relationship between interactive use and organizational learning. The relationship also holds in sub-group analysis for firm size, organizational culture, and environmental uncertainty.[337] Because performance measurement systems are an integral part of management accounting systems, it seems possible to transfer the results to the context of this study.

ABERNETHY AND BROWNELL took a closer look at the role of budgets in organizations facing strategic change. In an exploratory study of 63 large Australian hospitals, they find that the interactive use of budgets leads to enhanced performance when firms undergo strategic change.[338] For effective management during strategic change, top management requires prospective information and an increased information flow. The interactive use of budgets seems to serve as an integrative liaison device that breaks down the functional and hierarchical barriers that inhibit information flows.[339] This suggests that the interactive use of management accounting systems facilitates the learning and adaptation required when strategic change is underway.[340]

Research from BISBE AND OTLEY suggests that the interactive use of management accounting systems not only improves performance during strategic change, but also moderates the impact of innovation on performance. In a survey of 40 medium-sized, mature Spanish manufacturing firms, BISBE AND OTLEY tested whether the interactive use of management accounting systems makes companies more innovative, or whether it makes innovative companies more successful.[341] They did not find support for the postulate that the interactive use of management accounting systems favors innova-

---

[336] Ibid., p. 187.
[337] Henri (2006), p. 543. In context of low environmental uncertainty the relationship between interactive use and organizational learning is positive, but non-significant.
[338] Abernethy and Brownell (1999), p. 199.
[339] Ibid., p. 192.
[340] Ibid., p. 199.
[341] Bisbe and Otley (2004), pp. 710-711.

tion, but found that the relationship between product innovation and performance is more positive the more interactively management accounting systems are used.[342]

BISBE AND OTLEY suggest that the interactive use of management accounting systems provides direction, integration and fine-tuning to translate innovation into performance.[343] *Directions* signal preferences for search and provide the basis for a selection of initiatives. Thereby, interactive systems may help to shape the rich bottom-up process of emergence of patterns of action in highly innovative firms. *Integration* provides a forum and an agenda for organizational members to engage in face-to-face dialogue and debate about different interpretations of strategic issues. Similarly to ABERNETHY AND BROWNELL, BISBE AND OTLEY speculate that the interactive use of management accounting systems acts as an internal integrative capability in order to improve process efficiency and product effectiveness.[344] Finally, the interactive use of management accounting systems ensures that strategic uncertainties are given regular attention. This assists managers in *fine-tuning* strategies if needed, because of changing conditions of innovative contexts.[345]

BRUINING ET AL. provide some evidence of how the interactive use of controls helped two companies to sustain their innovation strategies after a management buy-out. The interactive use of planning helped to involve more key personnel at different levels of these companies in discussions with top management about strategic uncertainties relating to the intended strategy. These people contributed important private information through experience gained from their interactions and negotiations with customers. The interactive use became "an important part of a dynamic process of search and learning, to access insights and information that would be valuable in creating a competitive advantage in a changing market environment."[346]

A case study of two regional management teams at a large consumer goods company suggests that the interactive use of management accounting systems has some requirements in order to convert emergent strategies into useful action. OSBORN analyzed the impact of a new information system, introduced to analyze market trends and regional performance, on management collaboration and performance in two compa-

---

[342] Ibid., pp. 726-727.
[343] Ibid., p. 727.
[344] Ibid., p. 727. See also Verona (1999), p. 137.
[345] Bisbe and Otley (2004), p. 728.
[346] Bruining et al. (2004), p. 171.

rable management teams.[347] One team had been using the new information system for over a year and was heavily involved in specifying key characteristics of the information reports. The new tools helped them to understand causes for changes in regional markets. As a result their management discussions became increasingly anticipatory in nature.[348] The other team was just beginning to develop and use the system. OSBORN analyzed business performance review meetings and found that the dominant meeting activity of the former team was discussion, while in the later team it was presentation.[349] The increased use of the information system to filter and understand market trends helped the more successful first team to focus on building a shared interpretation of results, while the second team spent most of the meeting time presenting data to each other.[350] The information system helped to improve collaboration in the first team, as it "encouraged them to consider the profitability implications of their actions and enabled them to understand the challenges faced by their counterparts in other functions."[351] The study suggests that a flexible information system provides the basis for building interactive controls that encourage collaboration or learning across organizational boundaries.[352]

However, the focus on specific controls does not necessarily help to guide the strategic activity within a firm. In a case study of a British telecommunication company MARGINSON did not find evidence that emphasis on accounting-based targets helped in the development of new ideas and initiatives.[353] Top management often reprioritized key performance indicators through meetings, team briefs and weekly e-mails from the chief executive. MARGINSON even observed that pressure to achieve several performance measures simultaneously led to grass-roots decisions concerning the prioritization of measures.[354] It seems that frequent reprioritizations of measures provided only insufficient focus[355] and that not all managers at different organizational levels used the management accounting system in the same manner.

---

[347] Osborn (1998), p. 496.
[348] Ibid., p. 495.
[349] Ibid., p. 496.
[350] Ibid., pp. 498-499.
[351] Ibid., p. 501.
[352] Ibid., p. 504.
[353] Marginson (2002), p. 1026.
[354] Ibid., p. 1027.
[355] "Senior managers must also determine when to change the focus of interactive control systems. As competitive conditions and senior management vision changes, strategic uncertainties also change.

This suggests that not all management accounting systems can be used interactively. According to SIMONS five conditions are necessary for a management accounting system to be a candidate for interactive use:

- "To be used interactively, the management accounting system must require the *re-forecasting* of future states based on revised current information."[356] Any significant discrepancy between actual results and expectations triggers a search for understanding. An understanding of changed conditions allows managers to estimate the potential effect on current strategies and forces a dialogue about the underlying causes.

- "To be used interactively, the information contained in a management accounting system must be *simple* to understand."[357] Debate must focus on the causes and implications of information rather than on how the information was constructed and reported. As shown by OSBORN, managers' participation in the development of the information system helped them to understand the information in the system. This understanding allowed them to focus discussions on building a shared interpretation of results,[358] which is required to reduce equivocality associated with strategic issues.

- "To be used interactively, a management accounting system must be used not only by senior managers but also by managers at *multiple levels* of the organization."[359] Otherwise, the system will not serve as a catalyst for search activities. BRUINING ET AL.'s study shows how the interactive use of controls at multiple levels of the organization helped to gather important private information.[360] Managers in the telecommunication company as described by MARGINSON did not use the management accounting system in the same manner.[361] According to SIMONS this use would not classify as interactive use, which could explain the missing impact on strategic activity in that firm.

... On the other hand, changing signals too often can send conflicting signals and cause confusion and lack of focus in the organization." Simons (1995), p. 117.

356 Ibid., p. 108, italics added.

357 Ibid., p. 108, italics added.

358 Osborn (1998), pp. 498-499.

359 Simons (1995), p. 108, italics added.

360 Bruining et al. (2004), p. 171.

361 Marginson (2002), p. 1026.

- "To be used interactively, a management accounting system must *trigger revised action plans*."[362] Forecasts of changing conditions must provide input on how to adjust strategy to gain advantage. This type of information encourages participants to test new ideas and strategies in order to adapt in competitive markets. Learning requires action to create new stimuli to learn from. It also helps organizational members to create an enacted environment in order to make sense of strategic issues.[363]
- "To be used interactively, a management accounting system must collect and generate information that relates to the *effects of strategic uncertainties* on the strategy of the business."[364] Strategic uncertainties are unique to industries and business strategies, which makes design features (e.g., the types of measures used, the system focus, and the planning horizon) specific to the company.[365]

Although no research studied the direct relationship between interactive use and strategic sensemaking, there is enough evidence to suggest that the interactive use of management accounting systems has an impact on strategic sensemaking of managers.[366]

Firstly, the interactive use of management accounting systems seems to have an impact on observation by focusing attention on strategic uncertainties.[367] It provides directions to managers and signals which information is important for the business.[368] This should help managers to decide which environmental stimuli they need to attend to. The interactive use also helps managers to decide which private information, from their own experience, would be valuable for the company.[369] However, there is a risk in choosing the wrong interactive management accounting system. The interactive use may focus organizational search on the wrong strategic uncertainties. It may divert or-

---

362 Simons (1995), p. 109, italics added.
363 See also B2.5.1 Organizational Environments and Strategic Issues, pp. 5.
364 Simons (1995), p. 109, italics added.
365 Ibid., pp. 109-110.
366 "An effective learning organization is one in which employees at all levels continuously scan the environment, identify potential problems and opportunities, exchange environmental information candidly and openly ... in order to successfully adapt to the emerging environment. The main objective of interactive control is to facilitate the creation of a learning organization." Anthony and Govindarajan (2000), pp. 453-454.
367 Simons (1991), p. 50.
368 Bisbe and Otley (2004), p. 727.
369 Bruining et al. (2004), p. 171.

ganizational attention from other important stimuli and can prevent the observation of other opportunities.[370]

Secondly, evidence on the impact of interactive use of management accounting systems on interpretation is scarce. However, the reforecasting of future states based on revised current information, as postulated by SIMONS, should help managers to develop an understanding of changed conditions.[371] According to BISBE AND OTLEY the interactive use of MAS also provides the basis for selecting initiatives that maximize the impact on performance. It seems that the interactive use of management accounting systems focuses attention on the interpretation of strategic issues that relate to the identified strategic uncertainties.

Thirdly, the main impact of the interactive use of management accounting systems on strategic sensemaking seems to be on communication. SIMONS, ABERNETHY AND BROWNELL, BISBE AND OTLEY, BRUINING ET AL. and OSBORN report that the interactive use of management accounting systems increases interactions between organizational members and fosters discussions of information related to strategic uncertainties. The reduction of equivocality associated with strategic issues requires face-to-face discussions of interpretations by different organizational members. The interactive use of management accounting systems seems to provide a forum and agenda for such discussions.

SIMONS suggests that the interactive use of management accounting systems is a choice of managers.[372] Designers of management accounting systems also make choices, and therefore the next chapter will focus on the impact of management accounting system dimensions on strategic sensemaking.

---

[370] Simons (1995), pp. 113-114.
[371] Ibid., p. 108.
[372] "By choosing to use a control system interactively, top managers signal their preferences for search, ratify important decisions, and maintain and activate surveillance throughout the organization." Ibid., p. 102.

# C Management Accounting Systems and Strategic Sensemaking

*"The range of what we think and do*
*is limited by what we fail to notice.*
*And because we fail to notice*
*that we fail to notice*
*there is little we can do*
*to change*
*until we notice*
*how failing to notice*
*shapes our thoughts and deeds."*
*R.D. Laing*[373]

## 1. Impact of Management Accounting Systems on Strategic Sensemaking

In order to understand how management accounting systems can affect strategic sensemaking, it is necessary to gain a better understanding of management accounting system characteristics that can have an impact on cognitive processes in strategic sensemaking. This study draws on empirical and conceptual research from the following research areas: accounting, management information systems, general management, strategy, and organization behavior. Each of these areas provides fragmented descriptions of how management accounting system characteristics relate to sensemaking, decision-making, knowledge acquisition, change and learning.

Three iterative steps assisted the derivation of management accounting system characteristics that have an impact on individual managers' strategic sensemaking. Firstly, based on an extensive screening of relevant literature,[374] management accounting system characteristics, descriptions of observed effects, and arguments used to explain

---

[373] Goleman (1985), p. 24, cited in Starbuck and Milliken (1988), p. 45.

[374] Screening included *Accounting, Organizations & Society* (since 1991), *Management Accounting Research* (since 1994), *Academy of Management Journal* (since 1990), *Academy of Management Review* (since 1995), *Journal of Management Studies* (since 1994), *Strategic Management Journal* (since 1991) as the most relevant journals. Additionally the screening encompasses from accounting: *Behavioral Research in Accounting* (since 1991), *Journal of Accounting Research* (since 1991), *Journal of Management Accounting Research* (since 1989), from the field of management information system research: *Information Systems Research* (since 1990), *MIS Quarterly* (since 1994), from general management and strategy the *Administrative Science Quarterly* (since 1991) and from organization behavior: *Management Science* (since 1999) and *Organization Science* (since 1990). The literature review considers also contributions from other journals, which are especially promising.

their impact on strategic sensemaking, were extracted. Secondly, the described effects were assigned to strategic sensemaking process steps. Finally, management accounting system characteristics were clustered, in order to derive a preliminary hypothesis on how they can affect individual managers' strategic sensemaking.

The assignment of effects to strategic sensemaking process steps is based on the cognitive processes mentioned in the various articles. In cases where the authors did not provide a cognitive process explicitly, the assignment of variables depends on the information processing status: whether stimuli become accessible in the form of data, data becomes understandable through interpretation, or information forms the basis for individual's action (see Figure 7 below).[375]

The filtering of stimuli during acquisition of data relates to the *observation* step of sensemaking. According to the systems-structural perspective of information processing, data acquisition can be distinguished in two characteristic modes: scanning and focused search.[376] Scanning is when managers look broadly for new, unusual data without a specific question in mind. Focused search is the acquisition of data to answer specific questions.

The *interpretation* step involves the transformation of data into information through several cognitive sub-processes during problem solving. Cues in the observed data evoke a problem-space that activates a problem-solving process guided by a goal or an end state.[377] As already shown, research on the categorization of strategic issues, awareness during interpretation and intention to modify or delay messages is especially relevant for the interpretation step.[378]

Finally, the *action* step of strategic sensemaking involves the communication of information retained from the problem-solving process. Individuals have to communicate with other managers to resolve the equivocality of information about strategic issues, but also have to communicate their interpretations to the top management team, as a basis for further decision-making.

---

[375] Boisot and Canals (2004), pp. 46-48. See B4.1.2 Definition of Management Accounting Information, pp. 5.

[376] See B2.5.2.1 Systems-Structural Perspective, pp. 5.

[377] Gibbins and Jamal (1993), pp. 454-455.

[378] See B3.2 Interpretation in Strategic Sensemaking, pp. 5.

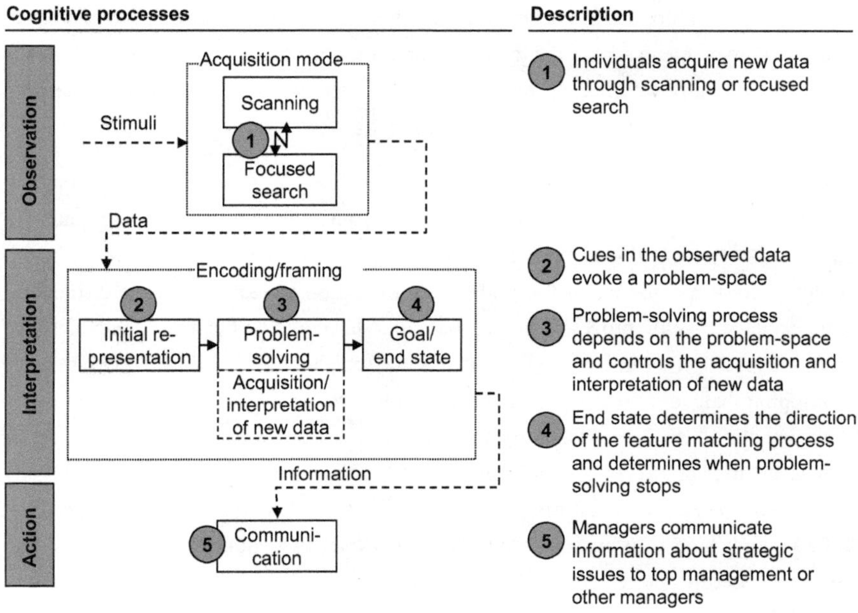


*Figure 7: Cognitive processes in strategic sensemaking*

Results of the literature review are presented in section C1.1 for observation, section C1.2 for interpretation, and finally section C1.3 for communication.

## 1.1 Impact of Management Accounting Systems on Observation

Managers acquire data for strategic sensemaking through focused search and scanning. Typical management accounting systems are designed with focused search in mind, in order to make decision-making more rational.[379] VANDENBOSCH AND HUFF conducted 36 interviews with users of executive information systems in seven North American companies and found that 30 interviewees exhibited focused search behavior, while only nine managers used their executive information system for scanning. Focused search seems much more frequent than scanning and scanning was only observed in conjunction with focused search.[380] In order to increase validity and general applicability of their findings, VANDENBOSCH AND HIGGINS conducted an additional survey with

[379] Vandenbosch and Higgins (1996), p. 203.

327 executive information system users in these companies. They found managers with the highest mean scores for focused search used management accounting systems that provided daily information on key operating metrics, but did not permit the integration of information from different sources.[381]

The availability of daily or real-time information from the competitive environment seems especially beneficial in fast changing environments like the microcomputer industry. EISENHARDT finds in her case studies on decision-making speed in eight microcomputer firms that the use of real-time information increases the pace of the strategic decision making process. She proposes that this could be due to a higher speed of issue identification or due to the fact that executives who use real-time information are developing their intuition, which enables them to react more quickly and accurately to changing stimuli in their firm or its environment.[382] LEIDNER AND ELAM took a closer look at the impact of executive information systems on decision-making. In their study of 91 users of executive information systems in 22 U.S. companies they found that systems with high information availability contribute to a higher problem identification speed. Easily accessible and timely information seems to help managers in the observation of strategic issues.[383] Four case studies by MOLLOY AND SCHWENK provide further support for the impact of information technology on the observation of strategic issues. Their analyses of eight strategic decisions support the argument that the use of information technology contributes to faster problem identification.[384] Decision makers even considered the use of information technology as critical for the identification activity in five out of the eight strategic decisions. Managers attribute timeliness, quality, and accuracy of data to the use of information technology for the observation of strategic issues.[385]

These three studies suggest that *timely*, *accurate* and *accessible* management accounting information can contribute positively to the observation of strategic issues through focused search. The availability of such management accounting information seems to contribute to faster problem identification in areas covered by the system. However,

---

[380] Vandenbosch and Huff (1997), p. 90.
[381] Vandenbosch and Higgins (1996), pp. 209-210.
[382] Eisenhardt (1989), p. 555. See also Sutcliffe (1994), p. 1364.
[383] Leidner and Elam (1995), p. 656.
[384] Molloy and Schwenk (1995), p. 293. They tested a proposition from Huber (1990), p. 63, but limited their analysis to the identification of problems. Huber's proposition of a better identification of opportunities was not tested.
[385] Molloy and Schwenk (1995), p. 296.

there is also a risk that management accounting systems focus on the wrong areas and that managers neglect other areas not covered by the system.

SMITH, in his study of outcome-related performance indicators in the public sector, uses the term "tunnel vision" to describe concentration on areas included in the performance measurement scheme, to the exclusion of other important areas.[386] In a similar manner, EDENIUS AND HASSELBLADH criticize the Balanced Scorecard as its use tends "to inhibit exploration and creativity, since the inadequacy of man's cognitive capabilities is repeatedly invoked and accepted."[387] They conclude from their case study at a large Scandinavian clothing company that the Balanced Scorecard, with its four perspectives, has the capacity to make things appear to be connected, including what is relevant and excluding the irrelevant with certainty.[388] "A number of key figures are accepted as 'wholeness'."[389] Based on 44 interviews with U.S. manufacturing and service firms, ITTNER AND LARCKER report negative consequences if management accounting systems focus attention on wrong objectives. Their study of quality planning and measurement practices suggests that incorrect performance measures can prevent the identification of the right quality-improvement projects.[390] Furthermore, they observed that inflexible management accounting systems can constrain managers to pre-specified plans and objectives and may keep them from identifying strategic issues.[391]

GILL provides with his case studies of Batterymarch Financial Management and Mrs. Fields Cookies examples how inflexible management accounting systems prevented the identification of strategic issues and led to the decline of these companies. Both companies relied on innovative information technology to automate responses to environmental changes. Initial success with these highly formalized systems reduced unstructured scanning of the environment as managers were preoccupied with achieving efficiency. Based on a review of research on the relationship between information technology and organizational learning, ROBEY ET AL. conclude that "information

---

[386] Smith (1993), pp. 140-141.
[387] Edenius and Hasselbladh (2002), p. 255.
[388] Ibid., p. 258.
[389] Ibid., p. 257.
[390] Ittner and Larcker (1997), p. 309.
[391] Ibid., p. 310.

technology may disable learning by supporting rigid systems that are not adaptable to changing conditions of use."[392]

It seems that *inflexible* and *formalized* systems can prevent the observation of strategic issues. The general management literature on strategic decision processes and information processing provides further support for the negative impact of formalization on managerial observation. In a literature review on the impact of organizational structure on the strategic decision process, FREDRICKSON suggests that rules and procedures dictate how various decision-making activities will be handled. Thus formalized search procedures increase the likelihood that information will be sought from previous sources and will thereby be constrained.[393] MILLER suggests that the more reliance is placed on highly formal, focused information systems, the less broadly targeted, informal scanning will take place.[394] According to ALDRICH AND AUSTER increasing formalization of information acquisition eventually constrains the information that decision makers can take into account. This lack of diversity in environmental perceptions reduces the ability to identify strategic issues.[395] Furthermore, SHANK ET AL. propose that "the accuracy of individual perceptions is negatively related to an organization's degree of formalization."[396]

However, formalization does not only have negative consequences. According to GALBRAITH formalization is a mechanism to increase the information processing capacity of an organization. Formalization makes information transmission more efficient and can help to avoid information overload for the decision makers.[397] Without such formalized systems managers who experience an information overload are likely to switch to an automatic processing mode in which they utilize old routines in order to attend to multiple stimuli simultaneously.[398] The automatic processing mode is not well suited for the identification of new strategic issues, since their ambiguity cannot be easily resolved with existing routines.[399] The reliance on old routines leads to a

[392] Robey et al. (2000), p. 145.
[393] Fredrickson (1986), p. 287. The increased bureaucracy associated with formalization will even reduce the time individuals can spend on other sources. Ittner and Larcker (1997), p. 309.
[394] Miller (1993), p. 133.
[395] Aldrich and Auster (1986), pp. 169-170.
[396] Shank et al. (1988), p. 38.
[397] Galbraith (1974), p. 32.
[398] Dutton (1993), p. 347. See also B3.1 Observation in Strategic Sensemaking, pp. 5.
[399] Ocasio (1997), p. 203.

greater selectivity of information attributes and can filter stimuli indicating new strategic issues.[400]

Overall, the review above suggests that *inflexible* and *highly formalized* management accounting systems can limit attention to areas covered by the system and thereby constrain the observation of strategic issues. In order to avoid a wrong focus of the management accounting systems, it is important to *regularly review* and realign them with current strategic uncertainties.[401]

Research from MILLER indicates that a regular review of the focus of management accounting systems is especially required in successful organizations, because success can discourage information processing within organizations.[402] He observed, in his longitudinal archival study of 36 companies, a greater decline in observation after successful periods than in periods following mediocre performance.[403] According to MILLER management accounting systems focus attention on what is thought to have mattered in the past, and such focused systems can institutionalize and routinize gaps in organizational intelligence. Success can engender overconfidence, which causes companies to allow scanning and control systems to deteriorate.[404]

VANDENBOSCH AND HIGGINS and VANDENBOSCH AND HUFF studied characteristics of information systems that overcome the narrowness of traditional management accounting systems by supporting managers' scanning behavior.[405] According to their research, scanning behavior is encouraged when management accounting systems *integrate data* from different sources, provide *analysis capability* and do not predefine the use of data.[406] Systems with analysis capability, the flexibility to define new reports and new metrics, are the most likely to support scanning, and therefore radical learning.[407] LEIDNER AND ELAM report a similar finding, that management accounting systems with analysis capability allow executives to identify and explore new relationships,

---

400 Dutton (1993), pp. 346-347.
401 See also Smith (1993), p. 141 and Kaplan and Norton (1996), p. 172.
402 Miller (1994), p. 329.
403 Ibid., p. 341.
404 Ibid., p. 330.
405 Vandenbosch and Higgins (1995) and Vandenbosch and Higgins (1996) use the term executive support system, while Vandenbosch and Huff (1997) use the term executive information system. However, the underlying definitions of the systems are the same.
406 Vandenbosch and Huff (1997), p. 93.
407 Vandenbosch and Higgins (1995), p. 124 and Vandenbosch and Higgins (1996), p. 210.

which help them to enhance their mental models.[408] According to VANDENBOSCH AND HIGGINS "providing executives with analysis capability to look at new and unusual information should take precedence over providing more accurate, timely and reliable versions of currently available information."[409]

However, this scanning behavior does not always lead to radical learning. It seems that some management accounting systems filter data and make it easier to absorb them, "because the filtered information fits more easily within preconceived conceptualizations."[410] According to FERRIS AND HASKINS management accounting systems that reduce ambiguity and remove redundancy show increasing traits of "standardisation, clarity, rationality and order."[411] They suggest that the availability of information, and the masking of uncertainty associated with this information, further limit search behavior, and that the most likely result will be routine learning.[412] Thus, *redundant*, *repetitive* or *inconsistent* information may be required for radical learning, as such information might appear as new and unusual during scanning.[413]

Overall, this review on the impact of management accounting systems on the observation of strategic issues suggests a complex relationship. It seems that *timely*, *accurate* and *accessible* management accounting information can contribute positively to the observation of strategic issues through focused search in areas covered by the system. In order to avoid a constraining of the observation of strategic of issues by inflexible and highly formalized management accounting systems with the wrong focus, it is important to *regularly review* the systems and to realign them with current strategic uncertainties. Furthermore, *flexible* management accounting systems that *integrate data* from different sources, and that provide *analysis capabilities,* may contribute to scanning behavior that increases the likelihood of observing strategic issues. It may be necessary for management accounting systems suitable for scanning to provide *redundant*, *repetitive* or *inconsistent* information.

---

408 Leidner and Elam (1995), pp. 660-661.
409 Vandenbosch and Higgins (1995), p. 124.
410 Vandenbosch and Higgins (1996), p. 203.
411 Ferris and Haskins (1988), p. 3.
412 Ibid., p. 3. See also Miller (1993), p. 126.
413 See also Vandenbosch and Higgins (1996), p. 203.

## 1.2 Impact of Management Accounting Systems on Interpretation

As already shown, the categorization of strategic issues, awareness during interpretation and message modification can affect the interpretation step in strategic sensemaking.[414] The following sections will describe how management accounting systems relate to these effects.

### 1.2.1 Categorization of Strategic Issues

Categorization theory posits that individuals form and use concepts to organize their world.[415] DUTTON AND JACKSON apply this general theory to the interpretation of strategic issues by decision makers. They propose that the initial categorization of issues can affect subsequent information processing and organizational decision-making.[416] Managers may withhold information that is incongruent with a superior's classification of an issue, or they may present ambiguous information in a way that fits with the current conception of the issue.[417] Two salient categories for strategic issues in extant literature are "threat" and "opportunity". Three attribute dimensions can differentiate these categories: positive-negative, gain-loss, controllable-uncontrollable.[418] The opportunity category describes a positive situation in which gain is likely, and over which one believes one has a fair amount of control. In contrast, the threat category implies a negative situation in which loss is likely and over which one has relatively little control.[419]

There is some empirical support for the impact of issue categorization on organizational actions. CHATTOPADHYAY ET AL. asked top executives from 117 manufacturing, healthcare and other service organizations to recall events that had triggered important actions within the previous six months.[420] Following categorization of the events, they found that control-reducing threats led to more conservative, internally-directed ac-

---

414 See B3.2 Interpretation in Strategic Sensemaking, pp. 5.
415 Dutton and Jackson (1987), p. 78. See also Dutton et al. (1983) pp. 310-317.
416 Dutton and Jackson (1987), p. 76.
417 Ibid., p. 82.
418 Ibid., p. 80 and Thomas and McDaniel (1990), p. 289.
419 Dutton and Jackson (1987), p. 80. Thomas and McDaniel (1990), p. 299 verified the relevance of these labels, but found that the positive-negative and gain-loss dimensions were operationally indistinguishable and were highly correlated.
420 Chattopadhyay et al. (2001), pp. 944-945.

tions[421] and that likely losses led to riskier externally-directed actions.[422] These findings are consistent with the threat-rigidity hypothesis and prospect theory. The threat-rigidity hypothesis proposes that executives will perceive reduced control and face the risk of a negative outcome when they are confronted with threats.[423] Therefore they may respond to control-reducing threats with risk-averse behavior and initiate internally directed actions, because they associate them with higher levels of control and lower levels of risk. "... threat-rigidity deals with the failure to consider alternative responses that are not well understood, whose outcome is highly ambiguous, and for which a probability distribution is not well-defined."[424] Prospect theory helps to explain why threats with likely losses lead to riskier externally-directed actions. Prospect theory argues that individuals in favorable conditions are risk-averse because they perceive that they have more to lose than to gain. However, individuals in unfavorable circumstances are risk seeking, because they have little to lose.[425] However, "the experimental results of prospect theory deal with the consideration of objectively risky but well-specified alternatives ..."[426] The ambiguity associated with strategic issues prevents the identification of well-specified alternatives. Therefore, it seems that the threat-rigidity hypothesis, with its emphasis on the controllability dimension of strategic issues, is more important for this research.

In a survey of 156 U.S. hospitals THOMAS ET AL. found that the interpretation of strategic issues as controllable had a positive effect on the externally-directed action product-service change. Furthermore, a high level of information use was associated with the interpretation of strategic issues as controllable.[427] According to THOMAS AND MCDANIEL managers in information-processing structures characterized by high formalization and low interaction will perceive only low levels of positive stimuli, because "these structures are designed to guard against threats, not to scan for opportuni-

---

[421] Internally-directed actions are aimed at adapting an organization to the pressures of the environment, e.g. by modifying the organizational structure or setting up an interdepartmental committee. Externally-directed actions are aimed more at modifying the environment, e.g. by developing a market niche or altering regulatory legislation. Externally-directed actions are often seen as less desirable than internally-directed actions, because they are seen as riskier and more difficult to implement and control. Ibid., p. 938.

[422] Ibid., p. 949.

[423] Ibid., p. 939 and Dutton and Jackson (1987), p. 84. See also Staw et al. (1981).

[424] Ocasio (1995), p. 297, cited in Chattopadhyay et al. (2001), p. 939.

[425] Chattopadhyay et al. (2001), p. 939. See also Hogarth (1993), p. 412 and Kahnemann and Tversky (1979).

[426] Ocasio (1995), p. 297, cited in Chattopadhyay et al. (2001), p. 939.

[427] Thomas et al. (1993), pp. 258-259.

ties."[428] THOMAS ET AL. suggest that organizations can increase the likelihood that managers will interpret issues as controllable by increasing interaction and decreasing the use of formalized scanning procedures.[429] The interactive use of management accounting systems increases interaction and therefore could improve the likelihood that managers interpret strategic issues as opportunities.

ASHMOS ET AL. provide further support for the relationship between formalization and categorization of strategic issues. They analyzed strategic issue participation and interpretation with the help of hypothetical decision situations in 55 hospitals and found that more rule-oriented organizations will be more likely to interpret strategic issues as threats, while less rule-oriented organizations tend to see the same issues as opportunities.[430] This is in line with FREDRICKSON's proposition that a higher level of formalization increases the likelihood that the strategic decision process will be initiated only in response to problems or crises that appear in variables monitored by the formal system.[431] He notes that management accounting systems can become so formalized that they drive out creative, proactive behavior and therefore "suggests that a formalized structure has the inherent ability to discourage the pursuit of opportunities."[432]

Overall, it seems possible to assume that management accounting systems with a high level of *formalization* discourage opportunities and increase the likelihood that strategic issues are interpreted as threats. The *interactive use* of management accounting systems can balance this effect by increasing information use, and thereby making the categorization of strategic issues as opportunities more likely.

### 1.2.2 Awareness during Strategic Issue Interpretation

The success of the interpretation of strategic issues depends to a great degree on managers' awareness and vigilance in questioning underlying assumptions and initiating further search for new data if required.[433] KUVAAS took a closer look at two theoretical perspectives of how information availability can affect strategic issue interpretation:

---

[428] Thomas and McDaniel (1990), p. 291.
[429] Thomas et al. (1993), p. 258.
[430] Ashmos et al. (1998), p. 43.
[431] Fredrickson (1986), p. 284.
[432] Ibid., p. 287. Smith (1993), p. 146 also notes that, "an excessively rigid performance measurement scheme can stifle innovation and suppress potentially healthy experimentation."
[433] See B3.2 Interpretation in Strategic Sensemaking, pp. 5.

the systems-structural perspective and the interpretive perspective.[434] The systems-structural perspective suggests that high information availability provides managers with the basis for interpretation and helps them "to realize the limitations of their organization's ability to control and manage ill-structured strategic issues."[435] This should decrease their perceived level of control over strategic issues and should encourage data search to improve their interpretation. However, in a survey of 162 top management team members in 73 Norwegian newspaper firms, KUVAAS did not find support for his hypothesis that the level of organizational information availability will be negatively related to top managers' control and manageability perceptions[436] and positively related to data search. Instead he found that information availability is positively related to controllability perceptions of strategic issues.[437] This provides some support for the interpretive perspective from behavioral decision making and social cognition, as this perspective argues "that information availability may increase managers' perception of control ... simply by their knowing that information is available or that information acquisition is being taken care of and institutionalized."[438] KUVAAS proposes that, "accurate interpretations may result from lower levels of perceived control ... and high levels of data search."[439]

In an archival study of 785 French manufacturing firms in 35 industries DURAND shows that higher levels of perceived control are associated with a positive forecast bias. However, organizational attention to external information reduces positive forecast biases and the magnitude of errors.[440] Therefore, management accounting systems that focus on external information may contribute positively to the interpretation of strategic issues.

In a literature review DENT notes that the impact of management accounting systems on strategic change depends very much on its design. "Information systems have the potential to filter away inconsistency, create a sense of security and engender faith.

---

434 See B2.5.2.1 Systems-Structural Perspective, pp. 5 and B2.5.2.2 Interpretive Perspective, pp. 5.

435 Kuvaas (2002), p. 981.

436 Controllability measures managers' perceptions of how difficult it is to control (capitalize on) a threat (opportunity) and whether they have the capability to do so. Manageability measures perceptions about sufficient knowledge and resources to understand and manage problems. Ibid., p. 994.

437 Ibid., p. 987. He did not find significant relationships between information availability and manageability perceptions or data search.

438 Ibid., p. 981.

439 Ibid., p. 990. See also Weick (1995). Kuvaas (2002), p. 988 found a negative association between controllability perceptions of threats and new data search.

440 Durand (2003), p. 833.

Such systems typically focus on small data sets, are integrated and have minimal redundancy."[441] Consistency in information sources can lead to increased confidence in judgments, but not to increased prediction accuracy.[442] "Alternatively, they [information systems] have the potential to create ambiguity and foster a sense of insecurity. Such systems typically embody competing data sets, are less integrated, and exhibit extensive redundancy."[443] According to DENT management accounting systems can promote a sense of clarity and comfort when they formalize isolated tasks and responsibilities. But when management accounting systems are used to challenge planning assumptions, and tasks and responsibilities are assigned to create tensions, they have the ability to increase awareness and experimentation.[444]

Overall, it seems that management accounting systems can increase awareness during issue interpretation, when they focus on *external data*, present *different perspectives*, *emphasize dependencies*, and allow *inconsistent/redundant data*. Otherwise, management accounting systems are likely to contribute to an informational context that has a comforting or confidence enhancing, rather than awareness increasing, effect on strategic issue interpretation.[445]

### 1.2.3 Short-term Orientation and Strategic Information Manipulation

The accounting literature provides evidence that management accounting systems can have a negative impact on strategic issue interpretation through the encouragement of a short-term orientation and strategic information manipulation.[446]

"Time is one of the most fundamental considerations in management decision-making and in organizations."[447] Organizations have to balance concerns for long-term positioning, growth and change with concerns for short-term performance, profitability and survival.[448] An excessive short-term orientation can increase the likelihood that manag-

[441] Dent (1990), pp. 18-19.
[442] See Hogarth and Makridakis (1981), p. 119 for a review of cognitive biases in forecasting and planning.
[443] Dent (1990), p. 19.
[444] Ibid., p. 19.
[445] Kuvaas (2002), p. 992.
[446] See Merchant (1990).
[447] Laverty (2004), p. 949.
[448] See Ibid., p. 949, Laverty (1996), p. 825 and Hoskisson et al. (1991), p. 307.

ers undervalue the long term.[449] This would have implications for the interpretation of strategic issues with long-term consequences.

In a study of 85 managers, LAVERTY found that management accounting systems can create temporal traps which contribute to an undervaluing of long-term consequences.[450] Temporal traps are situations in which the choice that is best for the long term is different from the choice that is best for the short term.[451] LAVERTY gives an example of a firm whose managers are required to constantly report on progress toward long-term strategic objectives while being judged on quarterly performance. This regularly reminds them of tradeoffs and can create temporal traps.[452] Furthermore, managers may decide against long-term opportunities if the required actions incur costs immediately, while the benefits are uncertain.[453] In order to reduce temporal traps, LAVERTY suggests a reduction in the reporting frequency of some financial items and the use of short-term indicators for developmental, instead of evaluative, purposes. This would still provide sufficient feedback on progress, but reduce the short-term focus.

VAN DER STEDE took a closer look at the impact of a rigid budgetary control style on managerial short-term orientation. His study of 153 Belgian business unit managers suggests an indirect relationship between rigid budgetary controls and short-term orientation through budget slack.[454] A general definition of organizational slack describes it "as the pool of resources in an organization that is in excess of the minimum necessary to produce a given level of organizational output."[455] The findings suggest that rigid controls reduce slack and make short-term budget more difficult to achieve.[456]

---

449 See Van der Stede (2000), pp. 609-610 and Hoskisson et al. (1991), p. 306.

450 Laverty (2004), p. 958.

451 Ibid., p. 951.

452 Ibid., p. 958.

453 See Anthony and Govindarajan (2000), p. 442, Smith (1993), p. 143 and Merchant (1990), p. 308. In addition, Merchant found that control systems do not discourage investments with a promising short-term payoff and therefore concluded that they support a short-term focus.

454 Van der Stede (2000), pp. 618-619.

455 Nohria and Gulati (1996), p. 1246. However, there is no generally accepted definition of slack. Because of conceptual and empirical difficulties with defining and measuring slack, some researchers limit their focus to budgetary slack. "A budget contains slack if the business unit managers have intentionally set their budget targets lower than their best guess forecast about the future so that the budget becomes easier to achieve." Van der Stede (2000), p. 615.

456 According to Lal et al. (1996), p. 490 the propensity to create budgetary slack can be positively related to the importance placed on meeting budget targets. It may be that the amount of budget slack is already so low that managers try to create budget slack during budgeting in order to make the targets more easily achievable. This seems to be a counter-reaction when budgetary control is too

This drives managers to become primarily concerned about short-term actions and deemphasizes the importance of long-term issues.[457]

In order to reduce dysfunctional behavior associated with an excessive short-term orientation it might be necessary to move to an evaluative style with a focus on flexible and long run targets. MERCHANT describes such an approach, where an organization changed from an evaluation based on very visible, quantitative performance measures with a strong focus on financial measures to a largely subjective evaluation of performance. However, he does not report results of this change.[458] Related to the use of management accounting information for evaluation are incentive schemes. COATES ET AL. found that incentive schemes can reinforce, narrow, modify or broaden the focus of performance measures. German multinational companies in particular tend to use incentives, like management by objectives-based incentive schemes, more than U.K. or U.S. multinationals to broaden the focus of performance indicators in order to balance the effect of short-term measures.[459]

Besides their impact on managerial short-term orientation, management accounting systems can also cause job-related tension that contributes to dysfunctional behavior.[460] "A subordinate's behavior is dysfunctional if he knowingly violates established control system rules and procedures."[461] JAWORSKI AND YOUNG summarize extant literature on dysfunctional behavior under the headings "gaming performance indicators" and "strategic information manipulation".

"Gaming performance indicators" are the behaviors that result from subordinates choosing actions to maximize their personal outcome, regardless of whether these actions jeopardize the company's long-term health. This happens when performance is measured only on a limited number of the subordinates' tasks, or on the wrong tasks.[462] Similarly to the observation step, it seems possible that a regular review of the focus of the management accounting system can reduce such behavior.

---

rigid and strongly linked to rewards, and does not rule out the possibility that short-term actions are still the main focus of managers' attention.

457 Van der Stede (2000), p. 617.

458 Merchant (1990), p. 310.

459 Coates et al. (1995), pp. 128-132.

460 Jaworski and Young (1992), p. 17 and p. 31.

461 Ibid., p. 18.

462 Ibid., pp. 18-19.

"Strategic information manipulation occurs when subordinates alter the natural flow of information, report only those aspects of an information set that is in their best interest, or in the extreme, falsify data and company records."[463] This behavior bypasses the causes of this information, and therefore complicates the interpretation of strategic issues. "Strategic information manipulation" can occur through smoothing, filtering or falsification of information. Firstly, *smoothing* happens "when a subordinate utilizes the information system to his benefit by altering the natural or preplanned flow of data without altering the actual activities of the organization."[464] MERCHANT found that managers under target pressure, and operating in high uncertainty environments, were more likely to transfer profits from the next period into the current period by deferring a needed expenditure.[465] Secondly, *filtering* of information occurs, when subordinates report only information that favorably reflects upon themselves, and withhold potentially threatening information.[466] MERCHANT describes a top management team that has become more willing to accept revised operating plans when the environment changes, in order to reduce managers' manipulative behavior.[467] It seems that in cases where the change of targets or plans is not discussible, managers are more likely to report favorable information and disguise potential issues as long as possible. Finally, the *falsification* of information, as a fraudulent act, is an extreme form of strategic information manipulation and involves the alteration of existing information.[468]

In a study of 348 marketing executives JAWORSKI AND YOUNG found that increased goal congruence, the adoption of values, goals and objectives of the organization as one's own goals, reduces dysfunctional behavior of subordinates through a decrease in person-role conflict and job-related tension.[469] As a specific management accounting system, KAPLAN AND NORTON propose that the Balanced Scorecard can be used to communicate and share the organization's vision and strategy. They suggest that the use of the Balanced Scorecard for target setting can help to increase goal congruence.[470] Job-related tension, as an antecedent to dysfunctional behavior, is also affected

---

[463] Ibid., p. 19.
[464] Ibid., pp. 19-20.
[465] Merchant (1990), p. 306. See also Anthony and Govindarajan (2000), p. 443.
[466] Jaworski and Young (1992), p. 20.
[467] Merchant (1990), p. 310.
[468] Jaworski and Young (1992), p. 20.
[469] Ibid., p. 31.
[470] See Kaplan and Norton (1996), p. 80 and Kaplan and Norton (2001), p. 5.

by the supervisory style of managers.[471] HOPWOOD's study of 167 managers in a North American manufacturing company suggests that a supervisory style with a rigid, short-term emphasis on budgetary information contributes to increased levels of job-related tension and dysfunctional behavior. This could be related to the fact that budgetary information captures only part of the information necessary to make an overall assessment of managerial performance.[472] In contrast, an evaluative style with a more flexible, longer-term use of budgetary information results in significantly less tension and dysfunctional behavior.[473]

Overall, it seems that *inflexible* management accounting systems with a focus on short-term performance measures are more likely to create a short-term focus and cause strategic information manipulation. Dysfunctional behavior may be reduced if financial items are reported *less frequently,* the performance evaluation is based on a *flexible* and long run use of targets and the focus of the management accounting system is *regularly reviewed.*

## 1.3 Impact of Management Accounting Systems on Communication

Communication is an essential part of strategic sensemaking, as the reduction of equivocality from strategic issues requires different points of view and the sharing of interpretations from different organizational members. The impact of management accounting systems on communication depends on their diagnostic or interactive use.

According to SIMONS, diagnostic management accounting systems are designed to conserve organizational attention so that action is only needed when critical performance targets are in danger.[474] Deviations are usually reported through highly codified exception reports with low media richness.[475] SUTCLIFFE notes that formal systems can constrain opportunities for interaction and communication between organizational members. Therefore, executives in organizations relying on formalized strategic planning or information systems are less likely to be aware of strategic issues than managers in organizations without such systems.[476] However, informal communication does

---

[471] Briers and Hirst (1990) (1990), p. 385.
[472] Otley and Fakiolas (2000), p. 500.
[473] Hopwood (1972), p. 175.
[474] Simons (1995), p. 70.
[475] Ibid., pp. 190-191.
[476] Sutcliffe (2001), p. 209 and p. 211.

not necessarily contribute to improved performance. In a survey of 230 top management team members in 53 high-tech and technology-intensive firms SMITH ET AL. found a negative association between informal communication and company performance. They suggest that there is a threshold level of formal communication needed to create opportunities for interaction and information sharing.[477]

Contrary to the diagnostic use, executives use interactive management accounting systems to increase interaction between organizational members and to foster discussions of information related to strategic uncertainties. Interactive management accounting systems serve "primarily as a catalyst to promote face-to-face dialogue and debate about the meaning of information and appropriate action plans."[478] Communication channels of high media richness are especially suited to transmit highly complex and/or tacit knowledge. Furthermore, they can support extensive problem solving as suggested by VICKERY ET AL.'s research on 113 customers of integrated logistical services providers in the U.S.[479] According to SIMONS, advances in information technology can potentially improve the interactive use of management accounting systems in three ways. Firstly, information systems have the capacity to transform and present complex data visually, which makes it easier to comprehend. Secondly, information technology allows the dissemination of relevant information more rapidly, or even in real-time, which contributes to a timely discussion of important information. Finally, advances in database management allow managers to do some analysis and support the re-forecasting of data and market dynamics.[480] These advances provide better data about strategic uncertainties, but the equivocality associated with strategic issues still requires face-to-face discussions of different perspectives. SIMONS suggests that particularly semi-coded information, which allows different interpretations but still remains simple to avoid discussions about calculations and transformations, is best suited to encouraging communication between managers.[481]

Overall, *very formalized* management accounting systems that contain *highly codified* information, and are used diagnostically with media of *low richness* are likely to constrain opportunities for interaction and communication. Interactive management accounting systems that transmit *simple* and *semi-coded* information for discussion in

[477] Smith et al. (1994), pp. 431-433.
[478] Simons (1995), p. 193.
[479] Vickery et al. (2004), p. 1118.
[480] Simons (1995), pp. 193-194.
[481] Ibid., p. 194.

channels with *high media richness* seem to improve communication and interaction in strategic sensemaking.

## 2. Management Accounting System Dimensions and Strategic Sensemaking

The literature review on the impact of management accounting systems on strategic sensemaking processes yields a set of tentative management accounting system characteristics that seems to have a positive or negative contribution (see Table 4 below).

| Strategic Sensemaking Process | | Management Accounting System Characteristics With … Positive Impact (Tentatively) | Negative Impact (Tentatively) |
|---|---|---|---|
| Observation | Focused search | Timeliness, accuracy, accessibility, regular review of focus | Inflexibility, high level of formalization |
| | Scanning | Flexibility, high level of data source integration, analysis capability, redundancy, inconsistency | No redundancy, no inconsistency |
| Interpretation | Categorization | – | High level of formalization |
| | Awareness | Focus on external data, different perspectives, emphasis on dependencies, inconsistency, redundancy | Focus on internal data, no inconsistency, no redundancy |
| | No short-term orientation and manipulation | Reduced financial reporting frequency, flexible evaluation, regular review of focus | Inflexibility, high financial reporting frequency |
| Communication | | High media richness, low level of formalization, semi-codification, simplicity | Low media richness, high level of formalization, high level of codification |

*Table 4: Tentative, theoretical impact of MAS characteristics on strategic sensemaking processes*

Previous management accounting research has focused mostly on a generic set of management accounting information characteristics or specific elements of management accounting systems. A frequently used set of information characteristics developed by CHENHALL AND MORRIS includes scope, timeliness, integration and aggregation of management accounting information.[482] Table 4 above suggests that most of these characteristics are also relevant for strategic sensemaking, but there are other important management accounting system characteristics that are more related to the production and delivery of management accounting information.

[482] Chenhall and Morris (1986), p. 17.

Information systems research has recognized that not only information characteristics, but also characteristics related to the production of information have an impact on the use and effectiveness of information systems. This research is relevant for this study because management accounting systems are formal systems that provide information to managers, and information systems are an integral part of this. Following a call from SHIELDS for more integrative research,[483] this study transfers results from information systems research to cluster the derived management accounting system characteristics into a comprehensive, but nevertheless parsimonious, set of management accounting system dimensions.

## 2.1 Quality Dimensions in Information Systems Research

Information systems research has dealt for a long time with the identification of factors that contribute to information systems success. However, as the concept of information system success is not clearly defined, researchers have developed many different measures, and this has prevented the building of a cumulative body of research. DELONE AND MCLEAN suggest that this could be related to the fact that information can be measured at the technical level, the semantic level and the effectiveness level. SHANNON AND WEAVER define the technical level as characteristics of the system that produces the information, the semantic level as the success of the information in conveying the intended meaning, and the effectiveness level as the effect of the information on the receiver.[484] In a review of 180 articles DELONE AND MCLEAN suggest a taxonomy of six aspects of information systems at these three levels. System quality, with its focus on the production of information, is related to the technical level; information quality as the product of an information system corresponds with the semantic level; and the effectiveness level can be measured by the categories use, user satisfaction, individual impact and organizational impact.[485]

The DELONE AND MCLEAN information systems success model suggests that information and system quality are antecedents to use and user satisfaction, which in turn lead to individual impact on users' work and collectively result in organizational impact.[486] In a study with 274 university users of an information system RAI ET AL. provide evi-

483 Shields (1997), pp. 28-29.
484 DeLone and McLean (1992), p. 61. See also Shannon and Weaver (1949).
485 DeLone and McLean (1992), p. 62.
486 DeLone and McLean (2003), p. 11.

dence for all of these relationships.[487] KHALIL finds a strong relationship between information quality and information system use in his study of 216 executive information system users in U.K. based organizations.[488] Furthermore, DELONE AND MCLEAN reviewed 16 studies that empirically validated individual or multiple relationships. Overall, this provides strong support for the information system success model.[489]

WANG AND STRONG took a closer look at information quality in order to understand dimensions of information quality that are important to information system users.[490] They conducted a two-stage survey and a two-phase sorting study to develop categories for organizing information quality dimensions.[491] According to this study *intrinsic information quality* considers properties of information largely in isolation from a specific user, task, or application. *Contextual information quality* highlights the requirement that information quality must be defined relative to the user, task, or application. Finally, *representational information quality* reflects the degree to which information presentation effectively facilitates interpretation and understanding.[492]

Based on the research of DELONE AND MCLEAN and WANG AND STRONG, NELSON ET AL. developed a set of information quality and system quality dimensions. In order to create a "good" set of information system dimensions they used four guidelines: the proposed dimensions should be complete, be relatively parsimonious, enhance under-

---

487 Rai et al. (2002), p. 61.

488 Khalil (2005), p. 84.

489 DeLone and McLean (2003), pp. 13-15. References from 300 articles in refereed journals provide evidence for the usefulness of this framework to integrate information systems research findings. The popularity of this framework led the authors to review and update their information systems success model. In order to reflect the increased importance of the IS function, and to measure the overall success of the IS department, they suggest that service quality should be added as a separate quality dimension. Furthermore, in order to reduce model complexity they combined all impact measures under the heading of net benefits. This research does not require the service quality dimension, because it does not intend to measure the success of the information systems department. Furthermore, this research will measure net benefits not directly but through the impact of management accounting system dimensions on cognitive processes in strategic sensemaking.

490 Wang and Strong (1996) use the term data instead of information. This research will continue to use the term information to describe data that has been processed by the information system (see B4.1.2 Definition of Management Accounting Information, pp. 5).

491 The first survey of 25 data consumers in the industry and 112 M.B.A. students at a large U.S. university elicited 179 attributes of information quality. A second survey of 355 alumni from this university provided ratings of the importance of the 179 attributes and allowed a grouping into 20 dimensions through an exploratory factor analysis. A two-phase sorting study with 30 subjects from industry helped to group these 20 dimensions into 4 categories.

492 Wang and Strong (1996), pp. 20-20. See also Strong et al. (1997), p. 104. Another category is accessibility, but along with Nelson et al. (2005) this research will associate this category with system quality as it describes the user's interaction with the system.

standing and be actionable.[493] Based on a survey of 465 data warehouse users NELSON ET AL. suggest four information quality and five system quality dimensions. *Scope*, *timeliness*, *format* and *accuracy* are suitable to measure information quality as the output of an information processing system.[494] Accuracy represents the intrinsic category of information quality, scope and timeliness the contextual category and format the representational category, as suggested by WANG AND STRONG. System quality reflects the information processing system required to produce the output measured by information quality. NELSON ET AL. found that *integration*, *flexibility*, *accessibility*, *response time* and *reliability* represent user perceptions of interaction with the data warehouse system over time.[495]

The comparison of these dimensions with the derived characteristics of how management accounting systems can affect strategic sensemaking shows that the system quality dimensions response time and reliability are specific to the data warehouse context.[496] *Response time* measures the degree to which a system offers quick or timely responses to requests for information. NELSON ET AL. show that response time has, in most cases, an insignificant impact on perceived system quality by data warehouse users.[497] Furthermore, response time is not meaningful for management accounting systems other than information systems, as hard-copy reports do not have a response time. Response time could also mean the timely provision of management accounting information, but this aspect is already covered by the information quality dimension timeliness. *Reliability* measures the degree to which a system is dependable, e.g., technically available over time. NELSON ET AL. show that the reliability of a data warehouse system is the most influential determinant of system quality perceptions.[498] However, reliability is not meaningful for hard-copy reports and the processes associated with the preparation of these reports. This research assumes that managers will replace an unreliable information system with other information sources, which makes this dimension less important to describe the impact of general management account-

493 Nelson et al. (2005), p. 202.

494 Ibid., pp. 202-204. The authors use the terms completeness and currency instead of scope and timeliness. However, scope and timeliness are related to the role of management accounting systems in strategic sensemaking and are already established terms in management accounting research, which justifies the renaming.

495 Ibid., pp. 205-207.

496 See Table 4, p. 5.

497 Nelson et al. (2005), p. 216.

498 Ibid., p. 218.

ing systems on strategic sensemaking. In addition, the literature review did not yield characteristics related to response time and reliability.[499] Therefore, this research will exclude the system quality dimensions response time and reliability.

However, the literature review on the impact of management accounting systems on observation, interpretation and communication processes of managers suggests two additional system quality dimensions: *formalization* and *media richness*. Formalization and media richness describe rules and channels for how organizational members interact with each other. They are less relevant for interactions between data warehouse users and their system and therefore were not considered by NELSON ET AL. However, because of their importance for strategic sensemaking, this research needs to incorporate formalization and media richness.

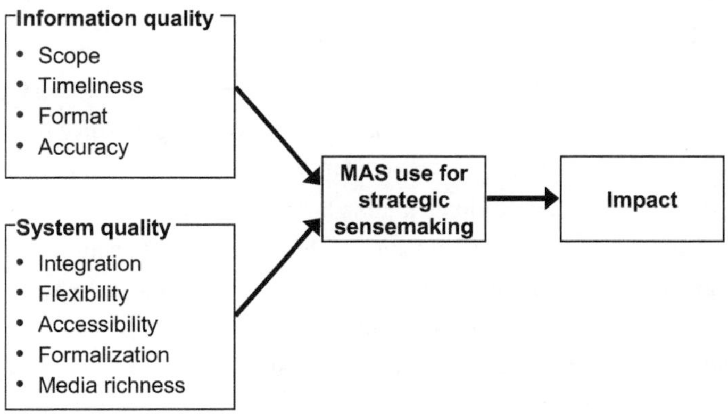


*Figure 8: Information and system quality as antecedents to MAS use*[500]

Figure 8 above summarizes the identified information quality and system quality dimensions as antecedents to system use and individual impact. The following sections describe the four information quality dimensions (scope, timeliness, format, accuracy) and the five system quality dimensions (integration, flexibility, accessibility, formalization and media richness) in more detail.[501] Furthermore, the findings from the litera-

[499] See Table 4, p. 5.

[500] Adapted from DeLone and McLean (1992), p. 87, DeLone and McLean (2003), p. 24 and Nelson et al. (2005), p. 208.

[501] See C2.2 Information Quality of Management Accounting Systems, pp. 5 and C2.3 System Quality of Management Accounting Systems, pp. 5.

ture review[502] will be used to develop tentative propositions how information quality and system quality dimensions have an impact on strategic sensemaking of individual managers.

## 2.2 Information Quality of Management Accounting Systems

### 2.2.1 Scope

The scope dimension, originally named completeness by NELSON ET AL., measures "the degree to which all possible states relevant to the user population are represented in the stored information."[503] Completeness belongs to the contextual category of information quality dimensions, and therefore needs to be defined relative to the task. Management accounting research has identified the scope dimension of management accounting information as relevant for strategic sensemaking.

In a study of 68 managers from Australian manufacturing organizations, CHENHALL AND MORRIS found that managers operating in uncertain environments perceive broad scope management accounting information as useful.[504] The scope dimension consists of the sub-dimensions focus, quantification and time horizon.[505] It can be viewed as a continuum ranging from narrow scope information to broad scope information. Narrow scope information is linked with traditional management accounting systems providing internally focused, financial, and historically based information. Broad scope information includes also externally focused, non-financial, and future-orientated information.[506] Broad scope management accounting information supposedly helps to focus on the sources of uncertainty and therefore increases the likelihood of identifying strategic issues.[507]

Other researchers have validated CHENHALL AND MORRIS' findings in different contexts. MIA AND CHENHALL conducted a study with 29 marketing and 46 production managers in five manufacturing companies and found that a higher usage of broad

[502] See C1 Impact of Management Accounting Systems on Strategic Sensemaking, pp. 5.
[503] Nelson et al. (2005), p. 204.
[504] Chenhall and Morris (1986), p. 30.
[505] Ibid., p. 19. In a study of 34 managers from U.S. companies, Gordon (1984), p. 40 show that external, non-financial, and future oriented management accounting information are strongly related to each other.
[506] Bouwens and Abernethy (2000), p. 223. See also Chenhall and Morris (1986), p. 20.
[507] Chenhall and Morris (1986), p. 20.

scope management accounting information was associated with enhanced performance for marketing activities but not for production activities.[508] It seems that broad scope information helps marketing managers in their boundary spanning activities to monitor and survey the external environment. Such information may help in understanding the complexity of markets, the nature of uncertainties and the potential impact of alternative decisions.[509] MIA shows that a higher level of perceived environmental uncertainty by managers leads to a higher level of management accounting information use, which contributes to improvements in their performance.[510] CHONG conducted a similar survey with 42 Australian manufacturing companies and found that managerial performance was high when managers used broad scope management accounting information under high task uncertainty situations. In addition, managerial performance was low when managers under low task uncertainty situations used broad scope information. CHONG suggests that managers might have suffered from an information overload, which had a negative effect on decisions and adversely affected performance.[511] GUL AND CHIA took a closer look at the relationship between perceived environmental uncertainty, decentralization and managerial performance. Their study of 48 Singaporean managers suggests that, under high levels of perceived environmental uncertainty in decentralized organizations, the use of broad scope management accounting information contributes to higher individual performance. Decentralization seems to increase information demands, as more managers are involved in making decisions. A management accounting system that satisfies this increased demand seems to enhance the decisions of managers, hence contributing to higher performance.[512]

However, research from BOUWENS AND ABERNETHY suggests that broad scope management accounting information is not suitable for all types of decisions. In a study of 170 production and sales managers in 85 business units of Dutch companies BOUWENS AND ABERNETHY focused on the impact of customization and interdependence on the use of management accounting information for operational decision making. They found that broad scope information is not important for operational decision-making.[513] Instead, research from ITTNER ET AL. suggests that broad scope information could be

---

[508] Mia and Chenhall (1994), p. 10.
[509] Ibid., pp. 3-4.
[510] Mia (1993), p. 281.
[511] Chong (1996), pp. 419-420.
[512] Gul and Chia (1994), p. 423. See also Chia (1995), p. 826.
[513] Bouwens and Abernethy (2000), p. 234.

important for strategic sensemaking. They conducted a survey with 140 U.S. financial services firms and found that companies that make more extensive use of broad scope performance measures than other firms with similar strategies or value drivers earn higher stock returns. In contrast, they did not find a significant relationship with short-term accounting measures.[514] It seems that managers use broad scope information for strategic decision making which has a long term impact captured by stock returns and not by accounting measures. The research results from BOUWENS AND ABERNETHY and ITTNER ET AL. suggest that broad scope management accounting information is particularly important for strategic decision making. Unfortunately, the research from CHENHALL AND MORRIS, MIA AND CHENHALL, GUL AND CHIA and CHONG did not explicitly specify the type of information use for decision-making. However, VAIVIO's case study of a British chemicals company provides some evidence for the strategic importance of broad scope information. Non-financial measurements helped to focus top management attention on areas with strategic relevance. It appears that non-financial measures became a vehicle of focused interactive control and helped to maintain a structured dialogue between top management and the organization.[515]

Overall it seems that broad scope management accounting information helps managers to observe and discuss strategic issues. Combined with DURAND's findings that external information may contribute positively to the interpretation of strategic issues, it seems likely that *broad scope* management accounting information will contribute *positively* to *observation*, *interpretation* and *communication* in strategic sensemaking.

### 2.2.2 Timeliness

The timeliness dimension of management accounting information, originally named currency by NELSON ET AL., measures "the degree to which information is up-to-date, or the degree to which the information precisely reflects the current state of the world that is represents".[516] Similar to the completeness dimension, currency belongs to the contextual category of information quality dimensions, which requires a definition relative to the respective task. This research will use the term timeliness, because its definition is similar to the currency definition by NELSON ET AL. and timeliness is already established in management accounting research. Management accounting infor-

[514] Ittner et al. (2003), p. 738.
[515] Vaivio (1999), p. 430.
[516] Nelson et al. (2005), p. 204.

mation is considered timely when information is provided frequently (i.e. on a daily or weekly basis) and when there is little delay between the point when an event occurs and the time when information concerning this event is provided to managers.[517]

CHENHALL AND MORRIS find that managers need to respond rapidly to environmental changes in uncertain situations, and therefore perceive timely information to be useful.[518] Furthermore, BOUWENS AND ABERNETHY show that customization and interdependence increase the importance of timely management accounting information for operational decision making.[519] The similarity of these findings with the scope dimension suggests that timely information could also be useful for strategic sensemaking.

In addition, the literature review on management accounting systems and strategic sensemaking processes provides evidence for the impact of timely management accounting information on observation and interpretation of strategic issues. EISENHARDT suggests that timely, or even real-time, information increases the speed of issue identification.[520] However, over-frequent reporting of financial items can lead to managers' short-term orientation,[521] which might have a negative impact on the interpretation of long-term strategic issues.

Overall this suggests that *timely* management accounting information can have a *positive* impact on *observation* and *interpretation* of strategic issues.

### 2.2.3 Format

Format measures "the degree to which information is represented in a manner that is understandable and interpretable to the user and thus aids in the completion of a task."[522] It belongs to the representational category of information quality dimensions. Since strategic issues are open to multiple interpretations, the format of management accounting information should encourage debate about its meaning. According to

---

517 Bouwens and Abernethy (2000), p. 224.
518 Chenhall and Morris (1986), p. 27.
519 Bouwens and Abernethy (2000), p. 233. Bouwens and Abernethy (2000) found a difference between sales and production managers concerning the impact of interdependence on the importance of timely information for operational decision-making. It seems that interdependence increases the importance of timely information for production managers, but not for sales managers. Bouwens and Abernethy (2000) do not provide an explanation for this difference.
520 Eisenhardt (1989), p. 555.
521 Laverty (2004), p. 958.
522 Nelson et al. (2005), p. 204.

SIMONS this is best achieved by semi-coded and simple information. Semi-coded information can contain graphical representations of complex data and qualitative comments or explanations. In addition, the information needs to remain simple, to encourage debate about the meaning and not about the performed transformations and calculations.[523]

Empirical research on the impact of semi-coded information on communication is scarce. In a study of 97 Danish and U.S. companies SCHULZ found that codification increases horizontal and vertical information flows. Vertical information flows transport knowledge from management to lower levels and from lower levels upwards, and thereby expose new knowledge to remote and different knowledge. "Such exposure reveals risks, threats, and opportunities that may arise when different kinds of knowledge are combined."[524]

This suggests that a management accounting information *format* with semi-coded and simple information can *improve communications* that help to develop a shared *interpretation* of strategic issues.

### 2.2.4 Accuracy

NELSON ET AL. define accuracy as "the degree to which information is correct, unambiguous, meaningful, believable and consistent."[525] The literature review provides mixed results concerning the impact of accuracy on observation of strategic issues.[526] The studies from EISENHARDT, LEIDNER AND ELAM and MOLLOY AND SCHWENK suggest that accurate management accounting information contributes to observation through focused search in areas covered by the management accounting system. However, FERRIS AND HASKINS suggest that management accounting systems with accurate information can mask uncertainty associated with the information and thus limit search behavior. It seems that managers who scan inaccurate management accounting information are more likely to identify strategic issues.

Concerning the impact of accuracy on interpretation of strategic issues, DENT suggests that consistency in information sources can lead to increased confidence in judgments,

---

[523] Simons (1995), pp. 193-194.
[524] Schulz (2001), pp. 674-675.
[525] Nelson et al. (2005), p. 204.
[526] See C1.1 Impact of Management Accounting Systems on Observation, pp. 5.

but not to increased prediction accuracy.[527] However, management accounting systems with competing data sets can create ambiguity and foster a sense of insecurity, which can increase awareness during issue interpretation.

Overall, a high level of information accuracy could contribute to observation through focused search in areas covered by the management accounting system. However, a low level of information accuracy seems to contribute to observation through scanning and can help to increase awareness during issue interpretation. Scanning is particularly important for the observation of new strategic issues. Therefore, this provides weak support for a *negative* impact of information *accuracy* on *observation* and *interpretation* of strategic issues.

## 2.3 System Quality of Management Accounting Systems

### 2.3.1 Integration

Integration measures "the degree to which a system facilitates the combination of information from various sources to support business decisions.[528] Management accounting systems can facilitate the integration of information from different functional areas, which is often complementary. According to VANDENBOSCH AND HUFF management accounting systems that integrate data from different sources encourage scanning behavior.[529] This increases the probability of observing new strategic issues. A longitudinal archival study of eight U.S. telecommunications companies by WILLIAMS AND MITCHELL provides further support for the impact of information infrastructure on strategic sensemaking. They studied how career paths of executives create information links between business units, and thereby affect market entry. The study shows that links between units can help to create an information-rich environment where the many perspectives available to managers enable innovation.[530] Information about different aspects of markets increases the probability of a firm entering a market.[531] Although WILLIAMS AND MITCHELL's empirical approach allowed them to investigate only informal networks as an indicator for the firm's information infrastructure, it

[527] See C1.2.2 Awareness during Strategic Issue Interpretation, pp. 5.
[528] Nelson et al. (2005), p. 206.
[529] Vandenbosch and Huff (1997), p. 93.
[530] Williams and Mitchell (2004), p. 1572.
[531] Ibid., p. 1571.

seems plausible to assume that integrated management accounting systems can contribute in a similar manner.

Another aspect of integrated management accounting systems is the integration between goals, strategies and operations. In a survey of 80 industrial organizations from Australia, CHENHALL found that strategic performance measurement systems with strategic and operational linkages increase the flexibility to adapt to market changes and support organizational learning.[532] Integrative strategic performance measurement systems, such as the Balanced Scorecard, can increase the strategic competitiveness of organizations "if they focus on how goals, strategies and operations are connected, and attempt to provide understanding of the interdependencies across the value chain."[533] This suggests that management accounting information from integrated management accounting systems can become a language for organizational members to discuss the impact of overarching strategic issues, and therefore can improve communication in strategic sensemaking. In addition, integrated management accounting systems can provide a shared framework to communicate the organization's strategy and vision[534] This can lead to increased goal congruence, which in turn can reduce dysfunctional behavior and thereby contribute to strategic issues interpretation.[535]

Overall, it seems that *integrated* management accounting systems can contribute *positively* to *observation*, *interpretation* and *communication* in strategic sensemaking.

### 2.3.2 Flexibility

Flexibility measures "the degree to which a system can adapt to a variety of user needs and to changing conditions."[536] Management accounting systems can limit the attention of managers to areas covered by the system. Therefore, it is important to regularly review the focus of the systems.[537] A study by BAINES AND LANGFIELD-SMITH of 141 Australian manufacturing firms suggests that changes in the competitive environment drive organizational changes, which in turn influence the reliance of managers on non-financial information. Finally, an increased reliance on non-financial measurements

[532] Chenhall (2005), p. 412.
[533] Ibid., p. 414.
[534] Kaplan and Norton (1996), p. 252. See also Chenhall (2005), p. 415.
[535] Jaworski and Young (1992), p. 31.
[536] Nelson et al. (2005), p. 206.
[537] Smith (1993), p. 141 and Kaplan and Norton (1996), p. 172. See also C1.1 Impact of Management Accounting Systems on Observation, pp. 5.

contributes to organizational performance.[538] This provides some evidence for the importance of a regular adaptation of management accounting systems to environmental changes.

According to VANDENBOSCH AND HUFF, flexibility exists if information is independent of the use to which it is put, and/or if the system provides analytic or modeling capability.[539] Management accounting systems that provide analytic capabilities are more likely to support scanning of a wide range of information and thereby increase the likelihood of identifying strategic issues.[540] Management accounting systems can become inflexible when their information is used in a rigid evaluative style. The rigid use of management accounting information for evaluation purposes can increase target pressure and result in dysfunctional behavior which complicates the interpretation of strategic issues.[541] This behavior can be prevented when management accounting information is used for evaluations in a flexible and long-run manner. However, management accounting information can also be used in a flexible manner when evaluations are complemented with other types of information.

Overall, we expect *flexible* management accounting systems to contribute *positively* to *observation* and *interpretation* of strategic issues.

### 2.3.3 Accessibility

Accessibility measures "the degree to which a system and the information it contains can be accessed with relatively low effort."[542] Access to information can be seen as necessary condition to system quality.[543] Accessibility is especially important when managers use analysis and retrieval capabilities of computerized management accounting systems. Easily accessible management accounting systems seem to help managers in the observation of strategic issues, and thereby contribute to a higher problem identification speed.[544] In case of hard-copy reports, earlier information quality research has

---

538 Baines and Langfield-Smith (2003), p. 692.
539 Vandenbosch and Huff (1997), p. 93.
540 Vandenbosch and Higgins (1996), p. 210.
541 Otley and Fakiolas (2000), p. 500.
542 Nelson et al. (2005), p. 206.
543 Ibid., p. 205.
544 Leidner and Elam (1995), p. 656.

assumed perfect accessibility. However, the increased use of computerized management accounting systems makes it necessary to take accessibility into account.[545]

Therefore, it seems that *accessibility* can have a *positive* impact on the *observation* of strategic issues.

### 2.3.4 Formalization

Formalization measures the degree to which a system contains rules or procedures. In order to coordinate activities, organizations establish procedures concerning how to react to stimuli from management accounting systems. This can involve reporting requirements, necessary deviation analysis and dedicated channels for interaction with other departments or superiors. As shown in the literature review, a high level of formalization can potentially increase focused search at the expense of scanning.[546] In addition, formalization increases the likelihood of interpreting issues as threats and discouraging the pursuit of opportunities.[547] SUTCLIFFE notes that formal systems can constrain opportunities for interaction and communication between organizational members.[548] However, SMITH ET AL. found that a certain level of formality in communication is associated with higher performance and suggest that there is a threshold level of formal communication needed.[549]

To summarize, a *balanced* level of *formalization* seems to have a *positive* impact on *observation*, *interpretation* and *communication* in strategic sensemaking.

### 2.3.5 Media Richness

Media richness measures the degree to which a system uses channels that enable a high level of personal interaction. Strategic issues are hard to quantify and require different points of view in order to create a shared interpretation. Face-to-face meetings and other rich media are best suited to exchange interpretations of strategic issues in order to reduce equivocality associated with them.[550] A management accounting system

---

[545] Wang and Strong (1996), p. 21.
[546] See C1.1 Impact of Management Accounting Systems on Observation, pp. 5.
[547] See C1.2.1 Categorization of Strategic Issues, pp. 5.
[548] Sutcliffe (2001), p. 209 and p. 211.
[549] Smith et al. (1994), pp. 431-433.
[550] See B2.5.2.2 Interpretive Perspective, pp. 5.

design that incorporates meetings for the discussion of reports provides a basis for creating a shared interpretation of strategic issues. According to SIMONS a process demanding frequent and regular attention by managers at all levels of the organization, which relies on the continual challenge and debate of underlying data, assumptions, and action plans in face-to-face meetings, characterizes an interactive use of management accounting systems.[551] The interactive use of management accounting systems provides a forum and an agenda for the regular, face-to-face dialogue and debate of non-routine issues.[552]

Therefore, it seems that management accounting systems with channels of *high media richness* can contribute *positively* to *interpretation* and *communication* of strategic issues.

## 2.4 Summary of Quality Dimensions and Strategic Sensemaking

Based on an extensive literature review of how management accounting system characteristics can affect cognitive processes in strategic sensemaking, this study proposes a set of information and system quality dimensions that seem to be useful for understanding the role of management accounting systems in strategic sensemaking. Table 5 below provides an overview of their tentative, theoretical impact on strategic sensemaking.

Most of the suggested theoretical relationships are tentative, because they are based only on limited empirical evidence. Furthermore, empirical evidence is missing for some relationships between quality dimensions and strategic sensemaking processes. Therefore, an in-depth empirical investigation is required before it is possible to develop hypotheses for the proposed relationships. To explore these complex relationships in their natural setting, this research draws on case study data of 30 top and middle level managers in seven large companies in Germany. The following chapter presents the research design of this study.

---

[551] Simons (1991), p. 50.
[552] Bisbe and Otley (2004), p. 727.

| | Quality Dimensions | Tentative Impact on Strategic Sensemaking … Observation | Interpretation | Communication | Overall |
|---|---|---|---|---|---|
| Information | Scope | + | + | + | + |
| | Timeliness | + | + | ? | + (?) |
| | Format | ? | + | + | + (?) |
| | Accuracy | – (?) | – (?) | ? | – (?) |
| System | Integration | + | + | + | + |
| | Flexibility | + | + | ? | + (?) |
| | Accessibility | + | ? | ? | + (?) |
| | Formalization | ± | ± | ± | ± |
| | Media richness | ? | + | + | + (?) |

Legend: + (positive); – (negative); ± (balanced); ? (unclear or not discussed)

*Table 5: Tentative, theoretical relationships between MAS dimensions and strategic sensemaking*

# D Research Design

This study aims to explore the role of management accounting systems in strategic sensemaking. In particular the study tries to improve understanding regarding how managers use management accounting systems for sensemaking and how management accounting system dimensions shape the role and use of management accounting system in strategic sensemaking. Due to the explorative nature of the research questions, and the objective of studying strategic sensemaking in its natural setting, the empirical approach is based on a multiple-case study design.

The following sections provide details on the research methodology. Section 1 discusses the reasons for choosing a case study design. Section 2 describes the approach for selecting 30 top and middle level managers and provides descriptions of the seven case companies. Section 3 describes the data collection procedure, which involved semi-structured interviews and a questionnaire. Section 4 provides the approach for analyzing the qualitative and quantitative data as the basis for explanation building. Finally, section 5 describes quality ensuring measures that were taken during the research design, data gathering and analysis phases.

## 1. Choosing a Case Study Design

According to YIN "a case study is an empirical enquiry that:

- investigates a contemporary phenomenon within its real-life context, especially when
- the boundaries between phenomenon and context are not clearly evident."[553]

Case research is therefore useful when a phenomenon is broad and complex, when an in-depth investigation is needed, and when a phenomenon cannot be studied outside the context in which it occurs.[554] A major strength of case studies is that they make it possible to develop novel, yet testable, relevant, and valid theory.[555] However, it is a misconception to believe that case studies are only appropriate for the exploratory

---

[553] Yin (2003), p. 13.
[554] Dubé and Paré (2003), p. 598.
[555] Eisenhardt (1989), p. 532 and p. 546.

phase in the early stages of research on a topic. Case studies can also be used for descriptive or explanatory purposes.[556] A 'critical case' can be used to falsify theory by providing an example of a set of phenomena that are inconsistent with underlying theory.[557] Another strength of case studies is that they allow the combining of quantitative and qualitative data from interviews, surveys, archives and other sources, in order to gain a more complete understanding of the phenomenon.[558] However, the case study approach is often considered inferior to other research methods because of insufficient precision, objectivity, and rigor.[559] Therefore, several researchers, such as YIN[560], EISENHARDT[561], OTLEY AND BERRY[562] and DUBÉ AND PARÉ,[563] address these stereotypes of case study research by highlighting its strengths and weaknesses in comparison to other methods. Furthermore, these researchers suggest several quality ensuring measures, which will be discussed throughout this chapter and specifically in section 5 on quality ensuring measures.

YIN suggests choosing a research strategy on three conditions: (1) the form of research question posed, (2) the focus on contemporary events as opposed to historical ones, and (3) the extent of control over behavioral events.[564]

*(1) The form of research question posed*: The objective of this study is to understand **how** managers use management accounting systems in strategic sensemaking. Furthermore, it is necessary to understand **how** management accounting system dimensions affect cognitive processes in strategic sensemaking and contribute to the use of management accounting systems. According to YIN case studies, experiments and histories are adequate research strategies for answering "how" and "why" questions, because they enable the researcher to explain complex relationships and interdependencies.[565] BOUWENS AND ABERNETHY propose a field study in a large organization to en-

---

556 Yin (2003), p. 3.

557 Otley and Berry (1994), p. 46.

558 Chetty (1996), p. 74.

559 Yin (2003), p. 10.

560 Ibid. provides a detailed assessment of the strengths and weaknesses of the case study method in social science research and suggest measures for how researchers can ensure high quality case study research.

561 Eisenhardt (1989) suggests an approach to build theory from case study research.

562 Otley and Berry (1994) review case study research in management accounting and control, in order to derive benefits and disadvantages of the approach.

563 Dubé and Paré (2003) investigate for the field of information systems research, the methodological rigor in case study research.

564 Yin (2003), p. 5.

565 Ibid., pp. 5-7.

hance our understanding of the complexities associated with the "whys" and "hows" of management accounting system design, which suggests that case studies are particularly suited for this research.[566] Furthermore, CHENHALL notes that aspects of management accounting systems should not be studied in isolation from each other when the system is not the sole source of information.[567] This is particularly true for this research, as strategic issues are often ambiguous and only the combination of information from different sources allows developing an understanding. Since there is no predefined set of systems used for sensemaking of strategic issues, it is useful to take a broad perspective on the different kinds of management accounting systems available in an organization. Only case studies provide enough flexibility to control for different management accounting systems.

*(2) Focus on contemporary events*: Case studies focus on contemporary events, which distinguish them from history. Many of the research techniques of case studies are similar to the historian's research strategy, but case studies can also include data from observation and systematic interviewing.[568] In addition, the focus on contemporary events can also avoid a possible "hindsight bias" where interviewees easily find plausible explanations for past events once they know the final outcome.[569]

*(3) Extent of control over behavioral events*: While case studies allow researchers to study phenomena in real-life settings, experiments can isolate individual drivers by controlling for all other remaining variables.[570] In order to study how management accounting systems are used for strategic sensemaking through experiments this would require the separation of individual management accounting system dimensions and sensemaking activities from their organizational context. However, strategic sensemaking is a very complex and iterative process that appears to be inseparable from other organizational processes and sometimes can even take place unconsciously. Furthermore, management accounting systems have usually evolved over a long period of time and are often adapted to specific organizational and environmental context factors. HOPWOOD notes that "Accounting has come to be recognized as a phenomenon whose form, functioning and consequences are interdependent with the context in

---

[566] Bouwens and Abernethy (2000), p. 235.
[567] Chenhall (2003), p. 135.
[568] Yin (2003), pp. 7-8.
[569] See Hogarth and Makridakis (1981), p. 120.
[570] Lee (1999), p. 54.

which it operates."[571] Therefore, it does not seem possible to isolate the phenomenon from its context in order to conduct experiments. The lack of evident boundaries for strategic sensemaking also excludes direct observation as a source of evidence for case studies.

Table 6 below summarizes the five research strategies along the three conditions suggested by YIN. Overall, case studies appear to be the most appropriate research strategy to study the role of management accounting systems in strategic sensemaking. With regard to the design of the case studies, it must be determined how much pre-structure is required and how many cases should be investigated.

| **Strategy** | **Form of Research Question** | **Focuses on Contemporary Events?** | **Requires Control Over Behavioral Events?** |
|---|---|---|---|
| Experiment | How, Why | Yes | Yes |
| Survey | Who, What, Where, How many, How much | Yes | No |
| Archival analysis | Who, What, Where, How many, How much | Yes/No | No |
| History | How, Why | No | No |
| Case study | How, Why | Yes | No |

*Table 6: Relevant research strategies for different research settings*[572]

Concerning the *amount of pre-structure* that should exist before entering the research field, researchers have developed two positions for building theory from case study research. GLASER AND STRAUSS, with their concept of grounded theory, suggest that researchers should build new theory by iteratively analyzing data and building explanations. Once a tentative theory or concept has started to form, the researcher should conduct a detailed literature review.[573] However, "nobody starts with a totally blank sheet."[574] Therefore, researchers like EISENHARDT propose that a priori specification of constructs can help to shape the initial design of theory-building research. It also permits researchers to measure constructs more accurately.[575] According to MCCUTCHEON AND MEREDITH "the necessary base may be available in the well-developed theories

571 Hopwood (1989), p. 1.
572 Yin (2003), p. 5.
573 See Glaser and Strauss (1967).
574 Goulding (2001), p. 23.
575 Eisenhardt (1989), p. 536.

from other fields."[576] For this research it was possible to draw tentative propositions from other research fields, which enabled the author to design semi-structured interviews and a questionnaire.

The other question relates to the *number of cases* that should be included in the research design. A single-case study can be appropriate to study a unique or critical case, in order to test well-formulated theory.[577] However, the evidence from a multiple-case design is often considered more compelling, and the overall study is therefore regarded as more robust.[578] Multiple cases can help the researcher to develop more elaborated theory as they often emphasize complementary aspects of a phenomenon.[579] However, a multiple-case design does not provide the basis for statistical generalization. Yin cautions that cases are not "sampling units" and should not be chosen for this reason.[580] The next chapter will discuss possible approaches to choosing cases in more detail. Case studies allow only for " 'analytic generalization', in which a previously developed theory is used as a template with which to compare the empirical results of the case study".[581] The literature review shows that there is no single theory to explain the role of management accounting systems in strategic sensemaking. Therefore, a single-case study seems not to be suitable and the author decided to employ a multiple-case study design.

Overall, a *pre-structured, multiple-case design* seems to be the most suitable empirical approach for this study. The next chapter will define the unit of analysis and present the chosen approach for case selection.

## 2. Case Selection

### 2.1 Unit of Analysis and Selection Criteria

The unit of analysis for this multiple-case study is the *individual manager,* because sensemaking happens on the individual level, as an organization can only learn

576 McCutcheon and Meredith (1993), p. 243.
577 Eisenhardt (1989), p. 47.
578 Ibid., p. 52.
579 Eisenhardt (1991), p. 620.
580 Yin (2003), p. 32.
581 Ibid., pp. 32-33.

through the individuals involved.[582] This research acknowledges that individual strategic sensemaking is only the first step in formulating a response strategy to strategic issues, as successful strategic decision-making requires sensemaking also at the organizational level.[583] However, this research assumes that it is primarily the individual manager who uses management accounting systems.

Of particular interest for strategic sensemaking are *middle managers*, because they are "usually the first to sense potential threats and opportunities in their own particular domain."[584] A number of researchers highlight middle managers as important sources of knowledge about the need for, and possibilities of, change.[585] In a survey of 259 middle managers from 25 organizations in various industries, FLOYD AND WOOLDRIDGE found that middle managers in boundary-spanning roles in particular exert upward strategic influence by providing top management with interpretations of emerging strategic issues and by proposing new initiatives.[586] The boundary-spanning role provides middle managers with access to external information and requires them to mediate between environmental uncertainty and internal organizational arrangements.[587]

However, *top managers* remain the most important individuals in an organization as they "bring together and interpret information for the system as a whole. Many participants play some part in scanning or data processing, but the point at which information converges and is interpreted for organizational level action is assumed to be at the top manager level."[588] Therefore, this study will focus both on middle and top managers as the unit of analysis.

As case studies strive for *analytical generalization*, rather then statistical, the case selection should support researchers in generating new theoretical insights that are helpful to generate, extend, or falsify a theory.[589] A multiple-case study requires the selection of cases according to replication logic. "In replication logic, cases which confirm

---

[582] Simon (1991), p. 125. According to Weick and Ashford (2001), p. 727 "Organizational learning is primarily about individuals learning within their organizations". Akgün et al. (2003), p. 856 defines sensemaking as an individual activity. See also B2.1 Level of Organizational Learning, pp. 5.

[583] Sutcliffe (2001), p. 205.

[584] Papadakis et al. (1998), p. 132.

[585] Huff et al. (2000), p. 31.

[586] Floyd and Wooldridge (1997), p. 477.

[587] Ibid., p. 469.

[588] Daft and Weick (1984), p. 285.

[589] Yin (2003), pp. 32-33 and Eisenhardt (1989), p. 542.

emergent relationships enhance confidence in the validity of the relationships. Cases which disconfirm the relationships often can provide an opportunity to refine and extend the theory."[590] YIN distinguishes between literal and theoretical replication logic. Cases selected according to literal replication logic should predict similar results, while cases chosen by theoretical replication logic should produce contrary results, but for predictable reasons.[591] As the design of a particular management accounting system is not observable from the outside, it was not possible to "choose cases such as extreme situations and polar types in which the process of interest is 'transparently observable',"[592] in order to limit case selection to the most promising cases. Therefore, case selection is based on external observable criteria like industry and organizational size.

Based on the assumption that management accounting systems play an important role in large, listed enterprises, the author first chose listed companies with more than 3,500 employees and with more than €1,000 million sales revenues in 2004. To reduce influence from national culture, the selection was further limited to German companies and German subsidiaries of multinational companies. Following *theoretical replication logic*, the author decided to include companies from different industries with either a long-term or a short-term time horizon concerning changes in their environment. The rationale for selecting companies from different industries is related to the findings of researchers like CHENHALL AND MORRIS that the design of management accounting systems is also dependant on external factors.[593] In addition MILLER AND CARDINAL found that the performance impact of strategic planning depends on industry effects and the level of environmental uncertainty.[594]

Companies with inflexible production technologies tend to have a *long-term planning horizon*.[595] These companies have complex development cycles for products with a long lifetime, and therefore need to identify and make sense of weak signals preceding strategic issues. Along *literal replication logic*, the author selected two companies from the aeronautics/space industry and one from the automotive industry. The se-

590 Eisenhardt (1989), p. 542.
591 Yin (2003), p. 47.
592 Eisenhardt (1989), p. 537.
593 See Chenhall and Morris (1986), p. 30.
594 Miller and Cardinal (1994), p. 1659.
595 Yasai-Ardekani and Haug (1997), p. 752.

lected manufacturing companies employed between 6,000 and 50,000 people and earned revenues between 1,500 and more than €20,000 million in 2004.

For companies with a *short-term horizon* concerning changes in their environment, this research focuses on companies in the information and communications technology sector. The information and communications technology sector witnesses intense competition, rapid changes in environmental factors such as technology and regulation, and ambiguous customer demands. Some authors refer to this as a hypercompetitive industry.[596] Companies operating in a hypercompetitive industry usually offer products with a short lifetime and need to adapt their product portfolio frequently. Therefore, they have a shorter planning horizon and need to make sense of more frequent changes. Following *literal replication logic*, the author selected two companies that provide information and communication technology services to business customers and two companies from the telecommunication industry, covering both service providers and equipment manufacturing. The selected companies employed between 3,500 and 40,000 people and earned revenues between 1,000 and more than €10,000 million in 2004.

| **Company** | **Industry** | **Company type** | **Employees (2004)** | **Revenues (2004, EUR million.)** | **Planning horizon (years)** |
|---|---|---|---|---|---|
| A | Information and Communications Technology | Service | 3,500 | 1,000 | 1-2 |
| B | Telecommunications | Service | 4,000 | 3,000 | 2-5 |
| C | Telecommunications | Manufacturing | 7,000 | 5,500 | 2 |
| D | Information and Communications Technology | Service | >40,000 | >10,000 | 3 |
| E | Aeronautics/Space | Manufacturing | 7,000 | 2,000 | 10 |
| F | Aeronautics/Space | Manufacturing | 6,000 | 1,500 | 10 |
| G | Automotive | Manufacturing | >50,000 | >20,000 | 5-15 |
| Pilot | Software development | Service | <500 | 40 | 2-3 |

*Table 7: Overview case companies*

In addition to the seven selected case companies, this research includes a pilot case study at a mature, mid-sized service company with less than 500 employees and sales revenues of €40 million in 2004. The privately owned pilot company develops soft-

[596] Bogner and Barr (2000), p. 212.

ware products and offers services related to the implementation of their software solutions. Table 7 above provides an overview for industry, company type, size and planning horizon of the selected case companies.

In order to get a broad overview of the general management accounting system setup, the author approached the chief controller, head of business development or head of strategic planning to understand the available management accounting systems and the most important functional managers in boundary-spanning roles. This helped to identify relevant functional managers as further interviewees. Following the procedure from EISENHARDT AND BOURGEOIS new managers were added until the incremental learning from new cases diminished.[597]

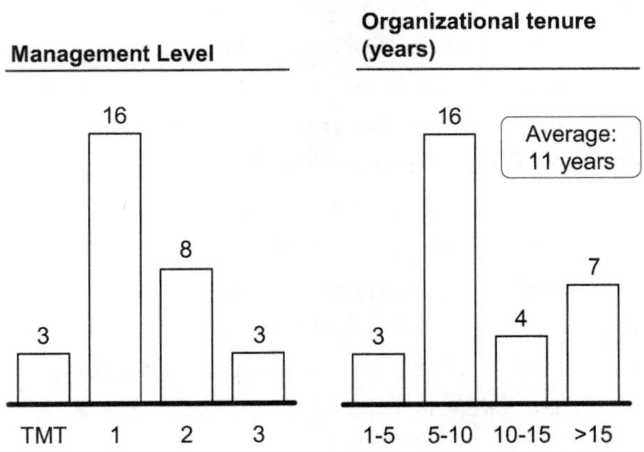


*Figure 9: Distribution of interview partners along management level and organizational tenure*

Overall, 30 top and middle managers were included in this multiple-case study design. The interviewees were experienced managers, with an average tenure of 11 years in their companies and 3 years in their current positions. The author interviewed 3 members of top management teams (TMT), 16 direct reports to the TMT, 8 managers who were 2 levels below the TMT, and 3 managers who were 3 levels below the TMT (see Figure 9 above). In addition, the CEO and 3 managers who were 2 levels below the TMT were interviewed for the pilot case study. Excluding the pilot study, the average

[597] Eisenhardt and Bourgeois (1988), p. 739.

age of the predominantly male interviewees was 40 years. Four interview partners from case company C were female.

## 2.2 Overview Case Companies

The following chapters provide a brief overview of the interview partners in each company. Additionally, descriptions of the relevant management accounting systems in use, and other information sources for strategic sensemaking, are provided.

### 2.2.1 Company A: Personal Networks and Informal Communication

*Introduction to company A*: Company A is the German subsidiary of a leading IT infrastructure service provider in Europe. It offers infrastructure integration, technology sourcing and managed infrastructure services to business customers. The company is a sales-driven organization that cooperates closely with its customers' IT departments. Key challenges for company A are continuing price erosion caused by a high level of competition in the IT infrastructure market and the ability to adapt quickly to changing customer requirements. For coping with pricing pressure, the company has set up a staff function responsible for conducting analyses and running projects that can further increase efficiency. The author conducted an interview with the head of this function (A1) and the chief controller of the company (A2). The author also interviewed a program director of strategic sales, responsible for datacenters (A3), and a key account manager (A4). A summary of interviewees including title, management level, tenure, age and interview duration can be found in Table 8 below.

| Case | Job title | Management level | Organizational tenure (years) | Age (years) | Interview duration (min) |
|---|---|---|---|---|---|
| A1 | Director Quality & Business Improvement | TMT - 1 | 2 | 36 | 60 |
| A2 | Manager Financial Planning & Analysis | CFO - 1 | 8 | 33 | 80 |
| A3 | Program Director Strategic Sales | TMT - 3 | 9 | 36 | 55 |
| A4 | Key Account manager | TMT - 3 | 8 | 33 | 70 |

*Table 8: Overview interview partners in company A*[598]

[598] The interviews A2 and A3 were conducted by telephone.

*Information sources for strategic sensemaking*: The most important sources concerning changes in the market environment are customers and suppliers. Managers maintain personal networks and share information concerning competitors and market changes, mostly informally. The chief controller explains that, "the only way to survive in this company is by having a good personal network. We have an open structure to support this." He provides the following example to illustrate the influence of personal networks: "When I used to work in one of our branches we had the network sales unit at one end of the corridor and the data center sales unit at the other end. As a result, the sales unit which was located next to the network unit had the highest market share in network sales, while the unit next to the data center unit had the highest share in data center related sales."

Company A does not have a customer relationship management system that allows a systematic tracking of opportunities, but a specific unit analyzes successful and unsuccessful bids in order to learn about areas for improvement. However, this is not a systematic process. According to manager A1, "We observe competitors and market changes only unsystematically. We get some information through our sales channels when we loose bids [...] but our management accounting systems do not provide this information." There were several attempts to introduce management accounting systems for improving the information flow from sales to management. These attempts failed, because management did not enforce their use and sales managers did not see the benefits of using these systems. The company distributes some market news through the intranet and via e-mail.

*Management accounting systems*: The most important management accounting system in company A is the data-warehouse. It provides up-to-date and historic information on financial and transaction data. The system provides analysis capabilities and allows access to detailed numbers for all areas of the business. Manager A1 and his department use this system to conduct analysis in order to identify improvement potential. The data-warehouse does not contain broad scope, especially not future-oriented management accounting information.

Company A does not have an explicit strategic planning process. The chief controller argues that the yearly planning process provides an opportunity to discuss strategic issues, but the planning information is not precise enough for deviation analysis during the period. "The yearly planning process adds value by making it possible to discuss potentials, chances and risks in different areas of the business. However, because of the high volatility in our business, planning information is only of limited use." Company A developed, for the first time in 2005, a three-year plan with a strong focus on the first and second year.

Finally, the company recently introduced a customer satisfaction survey in order to collect more systematic data from customers. The survey includes postcards, web-based feedback, onsite and telephone interviews. It provides management with a customer perspective on own strengths and weaknesses.

### 2.2.2 Company B: Analysis Capabilities for Operational Data

*Introduction to company B*: Company B is the German subsidiary of a European telecommunications company. It is a full service provider that owns and operates a telecommunications network. Key challenges for company B are increased competition from existing and new telecommunication providers, the introduction of competing technologies, and the fulfillment of changing and increasingly sophisticated consumer needs. The author conducted an interview with the chief controller (B1) in order to understand the planning processes and the overall management accounting system setup. Managers from the IT department (B2) and network department (B3 and B4) were able to provide information related to the technology and network area. In addition, the company has a business intelligence function that provides information for operational and strategic decision-making (B5). A summary of interviewees can be found in Table 9 below.

| Case | Job title | Management level | Organizational tenure (years) | Age (years) | Interview duration (min) |
|---|---|---|---|---|---|
| B1 | Vice President Controlling | CFO - 1 | 5 | 43 | 90 |
| B2 | Vice President IS Planning & Performance | CIO - 1 | 6 | 41 | 70 |
| B3 | Head of Network Development | CTO - 1 | 7 | 35 | 50 |
| B4 | Director of Network Operations | CTO - 1 | 8 | 54 | 70 |
| B5 | Vice President Business Intelligence | TMT - 1 | 8 | 43 | 90 |

*Table 9: Overview interview partners in company B*

*Information sources for strategic sensemaking*: Important sources for information about strategic issues are press releases, analyst reports, capital market information, fairs and conferences, discussions with strategic partners and suppliers, and personal networks. A close cooperation with major suppliers provides the company with timely information on application roadmaps and new technologies. Company B also has a staff function that regularly prepares reports and conducts analyses based on competitors' press releases. Furthermore, important sources for the network area are key performance indicators concerning network performance and utilization. The company increasingly focuses on key performance indicators from a customer perspective, in order to measure the fulfillment of customer needs. In addition, the business intelligence function regularly conducts analyses about new trends, markets and the potential impact of new products.

*Management accounting systems*: Company B has witnessed strong growth in recent years. It faces the challenge of finding the right level of control, necessary for a company with revenues of more than €3,000 million, without loosing the flexibility that allows it to adapt quickly to changes. The strategic planning process in company B has mostly been limited to discussions in the top management team with a few specialists. These discussions focus on general trends in the industry and have a time-horizon of five years at most. Functional managers are usually not involved in these discussions and perceive a lack of strategic direction for the company. To resolve this, the chief controller, B1, has recently introduced a monthly meeting with divisional directors to discuss forecasts, planning topics and issues for the next planning round, as he was unable to change the strategic planning process itself: "We have a formal strategic planning process that is limited to the executive board. Therefore, I have introduced another formal planning process at divisional director level, where we regularly discuss planning topics and also topics with a long-term horizon." The company has extensive planning and budgeting processes for the short-term horizon. Planning includes the development of scenarios in order to prepare for alternative developments. The planning process is highly iterative, as it involves bottom-up planning by functional units, while ancillary conditions are subject to frequent changes.

The first attempt at performance measurement in company B failed, and they have recently reintroduced a Balanced Scorecard. The first Balanced Scorecard provided only high-level indications of deviations and did not allow management to investigate reasons for these deviations. Now the key performance indicators are connected with underlying operational data, which allows managers to drill-down into more detail whenever necessary. Company B's IT department has developed its own Balanced Scorecard. Managers in the IT department use the Balanced Scorecard to measure progress for strategic projects and to discuss the initiation of new projects. Scorecard performance indicators are yearly aligned with the department strategy. Discussions during alignment ensure that the Balanced Scorecard focuses on the identified areas of uncertainty.

The business intelligence function of company B is responsible for providing up-to-date information on most operational data. The department maintains a data-warehouse that integrates data from all operational systems. This allows overnight updating of more than 1000 reports on all areas of the business with the latest transactional data. Each report has a business owner who defines, in cooperation with the business intelligence function, the content and presentation of the report. This ensures the relevancy of the reports. The systems not only provide pre-specified reports, but also have extensive analysis capabilities to conduct new analyses on request. The business intelligence function maintains forecast models that help business managers in capacity planning. Especially during the planning phase, managers ask the business intelligence to analyze the potential impact of different strategic options. Over the years, business intelligence managers have developed an extensive knowledge about interdependencies in the business model of the company. This allows them to proactively approach other managers with new reports or analyses that could be of interest to them.

### 2.2.3 Company C: Short-term Planning in a Dynamic Environment

*Introduction to company C*: Company C is an international telecommunication equipment manufacturer. Key challenges are the identification and fast adaptation to changing customer demands in a highly competitive environment. Because of short product lifecycles it is important to reduce time-to-market for new product development. The author was able to interview top and middle managers in the finance function. Interviewees include the managing director for finance and IT (C1), the head of the strategy department (C2), and the responsible controlling managers for research & development (C3), category management (C4), planning and controlling (C5 & C6) and marketing (C7). A summary of interviewees can be found in Table 10 below.

*Information sources for strategic sensemaking*: Both internal and external sources are important for strategic sensemaking in company C. The most important internal sources include daily information on key financials and volume data, monthly regional review meetings to discuss business developments and milestone reporting for new product development. External sources encompass market research, pricing intelligence, consumer behavioral analyses, trend scouts, and industry analysts.

| Case | Job title | Management level | Organizational tenure (years) | Age (years) | Interview duration (min) |
|---|---|---|---|---|---|
| C1 | Managing Director | TMT | 26 | 45 | 50 |
| C2 | Head of Strategy and Communications | TMT - 1 | 7 | 38 | 60 |
| C3 | Head of Controlling R&D | TMT - 1 | 5 | 47 | 90 |
| C4 | Head of Controlling Category Management | TMT - 1 | 2 | 33 | 65 |
| C5 | Director Planning and Controlling | TMT - 1 | 20 | 41 | 130 |
| C6 | Planning and Performance Controlling | TMT - 2 | 5 | 30 | see C5 |
| C7 | Head of Marketing Planning & Performance | TMT - 2 | 8 | 31 | 65 |

*Table 10: Overview interview partners in company C*

*Management accounting systems*: Company C has experienced declining performance in recent years. Changes to management accounting systems were being implemented when this research was carried out, so the research is based on the status of implementation at the time the interviews were conducted.[599]

In order to cope with frequent market changes, company C has established several interleaved planning processes. Strategic planning focuses on the next 18 months and includes major environmental trends. Manager C2 conducts a five forces analysis annually to identify industry transformation trends. Direct contacts with experts, suppliers and competitors along the value chain provide the necessary information. In addition, product volume planning is conducted at least quarterly, and more frequently when necessary, rather then annually, as in the past. According to manager C4 a regular planning process "forces managers to think constantly about the future, and to take relevant decisions at appropriate points in time. In the past this only happened at larger intervals. This has improved." In addition, C5 (planning and controlling) prepares monthly financial forecasts. These are not rolling forecasts, but have a time horizon until year-end. The preparation of these forecasts is a time-consuming task, because IT-systems are not standardized and provide only a poor data quality. This leaves little time for the interpretation of the financial information.

[599] Interviews in company C were conducted from November to December 2005.

For performance measurement company C has a management cockpit with the most important financial key performance indicators, including P&L items, cash-flow, and cost of capital. The cockpit provides also information on productivity, supply chain, order intake, and milestone achievements in the product development process. According to manager C2, top management does not use the cockpit sufficiently: "[Top management uses the cockpit] very differently, but overall too little. I think that we have a very good format that ideally allows top management to discuss supply chain issues, rolling order forecast and sales delivery situation in meetings. Top management could discuss the current situation, reasons for deviations and lessons learned … We do not have an optimal use of this instrument yet."

Reports in company C have grown over the years. Several reports are not discussed in meetings and their purpose is unclear. Manager C4 remarks: "Yes, it is information overkill. It is especially difficult for someone who is new, but also for people who have been around for quite some time. There is always a report where you ask yourself, 'what is the purpose and who is the receiver?' These reports are sent around and after a while you learn about what you really need. But it would be difficult if you started to look at every report."

### 2.2.4 Company D: Systematic Strategic Issue Management

*Introduction to company D*: Company D is an international provider of information and telecommunication services to enterprise customers. Key challenges include continuing price erosion, a high level of competition, and the introduction of new technologies. Unfortunately the author was only able to access the head of finance and controlling for large enterprise customers (D1). This manager's details are summarized in Table 11 below.

| **Case** | **Job title** | **Management level** | **Organizational tenure (years)** | **Age (years)** | **Interview duration (min)** |
|---|---|---|---|---|---|
| D1 | Head of Finance and Controlling | CFO - 1 | 14 | 42 | 85 |

*Table 11: Overview interview partners in company D*

*Information sources for strategic sensemaking*: Two types of information are particularly important for company D. On the one hand business development acquires external data about market developments from market research, analysts and other sources. On the other hand, company D monitors trigger points for new business opportunities.

This includes management or strategy changes at potential customers. Additionally, daily press clippings about competitors and suppliers help managers to stay up-to-date with latest developments in the industry.

*Management accounting systems*: Company D has a planning horizon of 3 years. Strategic planning consists of qualitative and quantitative elements. The qualitative side is mainly prepared by the business development function and includes overall discussions concerning the portfolio, overall topics, and strategic direction of company D. Manager D1 is responsible for quantifying the identified topics through analysis of customer developments in the different industries. This provides the basis for sales targets and the measurement of progression towards the strategic objectives.

Company D uses a Balanced Scorecard to communicate the strategy and make it executable. The Balanced Scorecard includes targets for financial and non-financial key performance indicators. Key performance indicators are connected with detailed reports that help to identify reasons for deviations and track the development of issues over time. A data-warehouse provides integrated data for a broad range of information. This allows for the creation of exception-based management reports that help to focus attention on specific customers and areas of the business.

In order to cope with increasing margin pressure, company D conducts a regular cost benchmarking with competitors. Discussions about the company's cost structure help to identify areas for improvement and to set targets for cost reduction efforts. Finally, a quarterly risk management process helps to collect strategic issues from the different areas of the business. It also ensures a regular monitoring of identified measures to deal with these issues.

### 2.2.5 Company E: Performance Measurement and Strategic Planning

*Introduction to company E*: Company E is an equipment manufacturer in the aeronautics and space industry. Key challenges are a high level of competition and very long product lifecycles. Company E tries to reduce related risks through a diversified product portfolio and partnerships for the development of new products. The author conducted interviews with commercial managers (E1 & E2), the responsible manager for maintenance and production (E3), managers from a central staff function for planning and controlling (E4 & E5) and the chief controller for the technical areas including research and development (E6). A summary of interviewees can be found in Table 12 below.

| Case | Job title | Management level | Organizational tenure (years) | Age (years) | Interview duration (min) |
|---|---|---|---|---|---|
| E1 | Senior VP Commercial Programs | TMT - 1 | 19 | 49 | 70 |
| E2 | Director Finance Commercial Programs | TMT - 2 | 7 | 47 | see E1 |
| E3 | Senior VP Maintenance | TMT - 1 | 18 | 44 | 65 |
| E4 | Head of Planning and Controlling | CFO - 2 | 6 | 36 | 80 |
| E5 | Planning and Controlling | CFO - 3 | 12 | 36 | see E4 |
| E6 | Director Controlling Operations | CFO - 2 | 13 | 41 | 120 |

*Table 12: Overview interview partners in company E*

*Information sources for strategic sensemaking*: Company E is particularly interested in information related to sales of existing products and development of new products. Contacts with customers and analysts, as well as industry databases provide information concerning new business opportunities. In addition, press releases are published on the intranet, in order to inform every manager of market developments and the situation of important customers. The development of new products is extremely complex and time consuming, and bears significant financial risks. Therefore, company E cooperates closely with development partners, with whom they openly share information concerning the new product development. Technology is a key success factor, and therefore the company has established a separate technology process. This involves the observation of new developments in the industry or related industries, and close cooperation with universities, research establishments and other external experts.

*Management accounting systems*: Long product lifecycles and inflexible production technologies make long-term and strategic planning especially relevant for company E. Therefore, strategic planning encompasses a time-horizon of ten years and operational planning three years. Business cases for new product developments even have a planning horizon of up to 40 years. In order to cope with the uncertainty associated with such long time-horizons, company E starts strategic planning with a discussion of core challenges. Top management uses market intelligence information to discuss major trends and developments in the industry. In addition, scenario and sensitivity analysis help to model these developments in order to understand their impact on the company. Commercial managers contribute particularly to strategic planning, with their information concerning market developments. Manager E1 describes this as an interactive process where strategy influences his actions and vice versa. "On the one hand we have an espoused strategy of the company, but on the other hand our actions contribute to the strategy in place, or the development of the strategy. That really is an interactive process. This does not happen daily or weekly, but yearly at strategic planning or during management conferences."

For performance measurement, company E has an on-line reporting system. Every month the system automatically provides the latest operational data, including financials, productivity and quality key performance indicators. The system provides drill-down functionalities to assist managers in the identification of reasons for deviations. It also highlights key performance indicators with severe deviations. In such cases, the responsible functional manager has to provide an explanation for the deviation and has to report suitable countermeasures including a timeline for its implementation. Information in this management cockpit is regularly discussed at different levels of the organization. In addition, a quarterly meeting is set up where every profit center manager with severe deviations in key performance indicators has to explain root causes for these deviations and to justify his countermeasures. Manager E6 explains, "We have a special presentation on a quarterly basis, where we use the on-line system to access all red flags. Each responsible profit center manager has to present and discuss things that went wrong, countermeasures he has taken, reasons for his choice, and when the measure will be effective." This process ensures constant focus on the achievement of targets.

Finally, company E established a risk management board to discuss potential risks and to monitor the implementation of countermeasures. The board also discusses long-term developments and feeds this information into the strategic planning process.

### 2.2.6 Company F: Long-term Planning and Performance Reviews

*Introduction to company F*: Company F is a division of an international space and aeronautics company. It is an equipment manufacturer that returned to profitable growth following restructuring efforts over the past few years. The key challenge for company F is to cope with pricing pressure caused by a highly competitive market. It is expected that an increasing concentration of customers in the market will further contribute to a high level of competition among equipment manufacturers. The author was able to conduct an interview with the CFO (F1) and the chief division controller (F3). A large part of the equipment is procured from external providers, which makes procurement an important lever to reduce costs. Therefore, an interview with the Senior Vice-President for Supply Management (F2) was conducted. An interview with the head of a product center (F4) concluded the interviews at company F. For a summary of the interviewees please see Table 13 below.

| Case | Job title | Management level | Organizational tenure (years) | Age (years) | Interview duration (min) |
|---|---|---|---|---|---|
| F1 | CFO | TMT | 16 | 42 | 40 |
| F2 | Senior VP Supply Management | TMT | 17 | 41 | 70 |
| F3 | Chief Division Controller | CFO - 1 | 7 | 31 | 70 |
| F4 | Head of Product Center | TMT - 2 | 25 | 52 | 75 |

*Table 13: Overview interview partners in company F*[600]

*Information sources for strategic sensemaking*: Managers in company F receive general information about the external environment from industry journals, conferences and technology workshops, and a regular distribution of analyst positions by the strategy department. Internal sources include marketing reports or regular meetings with marketing and sales, as well as contacts with subsidiaries. An important source of information concerning company F's competitiveness is feedback from tenders. Tenders provide an opportunity to derive cost targets for specific technologies and allow the definition of cost structures that need to be achieved. This can become the basis for strategic make or buy decisions.

*Management accounting systems*: Long product lifecycles highlight the importance of long-term strategic and operational planning for company F. Planning processes are very structured and begin with the preparation of a 10-year strategic plan. Strategic planning covers information about customer structures, sales potential, market environment, and changes in the competitive landscape including possible mergers and acquisitions. In addition, 10-20 leading banks provide macroeconomic data such as exchange rates and economic growth information. In order to cope with the uncertainty associated with a 10-year planning horizon, company F prepares a worst-case, high-probability and best-case scenario. Scenario planning helps managers to understand the impact of different developments on the company, and helps to identify the most important sources of uncertainty.

[600] The interview with F1 was conducted by telephone.

The 10-year strategic plan serves as an input for the operational planning, which has a 5-year planning horizon. The CFO (F1) provides basic assumptions and rough business growth and profitability targets to the business units as a starting point for their operational planning. The business units then have to prepare the profit and loss statement, cash-flow statement, balance sheet, order intake, and product development plan. One end product of the 5-year operational plan is the budget for the next year, which serves also as the basis for target-setting. Three forecasts during the year help to assess target achievement of each business unit and to define countermeasures when necessary. Each forecast contains a quantified assessment of risks and opportunities. A potential imbalance between risks and opportunities usually triggers top management to scrutinize the plan in order to understand the underlying issues.

Company F complements planning with quarterly performance reviews of selected business units. Each selected business unit has a whole day to present and discuss the most important projects with top management and the heads of all relevant internal suppliers. The review includes, for all relevant projects, not only financial information, but also the project schedule, technical issues, workload, resource utilization, quality, and procurement. These reviews provide top management with a good understanding of the current situation and potential issues at company F. In addition, a risk management process assesses and monitors identified risks. A quantification of the financial impact and occurrence probability helps top management to incorporate unavoidable risks, or risks with insufficient countermeasures, in reports, forecasts and plans.

The importance of continuous cost reductions makes benchmarking an important management accounting instrument for target setting. Benchmarking in combination with analyses of lost tenders helps to define a target cost-structure, and to identify areas for improvement. Permanent multi-functional teams consisting of engineering, finance and procurement develop solutions for how to close the identified gaps. These teams also develop options for top management as a basis for strategic make or buy decisions.

### 2.2.7 Company G: Comprehensive Information for Top Managers

*Introduction to company G*: Company G is an international car manufacturer. A key challenge is the development of innovative products in a highly competitive market. The author was able to interview the head of the staff function responsible for strategy and business development (G1). Other managers from this function possess different perspectives because of their functional focus or prior positions in the company. Manager G2 was able to provide more details on marketing and product development aspects, and manager G3 was able to provide more details on engineering and production. For a summary of interviews at this company please see Table 14 below.

| Case | Job title | Management level | Organizational tenure (years) | Age (years) | Interview duration (min) |
|---|---|---|---|---|---|
| G1 | Head of Strategy &Business Development | TMT - 1 | 4 | 36 | 75 |
| G2 | Strategy & Business Development | TMT - 2 | 9 | 38 | 90 |
| G3 | Strategy & Business Development | TMT - 2 | 14 | 51 | 90 |

*Table 14: Overview interview partners in company G*

*Information sources for strategic sensemaking*: Company G uses a wide variety of internal and external sources for sensemaking. External, impersonal sources include industry publications, press releases, the internet (especially on-line forums), and macroeconomic data from banks. However, more important are personal sources such as contacts at industry fairs (including fairs from adjacent industries), analysts and consultants, professional associations, suppliers and personal networks. Internal sources include marketing and sales (e.g., market shares, market developments and expectations), a regular newsletter from the company-owned research lab about new technologies, quality meetings, and analyses of products from competitors. The importance of innovation is highlighted by an annual innovations day, where the engineering department presents new technologies and research projects.

*Management accounting systems*: All management accounting systems provide information primarily to the top management team. Manager G1 describes this as, "all systems for information acquisition and preparation are adapted to the needs of the 15 top managers in our company. If you are manager 17, it is likely that you will only receive 50% of the information."

Company G conducts an annual formalized planning process with a rolling five-year time horizon. The planning process starts with top-level targets for financials (e.g., revenues, rate of return) and sales volume for each market. As a next step, managers prepare detailed plans for how to reach these targets. This requires a verification of the next four years from last year's planning and an update of the fifth year. Top managers use regular discussions with regional and sales managers to challenge their plans.

Because of long product life cycles it is not sufficient to focus only on the next five years, as this covers mainly the existing product portfolio. Therefore, the task of the strategy and business development department is to focus on developments that can have an impact on company G in 5-15 years. The department participates in the information flow directed at top management and uses all of the above-mentioned sources to conduct analyses and discuss them in strategy meetings with top management. Management accounting systems have only a supporting role and are used to assess the impact of potential developments on the company. Scenarios provide an instrument to analyze and discuss potential trends and their impact on the strategy of company G.

Company G has sophisticated management accounting systems that provide performance data for all areas of the business on a monthly basis. They include, in addition to financial data, sales volumes, market shares, competitor moves, quality indicators, customer satisfaction, and brand indicators. However, the interviewed managers use these systems mainly as a data source for specific analysis.

## 3. Data Collection

A major strength of case studies is that they make it possible to collect data from multiple sources.[601] YIN argues that, "the most important advantage presented by using multiple sources of evidence is the development of converging lines of inquiry, a process of triangulation ... Thus, any finding or conclusion in a case study is likely to be much more convincing and accurate if it is based on several different sources of information ..."[602] In particular, quantitative and qualitative sources can complement each other. Quantitative evidence can help the researcher to identify new relationships, which were not salient to him, whereas the qualitative data can be useful for understanding the rationale or theory for these underlying relationships.[603] "[Quantitative data] can also keep researchers from being carried away by vivid, but false, impressions in qualitative data, and it can bolster findings when it corroborates those findings from qualitative evidence."[604] THOMAS ET AL. suggest that the study of integrated cog-

---

601 Yin (2003), p. 97.
602 Ibid., p. 98.
603 Eisenhardt (1989), p. 538.
604 Ibid., p. 538.

nition-action-performance models in strategic sensemaking requires both qualitative and quantitative methods in individual studies.[605]

Data collection for this research followed this suggestion and focused on qualitative data from semi-structured interviews and quantitative data from a questionnaire. Between July 2005 and December 2005 the author conducted 30 interviews with top and middle managers. In addition, every interviewee was asked to complete a questionnaire. The following sections describe the content of the interview and questionnaire in more detail.

### 3.1 Semi-structured Interview

At the beginning of each interview the author described the background of this research. He clarified with the interviewee the broad definition of management accounting systems, which includes all formal systems that provide information about the company and its environment, through examples. Examples included regular reports, market reports, key performance indicators and scorecards, deviation analyses, plans and forecasts, computer based systems (e.g., SAP, enterprise resource planning systems, customer relationship management systems) and management/executive information systems. The author made explicit that management accounting information can be internal and external, quantitative and qualitative, financial and non-financial.

The interviews were conducted with the help of an interview guideline. They were semi-structured along the strategic sensemaking process of observation, interpretation and communication. Each interview started with open questions about the primary information sources for strategic sensemaking. In addition, the author asked each interviewee to describe the available management accounting systems and how they were used. This served as a starting point to uncover relevant management accounting systems and the processes associated with the use of these systems for strategic sensemaking. To reduce hindsight bias, and to allow for the identification of unconscious effects of management accounting systems in strategic sensemaking, the interviews focused only on systems actually used by the interviewee.

The second part of the interviews concentrated on the role of management accounting systems in observation of strategic issues. The author asked the interviewees to de-

---

[605] Thomas et al. (1997), pp. 321-322.

scribe how they use management accounting systems to observe strategic issues, and what triggers their information search. In addition, the interview partners had to rate how helpful their management accounting systems were for observing strategic issues on a scale from -3 (not helpful) to +3 (very helpful). The purpose of this rating was to provoke explanations for the underlying rationale.

Next, the impact of management accounting systems on the interpretation of strategic issues was investigated. The interviewees were asked to assess whether they perceived that management accounting systems suppressed or emphasized chances. The same question was asked in respect to risks. Again, both questions required the interviewee to rate the extent of suppression or emphasis on a scale from -3 (strong suppression) to +3 (strong emphasis) in order to provoke further explanations. To understand how management accounting systems contribute to interpretation of strategic issues the author asked questions like: (1) What kind of management accounting information catches your interest? (2) Is management accounting information sometimes contradictory or inconsistent? How do you deal with such information? (3) Does management accounting information improve your understanding of the business? Which information characteristics contribute to an improved understanding? (4) Is there a connection between management accounting information and corporate strategy? How is this achieved? (5) Do management accounting systems reduce or increase your awareness concerning changes in the company's environment (rated on a scale from -3 to +3)? (6) How do you decide whether to communicate information about potential strategic issues or not? (7) Have you ever taken measures to play down a potential problem?

Finally, the impact of management accounting systems on communication was discussed. This involved questions like: (1) What is the role of management accounting systems in communication? (2) Is management accounting information subject to frequent discussions? What makes this information so special? (3) Do management accounting systems suppress or promote communication with colleagues and superiors (rated on a scale from -3 to +3)? The interviews concluded with an open question on how to further improve management accounting systems for strategic sensemaking.

## 3.2 Questionnaire

In order to increase comparability across cases the author asked the interviewees to complete a questionnaire on the four information quality and five system quality dimensions, as well as the primary modes of information observation, interactive use, and the effectiveness of management accounting systems for strategic sensemaking. It took the respondents between 15 and 20 minutes to complete the questionnaire. Where there were severe time constraints the questionnaire was sent in advance, with a written introduction to the topic including examples of management accounting systems and management accounting information. In a few cases, the very senior positions of the interviewees left them with less time available than anticipated, and therefore the author asked them to return the questionnaire later, by fax or post.

Given the novelty of some management accounting system dimensions, the author tried to adapt whenever possible existing measurement instruments that had already proven their reliability and validity. The next sections provide descriptions of the chosen measurement instruments. A copy of the questionnaire is included in the appendix.

### 3.2.1 Measurement Instruments for Exogenous Variables

Exogenous variables are independent variables that are not explained by the research model. For this research exogenous variables encompass the four information quality and five system quality dimensions of management accounting systems. It seems plausible to assume that management accounting systems are not customized to individual users, but are adapted to context factors of the company and its environment.

The information quality dimension *scope* was measured by the scope instrument from CHENHALL AND MORRIS.[606] The author decided to reuse the identified sub-dimensions, but to adapt the initial question to the context of this study: "Do your management accounting systems provide enough of the following information for strategic sensemaking?" *Timeliness* was also measured by the timeliness instrument from CHENHALL AND MORRIS.[607] Since the original instrument focuses on the timely provisioning of management accounting information, two additional items for measuring whether the information itself is up-to-date and whether the most important information is available in real-time were included. The *format* instrument developed by NELSON ET AL. is too generic for the purposes of this research. However, SIMONS suggests that management accounting information that is used interactively should be both simple and semi-coded in order to encourage discussions about the meaning of the information.[608] Sim-

---

[606] Chenhall and Morris (1986), p. 32.
[607] Ibid., p. 32.
[608] Simons (1995), pp. 193-194.

ple information implies that the user knows how the information was created and what it means. Therefore, the author chose the user know-how instrument from SANDT.[609] An instrument from SCHULZ was adapted to measure the extent to which management accounting information includes qualitative information, like explanations, and presents quantitative information through tables and graphics.[610] Format was calculated as the average score of user know-how and semi-coding, since both conditions should be present. For *accuracy* the instrument from NELSON ET AL.[611] was complemented by one item to measure the consistency of information from different management accounting systems.

The system quality dimension *integration* consists of two different aspects: the integration of information from different areas of the company and the integration between goals, strategies and operations. The author decided to measure the integration of information from different areas with an instrument developed by NELSON ET AL.[612] Linkages between goals, strategies and operations were measured by an instrument from CHENHALL.[613] However, one item measuring the degree of codification was removed, because it belongs to the information quality dimension format. Integration was calculated as the average of these two instruments. Management accounting systems are flexible when they are regularly adapted to new strategic uncertainties, provide analysis capabilities and are used in a flexible and long-run-oriented evaluation style.[614] Therefore, for the *flexibility* dimension, the author chose the instruments adaptation from SANDT,[615] analytic capability from VANDENBOSCH AND HIGGINS[616] and the flexible and long-run use of targets as an evaluative style from OTLEY AND FAKIOLAS.[617] The score for the flexibility dimension was calculated as the average of these three instruments. *Accessibility* measures how easily managers can access management accounting information. It was measured by the accessibility instrument from NELSON ET AL.[618] For *formalization* the author created a new instrument based on ideas from

---

609 Sandt (2004), p. 142.
610 Schulz (2001), p. 680.
611 Nelson et al. (2005), p. 210.
612 Ibid., p. 211.
613 Chenhall (2005), p. 407.
614 See C2.3.2 Flexibility, pp. 5.
615 Sandt (2004), p. 140.
616 Vandenbosch and Higgins (1995), p. 130.
617 Otley and Fakiolas (2000), p. 509.
618 Nelson et al. (2005), p. 212.

MENON ET AL.[619] and BAUM AND WALLY.[620] The instrument measures the extent to which rules for deviation analyses exist, the presence of forms and templates and the existence of pre-defined channels for the communication of strategic issues. Finally, *media richness* is an original instrument and measures the extent to which rich media, such as group meetings and direct personal contact, are used to communicate strategic issues.

### 3.2.2 Measurement Instruments for Endogenous Variables

Endogenous variables are dependent variables that are supposedly affected by the exogenous variables of the research model. The literature review proposes that management accounting system dimensions can have an impact on observation, interpretation and communication of strategic issues. As interpretation is difficult to measure in a questionnaire, the author focused on measurement instruments for observation, communication and effectiveness of management accounting systems in strategic sensemaking.

*Observation* was measured with help of the instruments "focused search" and "scanning" from VANDENBOSCH AND HIGGINS.[621] These instruments evaluate the two primary information acquisition modes how managers can use their management accounting systems to observe changes in their company's environment. The author decided to measure the impact of management accounting systems on *communication* through their interactive use. The interactive use of management accounting systems increases interaction between organizational members and helps to foster discussions of information related to strategic uncertainties.[622] For the measurement of interactive use, the author decided to adapt an instrument from ABERNETHY AND BROWNELL to the strategic sensemaking context.[623] The instrument measures the extent to which management accounting information is used to discuss aspects of the business unit or changes in the company's environment, whether management accounting information causes managers to question basic assumptions of the business model, and the extent to which management accounting information demands frequent and regular attention of managers. The *effectiveness* of the use of management accounting systems in strate-

---

[619] Menon et al. (1999), p. 36.
[620] Baum and Wally (2003), pp. 1128-1129.
[621] Vandenbosch and Higgins (1996), p. 212.
[622] See C1.3 Impact of Management Accounting Systems on Communication, pp. 5.
[623] Abernethy and Brownell (1999), p. 202.

gic sensemaking was measured with the instrument scanning system effectiveness from YASAI-ARDEKANI AND NYSTROM.[624] The instrument focuses on the creation of awareness for relevant chances and risks, strengths and weaknesses, and general conditions of the environment through the use of management accounting systems. The author added two items that focus on the ability of management accounting systems to enable fast adoptions of product trends and the early identification of changing customer needs. In addition, the author used the instrument information acquisition scope from SIDHU ET AL. to measure the overall extent to which managers are aware of developments on the supply side, demand side and in other geographies.[625] The items for information acquisition scope do not distinguish between management accounting systems and informal sources. It is the intention of the author to capture the totality of available information for strategic sensemaking in order to have a second perspective on the contribution of management accounting systems.

## 4. Data Analysis

### 4.1 Analyzing the Interviews

In order to have a reliable data basis for analysis, all 30 interviews were fully taped and written out as verbatim protocols. The resulting 750 pages of qualitative data were imported into QSR NVivo for further analysis.[626] The author started the analyses by forming initial categories based on the literature review. As suggested by MILES AND HUBERMAN a coding guideline helped to define the categories and the conditions for assigning a text category to a text passage.[627] These categories or codes helped the researcher to organize the data and allowed him to retrieve text passages that belonged to a particular topic or hypothesis. The author used QSR NVivo to code the transliterated interviews in order to maintain consistency.

Codes were assigned along two primary sets of dimensions: steps of the sensemaking process and management accounting system dimensions. The assignment of categories

---

[624] Yasai-Ardekani and Nystrom (1996), p. 194.
[625] Sidhu et al. (2004), p. 922. The exact wordings for the items were obtained from Sidhu et al. (2004) by e-mail.
[626] QSR NVivo 2.0 is specialized software for the analysis of case study research data. It provides support especially for coding and analyzing of large amounts of qualitative data. See www.qsrinternational.com.
[627] Miles and Huberman (1984), pp. 54-56.

for the observation, interpretation or communication processes of strategic sensemaking followed the information processing status, whether stimuli became accessible in the form of data, data became understandable through interpretation, or information was communicated.

- *Observation*: Passages describing information acquisition were coded as "focused search" when the interviewee was looking for specific information in response to deviations, or to answer clearly defined questions. The code "scanning" was used when the interviewee described the search for new or unusual information without a specific question in mind. Furthermore, passages where the interviewee expressed opinions about the usefulness of management accounting systems for the observation of strategic issues were coded as "observation useful" or "observation not useful".

- *Interpretation*: Passages describing the impact of management accounting systems on the categorization of strategic issues were coded as "chance suppression", "chance neutral", "chance emphasis", "risk suppression", "risk neutral", and "risk emphasis". Statements that related to the level of awareness during interpretation were marked with "awareness increase" and "awareness decrease". Concerning dysfunctional side effects of management accounting systems, the author coded text passages describing the primary time-horizon of interview partners as "short-term", "mid-term" or "long term". Assignment to this category is based on a relative assessment with the planning horizon of the company. Furthermore, the presence of strategic information manipulation was coded as "manipulation present" and "manipulation not present".

- *Communication*: The impact of management accounting systems on communication was coded as "communication suppression" or "communication encouragement".

Whenever the interviewees explained steps in strategic sensemaking through management accounting system dimensions, the author used categories for the four information quality and five system quality dimensions to link management accounting systems to the respective sub process of strategic sensemaking.

- *Information quality dimensions*: Text passages describing comprehensive information from various sources, external information and future-oriented information were coded as "broad scope". Statements from interviewees about missing or incomplete information were marked as "narrow scope". Further coding for timeliness and accuracy were coded as "timeliness high", "timeliness low", "accuracy high", and "accuracy low". With respect to information representation, text passages where management accounting information was described as simple, well documented, comparable, standardized, understandable, and having qualitative components were coded as "format positive". Contrarily, text passages with descriptions like complex, different definitions, not comparable, not standardized, missing basis for comparisons, and a too high level of aggregation were coded as "format negative".

- *System quality dimensions*: Interview statements were coded with "integration high" when they referred to a high integration of different information sources and described the relationship between operational and strategic goals. "Integration low" was used when this integration was missing. Text passages that described a frequent adaptation of management accounting systems, the availability of analysis capabilities, and a flexible evaluation style were coded as "flexibility high". The category "flexibility low" was used for text passages with the opposite content. Easy accessible management accounting systems were coded as "accessibility high", while "accessibility low" was used for information that was difficult to obtain. The coding "formalization high" was used for statements of interview partners referring to prescriptions for processes, channels and reports while "formalization low" was used where such prescriptions did not exist. Finally, statements about interactions through personal channels were coded as "media richness high" and interactions solely through impersonal sources as "media richness low".

Data analysis of case study evidence is one of the least developed and most difficult aspects. There is no generally accepted model for the gathering or analysis of data for inductive research.[628] During the analysis of the interviews, the author found that some managers reported very different interpretation and communication processes. In order to explain the role of management accounting systems in strategic sensemaking it was necessary to distinguish three ways of using management accounting systems or management accounting information: adaptation, preparation and utilization. Adaptation is the alignment of management accounting systems with strategic uncertainties, preparations are the processes predominantly performed by middle management to prepare management accounting information, and utilization is the use of management ac-

[628] Yin (2003), p. 110 and Eisenhardt and Bourgeois (1988), p. 741.

counting systems mainly by upper management levels. This required the development of new categories and a recoding of all interviews.

- *Adaptation*: The coding "adaptation positive" was used when managers reported the review or adaptation of management accounting systems, discussions during the adaptation, the removal of reports or key performance indicators, or the use of management accounting systems to communicate the strategy and goals. A missing review of management accounting systems, too many reports, accounts about information overload, and a missing communication of the strategy were coded as "adaptation negative".

- *Preparation*: Text passages that describe interactions between different functions, the reconcilement of reports, discussions of challenges and planning assumptions, and benefits from preparing management accounting information were assigned the coding "preparation positive". Furthermore, a positive impact of management accounting systems on interpretation through their use for the development of strategic options, scenarios, forecasting of future states, but also their contribution to an improved understanding of the current situation, deviation analysis, and the development of countermeasures were also coded as "preparation positive". The coding "preparation negative" was used for statements related to discussions about data issues instead of discussions about root causes, a low level of interaction between managers, a missing use of management accounting systems for the assessment of future states, a low understanding of interdependencies, an insufficient interpretation of management accounting information, and missing benefits from preparing management accounting information.

- *Utilization*: Statements from managers that describe the interactive use of management accounting systems, their use to challenge managers and to provide regular feedback to them, the use of management accounting information for decision-making, and a broad distribution of management accounting information were coded as "utilization positive". Text passages that describe a low level of information use, reports without additional benefits, insufficient feedback to managers involved in the preparation of management accounting information, insufficient discussions about the meaning of information, and only narrow information distribution were assigned the coding "utilization negative".

The coding of the interview data provides not only qualitative data, but also quantitative data. Qualitative data contributes to the explanation of causal relationships and helps to understand the impact of management accounting systems on strategic sensemaking. Quantitative data, like the number of quotes and the percentage of interviewees who describe a certain relationship help to improve internal validity of the findings.

## 4.2 Analyzing the Questionnaires

The questionnaires provide quantitative data on the four information quality and five system quality dimensions, as well as the primary modes of information observation, interactive use, and the effectiveness of management accounting systems for strategic sensemaking. Analyses are based on 29 questionnaires from the interview partners.[629]

Missing data was not an issue for this study as only 0.7% of all data items were missing. Because of the small sample size, data sets with missing data were not excluded from further analyses. Instead, missing data items were replaced with the average of all other available data items for this construct.[630] At least two-thirds of all data items were available for constructs with missing data, which makes it unlikely that this procedure has introduced a bias. In order to verify the reliability of the measurements the author calculated the Cronbach alpha for all measurement instruments. Cronbach's alpha measures the internal consistency of a construct's items and is one of the most widely used indicators for the reliability of measurement instruments.[631] Values for Cronbach's alpha are between 0 and 1, with high values indicating high reliability. However, there is no general agreement on a value for Cronbach's alpha that indicates sufficient reliability. MALHORTA suggests a minimum value of 0.6 while NUNNALLY proposes a value of 0.7.[632] The exploratory nature of this research and the necessity to adapt or newly develop most of the measurement instruments justify a minimum value for Cronbach's alpha of 0.6. Table 15 below provides Cronbach alphas for all measurement instruments. It can show sample sizes of less than 29 data sets, because the calculation of Cronbach's alpha is based on the original data and eliminates data sets with missing values.

---

[629] Four questionnaires from the pilot case company were not used and one other questionnaire from company F was not returned by the interviewee.
[630] See also Allison (2001), pp. 11-12.
[631] Cronbach (1951), p. 332 and Peterson (1994), p. 382.
[632] Malhorta (1993), p. 308 and Nunnally (1978), p. 245.

| Category | Measurement instrument | | Data sets | Items | Cronbach alpha |
|---|---|---|---|---|---|
| Information quality | Scope | | 28 | 6 | 0.84 |
| | Timeliness | | 29 | 6 | 0.77 |
| | Format | User know-how | 28 | 3 | 0.87 |
| | Format | Semi-coding | 29 | 2 | 0.82 |
| | Format | Average | 28 | 5 | 0.88 |
| | Accuracy | | 28 | 4 | 0.89 |
| System quality | Integration | Source integration | 29 | 3 | 0.90 |
| | Integration | Strategic and operational linkages | 27 | 3 | 0.92 |
| | Integration | Average | 27 | 6 | 0.96 |
| | Flexibility | Adaptation | 29 | 4 | 0.85 |
| | Flexibility | Analytic capabilities | 29 | 2 | 0.63 |
| | Flexibility | Flexible, long run use of targets | 28 | 4 | 0.45 |
| | Flexibility | Average | 28 | 10 | 0.80 |
| | Accessibility | | 26 | 3 | 0.94 |
| | Formalization | | 28 | 3 | 0.85 |
| | Media richness | | 29 | 2 | 0.70 |
| Sense-making | Focused search | | 29 | 5 | 0.72 |
| | Scanning | | 29 | 4 | 0.58 |
| | Interactive use | | 29 | 4 | 0.85 |
| Effectiveness | Scanning system effectiveness | | 29 | 5 | 0.88 |
| | Information acquisition scope | | 28 | 13 | 0.86 |

*Table 15: Reliability of measurement instruments*

Overall, the measurement instruments of the questionnaire show a sufficient level of reliability, as indicated by high values for Cronbach's alphas. There are two notable exceptions. The construct 'flexible and long run use of targets' exhibits the lowest reliability with a Cronbach alpha of 0.45. The instrument is one factor of a larger instrument measuring also the rigid use of targets and non-use of targets for evaluation. OTLEY AND FAKIOLAS report a Cronbach alpha of 0.85 for their 10-item instrument.[633] The author also included the complete instrument in the questionnaire and calculated a

[633] Otley and Fakiolas (2000), p. 507. Otley and Fakiolas (2000) report 11 items in table 2 while the appendix shows only 10 items for this instrument. The author assumes that the Cronbach alpha was calculated for 10 items.

Cronbach alpha of 0.29 at a sample size of 26 for this instrument. Because of the small sample size it is not possible to draw conclusions on the overall reliability of this instrument. The low reliability of the instrument measuring the flexible and long run use of targets excludes it from an isolated consideration in this research. However, the instrument is treated as part of a larger construct measuring the overall flexibility of management accounting systems. A Cronbach alpha of 0.80 with 28 data sets for the 10-item instrument suggests a reliable measurement. The second exception is related to the instrument 'scanning' which has a Cronbach alpha of 0.58, slightly below the threshold of 0.60. Item-to-total correlations for the 4 items are between 0.61 and 0.71. However, a removal of the item with the lowest item-to-total correlation did not improve the reliability. Unfortunately VANDENBOSCH AND HIGGINS did not provide the Cronbach alpha for this instrument.[634] Because of the small sample size and the exploratory nature of this research, the author decided to use this instrument and pay particular attention to qualitative comments with respect to scanning behavior. Future research should especially improve the psychometric properties of the scanning instrument.

## 4.3 Within- and Cross-Case Analysis as Basis for Explanation Building

For all managers except one the author was able to compare qualitative data from the interview with quantitative data from the questionnaire. Combined with the tentative relationships derived from the literature review[635] this provided a first opportunity to understand how management accounting systems contribute to strategic sensemaking of each manager. The author looked for contradictory results between qualitative and quantitative data by comparing statements on management accounting system dimensions with the corresponding questionnaire results. Based on the quantitative data for each management accounting system dimension the sample was split at the median. Next, the author computed the percentage of all cases that made positive statements for the respective dimension and provided questionnaire results above the median. A value above 50% suggests coherent answers between interviews and questionnaires.[636] The

[634] See Vandenbosch and Higgins (1996). However, they found a high level of internal consistency with a measure developed by Fornell and Larcker (1981).

[635] See C2.4 Summary of Quality Dimensions and Strategic Sensemaking, pp. 5.

[636] A threshold of 50% indicates that an interviewee with questionnaire results above the median is more likely to provide positive than negative statements about the respective dimension. A higher threshold is not possible, because the quantitative data from the questionnaire allows only a relative

same procedure was applied to negative statements about management accounting system dimensions and questionnaire results below the median. Table 16 below provides the results for these analyses.

| **Management accounting system dimension** | **Percentage of matching cases for positive statements (number of cases)** | **Percentage of matching cases for negative statements (number of cases)** |
|---|---|---|
| Scope | 47% (7/15) | ***50% (2/4)*** |
| Timeliness | ***56% (5/9)*** | 40% (2/5) |
| Format | ***55% (6/11)*** | ***86% (6/7)*** |
| Accuracy | ***80% (4/5)*** | ***100% (5/5)*** |
| Integration | ***52% (11/21)*** | ***63% (10/16)*** |
| Flexibility | ***69% (11/16)*** | 38% (3/8) |
| Accessibility | ***64% (7/11)*** | 40% (2/5) |
| Formalization | ***57% (12/21)*** | ***57% (8/14)*** |
| Media richness | ***71% (12/17)*** | 25% (1/4) |

*Table 16: Correspondence of quantitative and qualitative data*

Table 16 shows that for eight out of nine management accounting system dimensions more than 50% (average 61%) of all cases that made positive statements for the respective dimension provided questionnaire results above the median. The only exception is the scope dimension, with 47% of corresponding cases. Results for the correspondence of negative statements for management accounting system dimensions with questionnaire results below the median are more mixed. Five out of nine dimensions show coherent answers between quantitative and qualitative data. However, there were also less negative statements than positive statements for management accounting system dimensions. In addition, some interviewees provided both positive and negative statements for different management accounting systems. This is a limitation of this research, as management accounting systems were very broadly defined as all formal systems that provide information to managers. Despite these limitations, on average 55% of all cases that made negative statements for the respective dimensions provided questionnaire results below the median. Overall, these analyses suggest coherent answers in the interviews and questionnaires.

assessment for each management accounting system dimension. Positive interview statements are not related to absolute values for the respective measurement instruments.

Coherent answers between quantitative and qualitative data provide the basis for cross-case analysis. Cross-case analysis is the search for patterns that go beyond the initial impressions. The use of structured and diverse lenses on the data particularly helps to improve the likelihood of accurate and reliable theory.[637] The analysis of quantitative data from the questionnaire provided a starting point in the search for patterns. The author conducted correlation analyses to identify relationships between management accounting system dimensions, strategic sensemaking processes and their effectiveness. Analyses of qualitative statements related to these relationships helped to explain them. In addition, the author performed a cluster analysis on the management accounting system dimensions and compared the use of management accounting systems for strategic sensemaking within and between the resulting groups. This further helped in understanding the differences in the use of management accounting systems and how information quality and system quality dimensions contribute to this.

After several iterations a more complete picture of the role of management accounting systems in strategic sensemaking emerged. Finally, the author prepared a report for each company, which included a comparison of their management accounting systems with other companies in their industry, a discussion of their strengths and weaknesses based on the research model and suggestions for improving the contribution of their management accounting systems to strategic sensemaking.

## 5. Quality Ensuring Measures

According to EISENHARDT there is no general set of guidelines for the assessment of case study research. However, case study research should contribute to theory that is parsimonious, testable, and logically coherent, which requires a careful analytical procedure.[638] "Because a research design is supposed to represent a logical set of statements, we also can judge the quality of any given design according to certain logical tests."[639] YIN suggests testing for construct validity, internal validity, external validity and reliability.[640] Table 17 below gives an overview of the measures taken to ensure

---

[637] Eisenhardt (1989), pp. 540-541.
[638] Ibid., p. 548.
[639] Yin (2003), p. 33.
[640] An application of these four tests to a case study in the accounting context can be found in Bruns and McKinnon (1993), p. 89.

quality for the four logical tests. The following sections describe the tests and contributing measures in more detail.

| Test | Quality ensuring measure | Research phase |
|---|---|---|
| Construct validity | • Use multiple sources of evidence (interviews, surveys)<br>• Establish a chain of evidence<br>• Let the interviewees review the results through a report | Data collection (section D3) |
| Internal validity | • Conduct within-case and cross-case analyses through data triangulation, correlation and cluster analysis<br>• Do pattern matching by comparing empirically based patterns with predicted ones<br>• Do explanation building | Data analysis (section D4) |
| External validity | • Use replication logic in multiple case-studies | Research design (section D2) |
| Reliability | • Use case study protocol<br>• Develop case study data base | Data collection (section D3) |

*Table 17: Quality ensuring measures and research phases*[641]

## 5.1 Ensuring Construct Validity

Construct validity tests whether the research establishes correct operational measures for the concepts being studied.[642] Researchers who criticize case studies often point out that the collection of data follows subjective judgment and does not contain a sufficiently operational set of measures. This research addresses construct validity by (1) using multiple sources of evidence, (2) establishing a chain of evidence, and (3) letting the interview partner review the results through a report.

*(1) Multiple sources of evidence*: This study draws on qualitative data from interviews and quantitative data from questionnaires. The use of multiple sources of evidence enables triangulation through the development of converging lines of inquiry.[643] Additional measures were taken to ensure construct validity of the measurement instruments in the questionnaire. First, existing constructs were used and translated to Ger-

[641] Adapted from Yin (2003), p. 34.
[642] Ibid., p. 34.
[643] Ibid., p. 98.

man whenever possible. Correspondence of the translation with the original constructs was verified by a professional translation service. Second, researchers who were familiar with the research topic and managers from the pilot case company reviewed the questionnaire. The modification of some questions further improved understanding.

*(2) Chain of evidence*: Following a suggestion of YIN this study established a chain of evidence by making explicit the method used by the researcher to analyze the data and reach conclusions and propositions.[644]

*(3) Review of results*: The author compiled the results of this research into a report for each company and sent it back to the interviewees. The reports included suggestions for the improvement of management accounting systems based on the propositions of this research. This enabled the interviewees to check even further for construct validity. Unfortunately it was not possible to introduce a second perspective during data collection through the use of a second interviewer. In order to further reduce a potential interviewer bias, the author regularly discussed the results with other researchers and practitioners. These discussions provided additional perspectives that helped to increase construct validity of the findings.

## 5.2 Ensuring Internal Validity

Internal validity tests whether the research establishes a sufficient causal relationship between dependent and independent variables.[645] This research addresses internal validity by (1) conducting within-case and cross-case analyses through data triangulation, correlation and cluster analysis, (2) pattern matching through comparing empirically based patterns with predicted ones, and (3) doing explanation building.

*(1) Within-case and cross-case analysis*: According to YIN a major threat to internal validity is the assumption of a causal relationship between two factors that actually occur coincidentally.[646] The author used correlation and cluster analysis to identify possible relationships between variables. In order to reduce the possibility of spurious effects, qualitative statements related to these relationships were investigated. This data triangulation helped to improve understanding of the relationships, and thereby in-

[644] Ibid., p. 105.
[645] De Vaus (2001), p. 27 and Yin (2003), p. 34.
[646] Yin (2003), p. 36.

creased the internal validity of the findings. In addition, the author verified the correspondence of quantitative and qualitative data through within-case analyses.[647]

*(2) Pattern matching*: Pattern matching compares an empirically based pattern with a predicted one. "If the patterns coincide, the results can help a case study to strengthen its internal validity."[648] Pattern matching is a specific application of cross-case analysis. This research is based on an extensive literature review about how management accounting systems can impact strategic sensemaking of individual managers. This review provided a set of tentative, theoretical relationships between management accounting system dimensions and strategic sensemaking. The author compared these theoretical patterns with empirical patterns. In case of deviations further analyses were conducted to understand the underlying rationale.

*(3) Explanation building*: The study further addressed internal validity by using explanation building during the analysis phase. This analytical strategy helped to explain the causal links for the different cases and contributed to the development of an overall research model.

## 5.3 Ensuring External Validity

External validity tests "… whether a study's findings are generalizable beyond the immediate case study."[649] Critics of case study research often implicitly compare case selection with statistical sampling in survey research and criticize a lack of generalizability. However, the goal of case study research is not statistical generalization, but analytical generalization. "In analytical generalization, the investigator is striving to generalize a particular set of results to some broader theory."[650] Following a suggestion from YIN the author chose a multiple-case study design in order to increase external validity of the empirical research.[651]

This study draws on 30 interviews with top and middle managers in seven large companies in Germany. Cases were replicated in two different industries with different requirements for strategic sensemaking. One industry is characterized by frequent changes in technology and customer demand, resulting in a short planning horizon.

---

[647] See D4.3 Within- and Cross-Case Analysis as Basis for Explanation Building, pp. 5.
[648] Yin (2003), p. 116.
[649] Ibid., p. 37.
[650] Ibid., p. 37.
[651] See D2.1 Unit of Analysis and Selection Criteria, pp. 5.

The other industry has long product lifecycles and an inflexible production technology that requires long-term planning. Cases were selected along literal and theoretical replication logic, which helped to increase the external validity of the findings from this research.

## 5.4 Ensuring Reliability

Reliability tests whether a different investigator following the same method would arrive at the same findings and conclusions. "The goal of reliability is to minimize the errors and biases in a study."[652] This research addresses reliability by (1) using a case study protocol and (2) by developing a case study database.

*(1) Case study protocol*: A case study protocol is a major tactic in increasing reliability of case study research and is intended to guide the researcher during the case studies.[653] The protocol for this research prescribed the use of a semi-structured interview guide, which ensured the use of the same opening and similar questions during the interviews.[654] Furthermore, a coding tree ensured a consistent coding of the interview data and thereby increased transparency of the analysis. The author conducted a pilot case study with four managers to test the interview guide and questionnaire.[655] Data from the pilot case study also provided an opportunity to verify the coding procedure and to conduct initial analyses.

*(2) Case study database*: The author decided to document the research thoroughly through field notes, interview tapes, verbatim protocols of the interviews, questionnaires, and additional documents collected from the interview partners. All documents were stored in a case study database, which also included the applied coding. As the interview protocols cannot be included due to the large amount of data, the data is accessible at the Chair of Management Accounting and Control of the European Business School (ebs), International University Schloß Reichartshausen.

---

[652] Yin (2003), p. 37.
[653] Ibid., p. 67.
[654] See D3.1 Semi-structured Interview, pp. 5.
[655] See Yin (2003), pp. 78-80.

# E Results of Case Study Research

The following chapters present the results from thirty top and middle managers in seven large companies. Firstly, section E1 describes the impact of management accounting systems on the strategic sensemaking processes of individual managers. It presents results on how management accounting system dimensions relate to observation (section E1.1), interpretation (section E1.2), and communication (section E1.3) in strategic sensemaking. A comparison of the findings with the literature review provides the basis for the development of propositions on the impact of management accounting system dimensions on the strategic sensemaking processes of individual managers (section E1.4).

Secondly, the case studies show that it is necessary to distinguish three different ways of using management accounting systems or information for strategic sensemaking: adaptation, preparation and utilization. Adaptation is the alignment of management accounting systems with strategic uncertainties (section E2.1), preparations are the processes predominantly performed by middle managers to prepare management accounting information (section E2.2), and utilization is the use of management accounting information, mainly by upper management levels (section E2.3). The interviews suggest that management accounting system dimensions contribute to different roles of management accounting systems in strategic sensemaking (section E2.4).

Thirdly, a summary of the derived propositions will be presented in section E3.

Quantitative data from the questionnaires provides a good starting point to identify relationships between management accounting system dimensions, strategic sensemaking and effectiveness. Table 18 below provides an overview of means, standard deviations and correlations between all dependent and independent variables.

| Variable | | Mean | s.d. | Information Quality | | | | System Quality | | | | | Impact | | | |
|---|---|---|---|---|---|---|---|---|---|---|---|---|---|---|---|---|
| | | | | I.1 | I.2 | I.3 | I.4 | S.1 | S.2 | S.3 | S.4 | S.5 | E.1 | E.2 | E.3 | E.4 |
| I.1 | Scope | 4.2 | 1.12 | | | | | | | | | | | | | |
| I.2 | Timeliness | 4.7 | 1.04 | .53** | | | | | | | | | | | | |
| I.3 | Format | 4.7 | 1.25 | .46** | .70† | | | | | | | | | | | |
| I.4 | Accuracy | 4.8 | 1.22 | .41* | .68† | .85† | | | | | | | | | | |
| S.1 | Integration | 4.2 | 1.47 | .61† | .72† | .73† | .76† | | | | | | | | | |
| S.2 | Flexibility | 4.8 | 0.92 | .46** | .58† | .75† | .76† | .80† | | | | | | | | |
| S.3 | Accessibility | 4.6 | 1.47 | .48** | .71† | .67† | .70† | .85† | .80† | | | | | | | |
| S.4 | Formalization | 3.3 | 1.41 | .28 | .50** | .38* | .37* | .35* | .15 | .15 | | | | | | |
| S.5 | Media richness | 5.7 | 1.14 | .25 | .52** | .41* | .48** | .64† | .58† | .47** | .31 | | | | | |
| E.1 | Scanning | 3.7 | 1.03 | .37* | .38* | .18 | .25 | .37* | .50** | .49** | .12 | .25 | | | | |
| E.2 | Focused search | 4.6 | 1.08 | .26 | .36* | .62† | .46** | .50** | .46** | .43** | .37* | .13 | -.11 | | | |
| E.3 | Interactive use | 5.4 | 1.12 | .52** | .51** | .52** | .46** | .65† | .54** | .58† | .44** | .45** | .31 | .61† | | |
| E.4 | Scanning system effectiveness | 3.8 | 1.14 | .78† | .61† | .62† | .59† | .70† | .58† | .61† | .42* | .41* | .42* | .39* | .61† | |
| E.5 | Information acquisition scope | 4.6 | 0.97 | .38* | .37* | .30 | .22 | .39* | .24 | .31 | .34* | .33* | .38* | .22 | .41* | .61† |

Note: All variables were measured on a 7-point Likert scale. Sample size: 29; one-tailed: * < .05; ** < .01; † < .001

*Table 18: Means, standard deviations and correlations for all variables*

# 1. Impact of Management Accounting Systems on Strategic Sensemaking

Management accounting systems play an important role in individual managers' strategic sensemaking. Results from the questionnaires indicate a strong correlation between scanning system effectiveness and the overall information acquisition scope ($r = .61$). Furthermore, this correlation is significantly higher than any other correlation between management accounting system dimensions and information acquisition scope (from $r = .22$ for accuracy to $r = .39$ for integration). This suggests that managers with effective management accounting systems gather more information and are more aware of developments in the company's environment. The following chapters will provide results on the impact of management accounting systems on observation (chapter E1.1), interpretation (chapter E1.2), and communication (chapter E1.3) in strategic sensemaking. Chapter E1.4 summarizes the impact of management accounting systems on strategic sensemaking.

## 1.1 Observation

The literature review suggests that managers use management accounting systems to acquire data for strategic sensemaking through focused search and scanning.[656] Results from the questionnaires show that both modes of information acquisition contribute to strategic sensemaking, as scanning system effectiveness has a similar association with scanning ($r = .42$) and with focused search ($r = .39$). In addition, managers seem to use their management accounting systems more intensively for focused search than for scanning (average score for focused search is 4.6 and for scanning 3.7; difference significant at $p = .001$). However, extant literature suggests a higher association with scanning, since scanning is the undirected search for new strategic issues and therefore should be more suitable for observation than focused search.

These findings can be explained by taking a close look at the role of management accounting systems in the observation step of strategic sensemaking. Several interviewees report that they learn about new strategic issues first through informal sources, and not through management accounting systems. Manager C2 describes the role of management accounting systems for the observation of strategic issues as follows: "I cannot observe chances and risks through management accounting systems alone. It is difficult to identify threats and opportunities with the help of a system. I need a lot of in-

---

[656] See C1.1 Impact of Management Accounting Systems on Observation, pp. 5.

teraction with the market and a good understanding about the industry in order to have a broad radar screen for opportunities. Operational risks are a bit easier to identify through management accounting information on operational performance, but strategic risks are as difficult as opportunities." A similar statement from A1: "Management accounting information indicates that sales are declining, but not much more. It does not help you to identify changes in technology or a different market positioning of competitors. This information is not part of management accounting systems." Managers receive information about new technologies through personal networks with specialists. As interview partner F4 remarks: "There are technicians that monitor the market and they permanently come up with new things that can further improve effectiveness. They are much more sensitive to new things."

Instead of using management accounting systems to observe new strategic issues, this research suggests that managers use their management accounting systems to look for specific information that helps them to substantiate information about strategic issues from informal sources. Manager G2 describes this: "At the beginning it is a creative process where highly qualified people from different functions discuss new ideas. They try to inspire others with their ideas. As a next step you use management accounting information, from various sources, to validate these ideas." Management accounting systems can help to validate gut feelings by providing additional facts, as mentioned by manager F3: "I like these gut feelings. If something seems strange, I try to substantiate my gut feelings through facts. Sometimes I am wrong, but if I can prove my gut feelings then we have to take corrective action." A similar statement is made by interviewee E3: "At the beginning it is a perception, or an issue that I have in my mind. But based on a press clipping I will not make an investment. At the end of the day it requires a sound business case, and I have not seen any press clippings in our business cases." It seems that an important role of management accounting systems in strategic sensemaking is to provide information that helps to make sense of already identified strategic issues, rather then to provide information about new strategic issues.

However, management accounting information can also help to identify operational issues. Manager D1 describes this as follows: "Developments in management accounting information over time are not helpful in identifying new strategic issues. However, they help in day-to-day decision making, in order to control certain business developments." Interviewee C1 argues in a similar way: "[Management accounting systems] help to identify operational issues, such as allocation problems or delayed sales. A rolling order forecast helps us to identify products that do not perform as expected." Manager B5 reports that sufficient performance information is available as an indicator for potential issues, but strategic sensemaking requires additional information to understand root causes and the expected impact: "There is enough information available to indicate that there is an issue. It is easy to say that we have a problem, but for strategic sensemaking it requires understanding of the root cause and its potential impact. [...] That requires additional effort."

Overall it seems that managers use management accounting systems in two different ways for the observation of strategic issues. Firstly, statements from the interviews and the overview of important sources for strategic sensemaking in section D2.2 indicate that informal sources are particularly important for the observation of potential strategic issues.[657] Managers use their management accounting systems to look for additional information in order to substantiate these issues. Secondly, for issues that already have an impact on performance it is the other way round. Management accounting information can indicate a problem and initiate the search for information from other sources. The top manager F2 puts this in a nutshell: "This is the topic of future or past orientation. The more you pay attention to past performance the more likely it is that management accounting information initiates the search for informal information. If you are sales- or action-oriented to achieve a certain goal, than it is more likely that you move from informal to formal information."

These findings suggest the following propositions:

> *PROPOSITION 1a: Managers are more likely to observe potential strategic issues through informal sources than through management accounting systems.*

> *PROPOSITION 1b: Managers use management accounting systems to search for additional information that helps them to substantiate potential strategic issues gleaned from informal sources.*

According to VANDENBOSCH AND HIGGINS focused search occurs when executives verify performance results or look up specific information.[658] This research shows that 91% of all managers that describe focused search behavior use their management accounting systems to identify reasons for deviations from key performance indicators,

---

[657] See D2.2 Overview Case Companies, pp. 5.
[658] Vandenbosch and Higgins (1996), p. 202.

or budget deviations from plans or forecasts. Manager A4 describes this as: "I use the data warehouse if I have specific information needs: I want to know about costs or want to understand how certain issues develop. I want to analyze raw data and drill down into detailed positions in order to understand why certain profit centers have deviations." Manager G2 adds specific questions from top management as an initiator of focused search: "I use the management accounting systems when I see deviations in monthly reports, or to answer specific questions from top management." Some interview partners also describe focused search in response to positive deviations, in order to understand whether these positive deviations are permanent. In such cases, they either intend to increase targets for the next planning round or try to learn from this situation in order to transfer it to other situations. According to interviewee F3, "positive deviations are very welcome, as they indicate that we can increase targets for the next year." Manager D1 states: "I look at positive deviations to understand where they come from. [...] With positive deviations we have to think about the mid-term and consider them during the next planning round."

In addition to deviations and specific questions, this research suggests that the interactive use of management accounting information can also initiate focused search. The questionnaires show a high association between focused search and interactive use ($r = .61$). This provides some evidence that the interactive use of management accounting information has an attention-focusing effect. Managers use management accounting systems to look for specific information that is of interest to upper level managers. Manager B4 provides an example to illustrate this: "There are important technical performance measures related to quality that receive special attention from top management. For these measures I conduct special analyses and I question their measurement. In addition we conduct benchmarks with our competitors to prove that our quality is sufficient."

This leads to the following propositions for focused search:

> PROPOSITION *1c: Managers use management accounting systems for focused search, in order to understand reasons for deviations and to answer specific questions.*

> PROPOSITION *1d: The interactive use of management accounting information initiates focused search to look for specific information that is of interest to upper level managers.*

In contrast to focused search, managers that exhibit scanning behavior browse through management accounting information without a particular problem to solve or question to answer.[659] In particular, pieces of information from different sources that appear inconsistent when brought together seem to draw the attention of managers. Interviewee A1 illustrates this: "We have key performance indicators for all areas of our service units. Last year the developments of certain indicators were not in line with developments in the financial statements. This initiated further analysis to understand the underlying reasons and to initiate counter-measures."

Scanning seems also to be associated with the availability of slack time. 12 Out of 20 managers (60%) from staff functions that are responsible for strategic projects, strategic planning or controlling have scores for scanning above the median, whereas only 2 out of 9 functional managers (22%) show high scanning behavior. Manager A1 states: "I scan management accounting information systematically, both opportunities and risks, to identify new projects." Interviewee A4, from the same staff function, relates his ability to have a different perspective, and to identify new issues to their organizational setup without operational responsibilities: "It is important to have an external or different perspective to see things differently. I think it is because of our organizational setup. We are trained to think analytically and have the ability to understand basic dependencies without knowing the operational work in detail. This gives us a different perspective and avoids blind spots." Manager G3 adds: "When you are not involved in day-to-day business you can ask questions that others might classify as stupid. But you can ask every question and provide a different perspective that might help to do things differently." Managers in staff functions have sufficient time to scan management accounting information and to compare it to their own experience. Manager C3 illustrates this: "I can identify issues relatively early, just by looking at the cost development, but of course this is related to my experience."

This suggests the following proposition for scanning:

> *PROPOSITION 1e: Managers in staff functions are more likely to use their management accounting systems for scanning than managers with operational responsibilities.*

---

[659] Ibid., p. 202.

In order to understand the impact of specific management accounting system dimensions on observation, the author triangulated questionnaire results on system dimensions with interview statements. For each management accounting system dimension the cases were split into two groups at the median, and the percentages of cases with statements related to observation helpful, observation not helpful, scanning and focused search were computed (see Table 19 below). Combined with results from correlation analysis between management accounting system dimensions and focused search, as well as scanning (see Table 18 above) this provides indications of relationships. The following section provides a discussion of the findings for each management accounting system dimension and will conclude with a formulation of propositions.

*Scope* has a consistent positive association with observation through scanning (r = .37) and focused search (r = .26). Although the association with focused search is not significant, 69% percent of all statements about focused search are from managers who report broad scope information. This suggests an important relationship between scope and focused search. Manager A2 emphasizes the importance of future-oriented information: "I would not say that we do not have any information related to future issues, but it is definitely an area which requires improvement. [...] I have some basic information but its time-horizon is very limited." In addition, interviewee G3 stresses the importance of a broad range of information: "If you have a broad range of information you can identify new things and put them on your radar screen. The next time, you pay more attention to these things even if you do not know what it means for the company. But you have a picture in your mind and you know that there is some information. You can work in a very structured manner, but I think that a lot of relevant information comes up by chance. I am not sure that I would have found such information if I had been looking for it."

*Timeliness* has a consistent positive association with observation through scanning (r = .38) and focused search (r = .36).

*Format* has a consistent positive association with observation through focused search (r = .62). The high correlation, combined with the previous statements on focused search, suggests that management accounting information in a format that includes graphical representations, tables and qualitative comments helps managers to identify deviations and to look for underlying reasons. Manager C5 stresses the importance of a standardized format to find important information: "We do not have a standardized format. We have to standardize it so that everybody can identify issues, not only people who know how to read these reports."

Note: Ratings for usefulness of observation are centered at the median. Consistent positive results are indicated by (1) higher values on both elements of the main diagonal for observation compared to the corresponding elements of the secondary diagonal and (2) higher percentage of cases that describe scanning or focused search and have provided questionnaire results above the median for the respective dimension. Rows for usefulness of observation do not add to 100% because of missing values. Sample size is n=26, because 3 interviews were conducted with 2 interviewees each and 1 questionnaire was not returned.

*Table 19: Relationships between MAS dimensions and observation*

*Accuracy* has a consistent positive association with observation through focused search (r = .46) but not with scanning (r = .25, not significant). The interviews provide some support for a negative association between information accuracy and scanning. In particular, information inconsistencies as described in previous interview statements seem to contribute to the observation of strategic issues through scanning. However, a median split along accuracy and a correlation analysis for both groups shows only insignificant positive correlations between scanning and accuracy (r = .36 at p = .11 for low accuracy and r = .31 at p = .12 for high accuracy). Overall, this suggests that accuracy has a positive association with observation.

*Integration* has a consistent positive association with observation through focused search (r = .50). Interviews do not provide a clear indication for a relationship between integration and scanning. However, the questionnaires suggest a low, but significant positive correlation (r = .37). In addition, integration is highly correlated with scope (r = .61), which suggests that the integration of information sources contributes to the usefulness of a broad range of information as described by manager G3 in the scope section. Overall this suggests a positive relationship between integration and scanning.

*Flexibility* and *accessibility* are both positively associated with scanning (r = .50 and r = .49) and focused search (r = .46 and r = .43, respectively). These high correlations outweigh the mixed picture concerning their impact on observation in Table 19.

*Formalization* has a consistent positive association with observation through focused search (r = .37). The literature review suggests that a high level of formalization has a negative impact on scanning.[660] To verify this, a median split was conducted for the formalization dimension and the correlation between scanning and cases with a high level of formalization was computed. A correlation of r = -.49 (significant at p = .06) provides support for a negative impact of a high level of formalization on scanning. However, managers are more likely to use management accounting systems for focused search, which has a positive association with formalization. This suggests that a balanced level of formalization is most suited to the observation of strategic issues.

*Media richness* has an inconsistent association with scanning and focused search. Furthermore, correlations are not significant. Combined with missing theoretical propositions from the literature review this suggests that media richness has no impact on the observation of strategic issues.

A pattern matching with tentative propositions developed from the literate review[661] provides consistent results for the impact of scope, timeliness, integration, flexibility, accessibility and formalization on observation. The literature review did not provide suggestions for the role of format and tentative propositions for accuracy were unclear. This research shows a strong positive association between format and observation

---

660 See C2.3.4 Formalization, p. 5.
661 See Table 5, p. 5.

through focused search. For accuracy it provides evidence for a positive association between accuracy and focused search that is in line with the literature. It was not possible to confirm the expected negative impact of accuracy on scanning.[662] Overall the impact of management accounting system dimensions on observation can be summarized in the following propositions:

> *PROPOSITION 1f: The information quality dimensions scope, timeliness, format, and accuracy, and the system quality dimensions integration, flexibility, accessibility, and formalization contribute positively to the use of management accounting systems for the observation of strategic issues. High levels of formalization have a negative impact on observation.*

> *PROPOSITION 1g: The dimensions scope, timeliness, format, accuracy, integration, flexibility, accessibility, and formalization contribute positively to the use of management accounting systems for focused search.*

> *PROPOSITION 1h: The dimensions scope, timeliness, integration, flexibility and accessibility contribute positively to the use of management accounting systems for scanning. High levels of formalization have a negative impact on scanning.*

## 1.2 Interpretation

Results concerning the impact of management accounting systems on interpretation are mainly based on interview statements and interviewees' ratings on the suppression or emphasis of chances and risks, as well as ratings on their awareness during interpretation. Questionnaire results on management accounting system dimensions were triangulated with ratings from interview partners through sub-group comparisons. These sub-groups were created through median splits along system dimensions and interviewer ratings. Table 20 provides the percentage of respondents in each group.

The author asked the interviewees to rate the extent to which they believe that management accounting systems emphasize or suppress chances and risks. On average the respondents perceive that management accounting systems emphasize risks (average 1.4 on a scale from -3 to +3), while the effect on chances seems to be balanced (average -0.1 on a scale from -3 to +3). Table 20 below shows that the management accounting system dimensions scope, timeliness, format, accuracy and flexibility con-

---

[662] See C2.2.4 Accuracy, pp. 5.

tribute to the emphasis of management accounting systems on risks. This suggests that mainly information quality dimensions, with the exception of flexibility, contribute to the emphasis on risks. On the contrary, it seems that the system quality dimensions integration, accessibility, formalization and media richness particularly contribute to the emphasis of management accounting systems on chances.

| | | | **Percentage of respondents in each group with ratings related to ...** | | | | | | |
|---|---|---|---|---|---|---|---|---|---|
| | | | ***Chance*** | | ***Risk*** | | ***Awareness*** | | |
| **Median split along MAS dimension** | | **N** | ***Em-pha-sis*** | ***Sup-pres-sion*** | ***Em-pha-sis*** | ***Sup-pres-sion*** | ***Incr-ease*** | ***Decr-ease*** | **Comment** |
| Scope | Broad | 13 | **54%** | 31% | **54%** | 38% | **46%** | 23% | Consistent positive results for risk emphasis and awareness increase |
| | Narrow | 13 | 15% | 23% | 31% | **46%** | 23% | **38%** | |
| Timeli-ness | High | 13 | **46%** | 31% | **69%** | 23% | **62%** | 15% | Consistent positive results for risk emphasis and awareness increase |
| | Low | 13 | 23% | 23% | 15% | **62%** | 8% | **46%** | |
| Format | Pos. | 13 | **46%** | 31% | **62%** | 31% | **38%** | 23% | Consistent positive results for risk emphasis and awareness increase |
| | Neg. | 13 | 23% | 23% | 23% | **54%** | 31% | **38%** | |
| Accu-racy | High | 14 | **50%** | 29% | **57%** | 36% | **36%** | 21% | Consistent positive results for risk emphasis and awareness increase |
| | Low | 12 | 17% | 25% | 25% | **50%** | 33% | **42%** | |
| Integra-tion | High | 13 | **62%** | 15% | 46% | 46% | 38% | 31% | Consistent positive results for chance emphasis |
| | Low | 13 | 8% | **38%** | 38% | 38% | 31% | 31% | |
| Flexi-bility | High | 13 | **38%** | 31% | **54%** | 38% | **38%** | 31% | Consistent positive results for risk emphasis |
| | Low | 13 | 31% | 23% | 31% | **46%** | 31% | 31% | |
| Acces-sibility | High | 14 | **50%** | 21% | **50%** | 43% | **43%** | 36% | Consistent positive results for chance emphasis |
| | Low | 12 | 17% | **33%** | 33% | 42% | 25% | 25% | |
| Formal-ization | High | 14 | **57%** | 14% | **50%** | 43% | **50%** | 14% | Consistent positive results for chance emphasis and awareness increase |
| | Low | 12 | 8% | **42%** | 33% | 42% | 17% | **50%** | |
| Media richness | High | 18 | **44%** | 22% | 44% | 44% | 28% | **39%** | Consistent positive results for chance emphasis and consistent negative impact on awareness |
| | Low | 8 | 13% | **38%** | 38% | 38% | **50%** | 13% | |

Note: Ratings are centered at the median. Consistent positive results are indicated by higher values on both elements of the main diagonal compared to the corresponding elements of the secondary diagonal. Rows for chance, risk and awareness categories do not add to 100% because of missing values. Sample size is n=26, because 3 interviews were conducted with 2 interviewees each and 1 questionnaire was not returned.

*Table 20: Relationships between MAS dimensions and interpretation*

Some interviewees relate the emphasis of management accounting systems on risks to regular comparisons of management accounting information against plans and targets and the explicit reporting of risks. Managers are often required to perform monthly deviation analyses in order to explain trends or reasons for underperformance, while the identification of opportunities is carried out less rigorously. Manager E4 emphasizes the focus on risk management: "I would say that we emphasize risks and suppress chances. It is a bit as though you keep chances up your sleeve and you want to identify risks as early as possible. Therefore we have a risk management process, to be on the safe side. I am sure that our planning process contributes to the focus of our managers on risks. ... We also maintain a risk portfolio. There is a regular collection of identified risks from risk managers in each center. We filter these risks along occurrence probabilities and financial impact, and report them to top management, who regularly discuss them. We have an improvement map for smaller chances. But this is for smaller things as we do not include big opportunities." However, cultural context factors and prior performance also contribute to an emphasis on risks. Interviewee F3 remarks: "Because of our past experiences we have a tendency to focus too much on risks. We are very risk-oriented and report all risks immediately." Manager E1 refers to the criticality of risks for the business model of company E: "It is difficult to revise mistakes. They are not forgotten after a few years; it takes much longer. This has a strong impact on our culture. Our most important skill is risk control." A financial controller relates his emphasis on risks to his position: "We focus too little on chances. There is almost exclusively a focus on risks. Probably this is also related to the mentality of the controller. I am a cautious person and I will consider positive effects in our planning only when I am fully convinced that they will materialize."

Often, management accounting systems provide a special focus on opportunities only during planning and forecasting. The senior manager F2 from company F states that their planning process helps, in a sense, to ensure that they do not miss chances: "Business planning and sales planning ensure that we identify all available opportunities. We evaluate opportunities also through occurrence probabilities. This makes sure that we do not forget opportunities and helps us to put changes into perspective." Company F has an extensive bottom-up planning process that requires strong participation from middle managers. They develop strategic options at middle management levels and only present them to top management in decision meetings. This suggests that formalized management accounting systems can force managers to prepare initial interpretations of existing issues. Formalized management accounting systems can also ensure a sufficient representation of opportunities. Manager F3 describes how a balanced representation of risks and opportunities contributes to a stronger focus on chances: "There is a strong focus also on chances. In our monthly report we focus explicitly on opportunities. The same is true for our forecasts. Top managers question our planning when chances and risks are not balanced. If your chances amount to 20 million and risks to 100 million then there must be something wrong." The literature review suggests that a high level of formalization can discourage opportunities and emphasize threats.[663] A median split along the formalization dimension shows that management accounting systems with a lower level of formalization contribute to a slight suppression of chances (-0.6 on a scale from -3 to +3) and a weak emphasis of risks (0.9 on a scale from -3 to +3). However, a high level of formalization contributes to a slight emphasis of chances (0.6 on a scale from -3 to +3) and a strong emphasis of risks (2.1 on a scale from -3 to +3). A t-test shows significant differences for chances ($p = .02$) and risks ($p = .01$). This suggests that formalized management accounting systems emphasize both chances and risks. Even higher levels of formalization do not lead to a suppression of chances.

A few interview partners relate the suppression of chances through management accounting systems to the representation format of management accounting information. Interviewee A2 mentions a missing possibility of representation in their systems: "There is a slight suppression of chances, because we do not have information that can be aggregated." However, a high level of aggregation can also prevent the identification of strategic issues. Manager C4 refers to a high level of aggregation: "... nobody knows anymore what risks are reported by other units. Risks are presented to top management on a very high level of aggregation. You cannot understand anymore what is behind the numbers and whether there are overlaps in the reported risks. It does not help anymore." A median split along the format dimension suggests significant differences concerning the emphasis on risks (0.7 for negative format and 1.9 for positive format on a scale from -3 to +3, t-test significant at $p = .01$), but not for the emphasis on chances. This suggests that management accounting information format contributes especially to an emphasis on risks.

Interviews further suggest that management accounting systems emphasize chances through broad scope information and channels with high media richness. Manager F4 explains the importance of external information from benchmarking: "We are aware of all levers for cost reduction. But external benchmarking helps us to identify long-term opportunities. We depend largely on the internal market, but I need the comparison with external sources in order to identify targets and things that can be done. I need external benchmarking to see what competitors are doing." Furthermore, face-to-face discussions help to identify new chances, as suggested by interview partner G1: "We

---

[663] See C1.2.1 Categorization of Strategic Issues, pp. 5.

need to strengthen our ability to identify new chances. We cannot learn much from our competitors. Instead we have to identify our own chances. This is the reason why we focus on the future during our off-site management meetings."

Overall, these findings suggest the following propositions for the impact of management accounting systems on the categorization of strategic issues:

> PROPOSITION *2a: The information quality dimension scope and the system quality dimensions integration, accessibility, formalization and media richness contribute positively to an emphasis of management accounting systems on chances.*

> PROPOSITION *2b: The information quality dimensions scope, timeliness, format and accuracy, and the system quality dimensions flexibility and formalization contribute positively to an emphasis of management accounting systems on risks.*

> PROPOSITION *2c: Formalized management accounting systems do not lead to a suppression of chances.*

The second important area for how management accounting systems contribute to the interpretation of strategic issues is related to their impact on the awareness of managers concerning changes in the environment. Interview partners perceive that management accounting systems can increase their awareness concerning potential strategic issues (average 1.6 on a scale from -3 to +3). Managers who report an increased awareness explain this through the ability of management accounting systems to give an impetus for further information search. Management accounting information can become an initiator for the consideration of other information sources, as described by manager G3: "Management accounting information provides a basis. But it is only an indicator and other information must be taken into account". Broad scope management accounting information like external information (e.g., analyst reports, market reports), or future-oriented internal information related to targets or trends, can especially help to increase awareness. Furthermore, qualitative statements can have an awareness-increasing effect, as suggested by interview partner F3: "It makes a difference whether a manager describes an issue or just enters a number into the system that says 5% deviation from plan. That is an important assessment that we ask for." This suggests that management accounting information in a semi-coded format can increase awareness, because it can be adapted to the specific case and leaves room for multiple interpretations.

There are mixed results regarding the impact of information accuracy on awareness. This research provides some support for increased awareness through a low level of information accuracy as suggested by the literature review.[664] Manager C7 describes this as: "I would say more the former [awareness increase], with this information I need to get further qualification, I have questions, primarily related to the [poor] quality of the information." However, results from sub-group comparisons on information accuracy suggest an awareness increase through accurate management accounting information. Managers who report a higher level of information accuracy rate the contribution of management accounting systems to increased awareness at 1.7 compared to 1.4 from managers who report a lower level of information accuracy (both on a scale from -3 to +3). A t-test shows insignificant differences between these two groups ($p = .26$). This provides no support for the negative effect of information accuracy on interpretation through decreased awareness of managers.

Several interview partners suggest that also the processes of preparing management accounting information can increase awareness. The chief controller from company F (F3) states that the company's systematic planning process, which covers all relevant internal and external areas, is able to increase his awareness concerning strategic issues: "Our management accounting systems definitely increase awareness, because they include systematic processes that focus on the company, its environment and the customers. These processes distribute financial and non-financial information that increase one's awareness. There is little to improve." A highly significant difference (t-test significant at $p = .02$) between awareness ratings of mangers with less formalized and more formalized management accounting systems (1.1 and 1.9 respectively, on a scale from -3 to +3) provides further support that formalized management accounting systems can increase and focus awareness on already identified sources of uncertainty.

Table 20 contains a surprising finding concerning the impact of media richness on awareness. It suggests that the use of communication channels with high media richness has a negative impact on managers' awareness. However, an additional t-test shows only an insignificant relationship ($p = .23$) and the interviews do not provide evidence for this effect. Therefore, it seems that this is a spurious finding.

[664] See C1.2.2 Awareness during Strategic Issue Interpretation, pp. 5.

Overall this leads to the following propositions for the impact of management accounting systems on managers' awareness during issue interpretation:

> PROPOSITION *2d: The information quality dimensions scope, timeliness, and format and the system quality dimension formalization contribute positively to awareness during issue interpretation.*

Finally, the literature review suggests that management accounting systems can contribute to a short-term orientation and strategic information manipulation.[665] The respondents in this study report only low levels of dysfunctional behavior. To verify these statements, the author included the measurement instrument "dysfunctional behavior" from JAWORSKI AND YOUNG in the questionnaire.[666] The instrument focuses on strategic information manipulation, the selective presentation of information and the ignorance of activities not monitored by superiors. The average score for dysfunctional behavior is 2.1 (on a scale from 1 to 7; standard deviation .86) which supports the low level of dysfunctional behavior observed in the interviews. On the one hand, the low level of reported dysfunctional behavior could be an indication for a potential response bias, since the author asked for a self-assessment and did not conduct crosschecks with other managers. On the other hand, the interview partners also report a flexible evaluation style, which should compensate for target pressure and the related dysfunctional behavior associated with attempts to improve performance. Several managers mention that criteria for their advancement are based on a subjective assessment of their long-term contributions. Furthermore, most of the interviewees are pursuing a long-term career with their current employer and have reached high management positions already. It is unlikely that these managers would be able to hide dysfunctional behavior for a longer period of time.

One manager from the pilot case company who reports a particularly low level of dysfunctional behavior states that formalized reporting processes with face-to-face meetings ensure that he forwards important information concerning strategic issues:[667] "The decision to forward important information has already been taken, because we have a management meeting to discuss exactly this kind of information. It is a fact-based discussion, where we do not want to hide information or have political influences. We are

---

[665] See C1.2.3 Short-term Orientation and Strategic Information Manipulation, pp. 5.

[666] Jaworski and Young (1992), p. 35.

[667] This statement from a manager in the pilot case company is included because it best describes the suggested relationship.

required to report truthfully and this is what I do." The chief controller from company F (F3) explains that he aims to prevent dysfunctional behaviors by other managers through using management accounting systems with structured processes that include personal on-site visits, in order to speak to employees in the vicinity of this manager: "The only way to identify dysfunctional behavior is to have a structured process and always be on-site in order to access all possible information sources, including chartered accountants and people in the vicinity of the manager. If I looked only at my spreadsheets I would not be able to identify such behavior."

This research does not provide evidence for the potential negative impact of inflexible management accounting systems with a high reporting frequency of financial items on dysfunctional behavior, but it suggests the following proposition:

> *PROPOSITION 2e: Formalized management accounting systems that include communication channels with high media richness can ensure sufficient information flows and increase the likelihood of identifying dysfunctional behavior.*

The combination of propositions for the impact of management accounting systems on categorization of strategic issues, awareness during issue interpretation and dysfunctional behavior suggests the following proposition:

> *PROPOSITION 2f: The information quality dimensions scope, timeliness, format and, accuracy, and the system quality dimensions integration, flexibility, accessibility, formalization and media richness, contribute positively to strategic issue interpretation.*

## 1.3 Communication

Results concerning the impact of management accounting systems on communication are based on interview statements, ratings of the interview partners on the promotion or suppression of communications through management accounting systems, and questionnaire results on their interactive use. Again, questionnaire results on management accounting system dimensions were triangulated with ratings from interview partners through sub-group comparisons. Median splits along system dimensions and interviewer ratings yielded the sub-groups. Table 21 below provides the percentage of respondents in each group. It shows that all management accounting system dimensions have a consistent positive association with the promotion of communication.

| Median split along MAS dimension | | N | Percentage of respondents in each group with statements related to ... Communication Promotion | Communication Suppression | Comment |
|---|---|---|---|---|---|
| Scope | Broad | 13 | **54%** | 38% | Consistent positive results for communication promotion |
| | Narrow | 13 | 38% | **46%** | |
| Timeliness | High | 13 | **62%** | 23% | Consistent positive results for communication promotion |
| | Low | 13 | 31% | **62%** | |
| Format | Positive | 13 | **69%** | 15% | Consistent positive results for communication promotion |
| | Negative | 13 | 23% | **69%** | |
| Accuracy | High | 14 | **57%** | 29% | Consistent positive results for communication promotion |
| | Low | 12 | 33% | **58%** | |
| Integration | High | 13 | **69%** | 23% | Consistent positive results for communication promotion |
| | Low | 13 | 23% | **62%** | |
| Flexibility | High | 13 | **69%** | 23% | Consistent positive results for communication promotion |
| | Low | 13 | 23% | **62%** | |
| Accessibility | High | 14 | **64%** | 29% | Consistent positive results for communication promotion |
| | Low | 12 | 25% | **58%** | |
| Formalization | High | 14 | **57%** | 36% | Consistent positive results for communication promotion |
| | Low | 12 | 33% | **50%** | |
| Media richness | High | 18 | **50%** | 39% | Consistent positive results for communication promotion |
| | Low | 8 | 38% | **50%** | |

Note: Ratings are centered at the median. Consistent positive results are indicated by higher values on both elements of the main diagonal compared to the corresponding elements of the secondary diagonal. Rows do not add to 100% because of missing values. Sample size is n=26, because 3 interviews were conducted with 2 interviewees each and 1 questionnaire was not returned.

*Table 21: Relationships between MAS dimensions and communication*

The literature review suggests that the impact of management accounting systems on communication depends on their interactive use.[668] Table 18 above provides the correlation coefficients of management accounting systems dimensions with interactive use. All management accounting system dimensions are correlated with interactive use (from r = .44 to r = .65), which provides further support for the relationships as suggested by Table 21 above. Interactive use has a very high association with management accounting system scanning effectiveness (r = .61) that underlines its importance for effective strategic sensemaking. Most importantly, interactive use has a higher as-

[668] See C1.3 Impact of Management Accounting Systems on Communication, pp. 5.

sociation with scanning system effectiveness than scanning (r = .42) or focused search (r = .39). This suggests that the interpretive perspective of information processing, with its emphasis on the construction of meaning through interactions between managers, is important in explaining how organizations can reduce equivocality associated with strategic issues.[669] The systems-structural perspective focuses on the acquisition, as well as the distribution of data.[670] The lower correlations for the information acquisition modes scanning and focused search with scanning system effectiveness suggest that it is not sufficient to provide only "the facts" in order to make sense of strategic issues. Instead, the high association between focused search and interactive use (r = .61) suggests an indirect relationship between focused search and scanning system effectiveness through interactive use. Therefore, both information-processing perspectives are required to explain the impact of management accounting systems on strategic sensemaking. This leads to the following propositions:

> *PROPOSITION 3a: The systems-structural perspective of information processing, with its focus on information acquisition, is not sufficient to explain the impact of management accounting systems on strategic sensemaking.*
>
> *PROPOSITION 3b: The interactive use of management accounting systems contributes to strategic sensemaking by facilitating interactions between managers and by focusing attention on strategic uncertainties.*
>
> *PROPOSITION 3c: The systems-structural and interpretive perspectives of information processing are both required to explain the impact of management accounting systems on strategic sensemaking.*

Most interviewees report that management accounting systems promote communications in strategic sensemaking (average rating 1.5 on a scale from -3 to +3). Managers describe management accounting systems as communication platforms, because they can enforce discussions. This research suggests that both the preparation of management accounting information and the information itself can form the basis for discussions about strategic issues. Managers report two kinds of interaction when asked about the role of management accounting information in discussions.

---

669 See B2.5.2.2 Interpretive Perspective, pp. 5.

670 See B2.5.2.1 Systems-Structural Perspective, pp. 5.

The first kind of interaction relates to discussions about the meaning of management accounting information. Manager A1 states that these discussions cause him to think about what can be learnt from certain developments, how things can be improved and how this learning can be further developed: "Our data-warehouse promotes communications because it provides opportunities to discuss positive or negative business developments. This information serves as a basis to talk about reasons for certain developments, what we can do about them and how we can benefit from them." Manager B2 emphasizes the importance of management accounting information as a fact basis in discussions: "Management accounting systems promote communications. They provide an opportunity to distinguish fact from fiction and reduce the possibility of managers covering things up." In addition, interview partner A4 suggests that management accounting systems force the discussion of issues: "Management accounting systems promote discussions. I would say that they institutionalize communications. In our meetings, management accounting information serves as a basis for discussions. It makes sure that certain issues get covered." Other managers who report regular discussions also mention that their management accounting systems provide easily readable reports with graphic representations, comparisons over time and written descriptions of personal interpretations. Manager F2 mentions a certain degree of flexibility in standardized reports as an initiator for discussions: "Four times a year we have these key performance reviews that cover everything from the market side to the internal cost structure and headcount, in a standardized format. But there is a certain degree of flexibility to add own comments and interpretations. This often initiates discussions." Interviewee C3 also stresses the importance of comments in reports: "I require my subordinates to add comments to our monthly reports. It is not sufficient to provide a number or a table to our developers. Instead we want to point out that we see certain risks or problems. These comments serve as a basis for discussions with the developers." A good format also includes simple information to ensure that discussions focus on the underlying issues and not on understanding of the data, as described by manager C5: "Sometimes it was not clear who had provided certain information. Then I had to go around and ask everybody in order to find the right person. After a while I gave up. Management accounting systems did not improve communications. Maybe it was because I only asked for highly aggregated data." These findings are further supported by a high correlation between format and interactive use ($r = .52$) and suggest that well-formatted management accounting information encourages discussions about strategic issues. This is in line with the literature review[671] and leads to the following proposition:

> *PROPOSITION 3d: Semi-coded and simple management accounting information helps managers to share interpretations of strategic issues.*

The second kind of interaction as reported by some interviewees relates to discussions about the correctness of measurements and whether the measurement is useful at all. These discussions seem to be a kind of defensive behavior, which occurs particularly in the case of negative deviations from plans. As manager E1 states: "If you have to defend poor figures it is very easy to resort to a questioning of the measurement method." This is particularly easy with management accounting information of low accuracy. Discussions about inconsistent data can prevent discussions about the underlying reasons of deviations as suggested by manager C4: "Inconsistent data is not trustworthy and therefore gets questioned by managers. ... Discussions are not goal-oriented, because we talk about the shortcomings of our systems and question deviations that nobody can explain, instead of discussing the relevant issues underneath." Interview partner B4 refers to conflicts because of inaccurate management accounting information: "The validity of numbers is one of the most frequent reasons for conflict. There are differences because of inconsistent time intervals and different ways to look at the data. One of our issues is that we do not have a consistent IT system for our financials." Furthermore, the association between interactive use and accuracy ($r = .46$) suggests that accurate data contributes to interactive use and thereby helps to focus discussions on the meaning of information. This results in the following proposition:

> *PROPOSITION 3e: Accurate management accounting information contributes to interactive use and helps to focus discussions on the meaning of information by minimizing discussions about the measurement method.*

Interviews suggest that the preparation of management accounting information can also improve the communication of strategic issues. At company F reports and strategic options are developed bottom-up. Extensive discussions are required to coordinate strategic options with all relevant managers before they are presented to top management in a decision meeting. Company F is under high cost-pressure and needs to in-

---

[671] See C1.3 Impact of Management Accounting Systems on Communication, pp. 5.

corporate local engineering knowledge in order to find the most cost-efficient solution. Manager F2 explains this as follows: "The multifunctional teams develop a commodity strategy for the product. They also develop options for tenders that have a different cost structure and therefore potentially can decrease our costs. ... The teams are very focused on technical issues. Planning provides them with improvement targets as an input for their work. They have to solve the problem of how to reduce costs." Interviewee F4 adds: "We have multifunctional teams and meet regularly. We have a weekly jour-fix with our executives, including procurement, to discuss current projects. We align all activities with procurement, quality, finance and our managers."

It seems that integrated management accounting systems especially promote communications, because they provide information at the interface between functions. Such information encourages discussions to align activities or to jointly resolve issues. Manager B5 provides the following example: "A typical example is our product-channel matrix. Product managers look at channels and sales managers look at products. Everybody is watching the other and as soon as something unexpected happens they ring the alarm bells. That is a very strong communication, because of the common data." In addition, processes to prepare information can also support the integration of different functions and promote the discussion of issues, as described by interviewee B1: "The process enforces alignment. For the preparation of a business case it is not sufficient to provide only ideas for a new product. The process requires that you also include information about the technical requirements to operate the product. Therefore, you have to speak to the responsible managers and they estimate the cost of operations. This creates alignment between the functions." A high correlation between integration and interactive use ($r = .65$) provides further support for the contribution of integrated management accounting systems to improved communication in strategic sensemaking.

> *PROPOSITION 3f: Integrated management accounting systems improve communications about strategic issues between different functions.*

In strategic sensemaking it is important that information concerning strategic issues is communicated to managers who have additional information to better understand the issues, or who are able to take action. In company G most reports are only available to the top management team, meaning that the company relies on senior managers to forward information about strategic issues, through meetings in their functional areas. In addition to the normal reporting structures, this company has established an integrative staff function with dedicated personnel to interface with the functional areas. Manager G2 emphasizes the advantage of a formalized process to ensure that information reaches the right recipient: "That is quite formalized, because we have a dedicated person for each functional area. In my area of responsibility, everybody communicates with me and this process ensures that important information gets considered. If you always speak to different people it is not possible to ensure that information reaches the right management committee. The information that is out there would not be taken into account." The interviewed managers from company G report that they are well informed about potential strategic issues. In contrast company A does not have formal channels or processes to communicate information about strategic issues. Information is passed mainly to people within the personal network, or to people referenced by other colleagues. Interviewee A3 describes a situation where he passed information by e-mail to other colleagues, but did not receive feedback, and no discussion developed around this issue: "Last week I distributed an article on channel conflict to the management team via e-mail. I referred to a certain paragraph as a discussion starter. I sent the e-mail to 11 people and only got feedback from one manager, who stated that he already knew the article. ... Sometimes there are even people that assume that you have too much time." The author gained the impression that this manager was unsatisfied by this, and therefore less likely to forward information about issues in the future.

This research suggests that it is necessary to complement formalized processes with face-to-face meetings, in order to discuss reports and provide feedback. Manager F3 stresses the importance of meetings: "Communication is extremely important, because it makes a difference whether a manager describes his problem or just provides a number in a report." Interview partner C5 mentions missing feedback in reporting processes: "Reporting is paper-based. There is no direct feedback. Sometimes there are additional reviews where you discuss performance, but you cannot find the reported information in there. Maybe it is included somewhere." Reports are a good preparation for face-to-face meetings and allow managers to focus on business developments and strategic measures in the meeting. Manager F1 describes this as follows: "We have detailed forms that need to be completed before the meeting. They help us to ensure completeness, to conduct plausibility checks and to consolidate information from different business units. We use the presentations in these meetings to discuss business developments and strategic measures with the managers responsible. Because of the forms we do not need to get back to the business units for details."

Interview partner G3 suggests that reports are also useful to gather opinions on issues from several departments, prior to discussing them in a final face-to-face meeting: "Reports provide the opportunity to distribute interpretations of facts and to work on them asynchronously. We cannot wait until everybody has time for a meeting. Therefore we write our comments and send them on to the next person, so that the information gets distributed quickly ... Finally, we have a meeting to discuss the different opinions of the departments involved. We combine all interpretations to develop a common picture of the situation. Jointly we draw conclusions and develop an understanding of the interdependencies. ... It also helps to ask clarifying questions." Manager B3 suggests that a formalized process including communication channels of high media richness helps to integrate information from different functions and improves mutual understanding of issues: "Forecasts are still not timely and of sufficient quality. They tried to deal with this problem through tools, but this is not sustainable. The only effective solution is to involve the required departments in a process and to synchronize things. ... This process contributes now to an exchange of different perspectives. It has improved the mutual understanding of each others' problems and challenges." A regular process ensures a frequent discussion of issues. Manager F2 mentions: "I think that our rolling planning processes and our regular performance reviews contribute to regular discussions about performance, not only retrospectively, but also about current issues and future utilization."

A median split along the formalization dimension shows that management accounting systems with a high level of formalization contribute stronger to communication (2.1 on a scale from -3 to +3) than systems with a low level of formalization (1.1 on a scale from -3 to +3). The difference is significant (t-test $p = .04$) and provides no evidence that formalized management accounting systems constrain opportunities for interaction and communication. However, the correlation between formalization and interactive use for the group with more formalized management accounting systems is significantly negative ($r = -.45$, significant at $p = .08$). Although the interviews did not provide statements related to a too high level of formalization, this provides some evidence that formalized management accounting systems contribute positively to communication, unless they are too highly formalized.

Overall this suggests that formalized management accounting systems with regular face-to-face discussions are best suited to promote communication in strategic sensemaking. The correlations of interactive use with formalization ($r = .44$), with media richness, (r = .45) and with timeliness (r = .51) provide further support for these relationships. This leads to the following proposition:

> PROPOSITION *3g: Management accounting systems with a balanced level of formalization that require a regular communication of management accounting information through channels of high media richness encourage discussions about strategic issues.*

A combination of prior propositions in this chapter with the consistent positive relationships between all management accounting system dimensions and communication, as indicated in Table 18 above and Table 21 above, suggests the following propositions:

> PROPOSITION *3h: The information quality dimensions scope, timeliness, format, and accuracy, and the system quality dimensions integration, flexibility, accessibility, formalization, and media richness contribute positively to communication in strategic sensemaking. Overly high levels of formalization have a negative impact on the communication of strategic issues.*

> PROPOSITION *3i: The information quality dimensions scope, timeliness, format, and accuracy, and the system quality dimensions integration, flexibility, accessibility, formalization, and media richness contribute positively to the interactive use of management accounting systems. Overly high levels of formalization have a negative impact on the interactive use of management accounting systems.*

## 1.4 Intermediate Results of Quality Dimensions and Sensemaking

Based on the propositions developed in the previous sections, Table 22 below provides an overview of the impact of management accounting system dimensions on strategic sensemaking processes of individual managers. Overall, management accounting system dimensions seem to have a consistent positive impact on individual managers' observation, interpretation and communication processes in strategic sensemaking. To the knowledge of the author this is the first study to analyze the impact of a comprehensive set of management accounting information quality and system quality dimensions on strategic sensemaking processes.

| Quality Dimensions | | Impact on Strategic Sensemaking ... Observation | Interpretation | Communication | Overall |
|---|---|---|---|---|---|
| Information | Scope | + (1f, 1g, 1h) | + (2a, 2b, 2d, 2f) | + (3h, 3i) | + (4a) |
| | Timeliness | + (1f, 1g, 1h) | + (2b, 2d, 2f) | + (3g, 3h, 3i) | + (4a) |
| | Format | + (1f, 1g) | + (2b, 2d, 2f) | + (3d, 3h, 3i) | + (4a) |
| | Accuracy | + (1f, 1g) | + (2b, 2f) | + (3e, 3h, 3i) | + (4a) |
| System | Integration | + (1f, 1g, 1h) | + (2a, 2f) | + (3f, 3h, 3i) | + (4a) |
| | Flexibility | + (1f, 1g, 1h) | + (2b, 2f) | + (3h, 3i) | + (4a) |
| | Accessibility | + (1f, 1g, 1h) | + (2a, 2f) | + (3h, 3i) | + (4a) |
| | Formalization | ± (1f, 1g, 1h) | + (2a, 2b, 2c, 2d, 2e, 2f) | ± (3g, 3h, 3i) | ± (4a) |
| | Media richness | ? | + (2a, 2e, 2f) | + (3g, 3h, 3i) | + (4a) |

Note: Corresponding propositions in parenthesis
Legend: + (positive); ± (balanced); ? (no impact observed)

*Table 22: Proposed relationships between MAS dimensions and strategic sensemaking*

Extant literature provides only fragmented theoretical relationships based on limited empirical evidence.[672] This study contributes to existing research in two ways: (1) by closing research gaps in the relationships between management accounting system dimensions and strategic sensemaking processes of individual managers, and (2) by verifying previous findings from various research disciplines in the strategic sensemaking context.

*(1) Closing of research gaps*: The literature review on the relationship between management accounting system dimensions and strategic sensemaking processes revealed several neglected areas.[673] This research provides propositions to close these gaps.

Firstly, a semi-coded and understandable management accounting information format does not only improve communications and contribute to the interpretation of information. Managers are also more likely to use their management accounting systems for focused search when information is presented in such a format (proposition 1g). Focused search helps them to understand reasons for deviations and to answer specific questions (proposition 1c).

Secondly, the literature review suggests a negative impact of information accuracy on observation and interpretation. It does not provide indications for the impact of infor-

[672] See C2.4 Summary of Quality Dimensions and Strategic Sensemaking, pp. 5.
[673] See Table 5, p. 5.

mation accuracy on communications. A low level of information accuracy supposedly contributes to observation through scanning and helps to increase awareness during issue interpretation. This research was not able to support the expected negative relationship between accuracy and scanning, but it was also not possible to confirm a positive relationship. However, the importance of focused search for observation and the positive relationship between accuracy and focused search provide evidence for an overall positive impact of accuracy on observation (proposition 1f). In addition, this study provides mixed evidence for a negative impact of accuracy on awareness during issue interpretation. Along with the literature review there are some statements that report an awareness increase, because a low level of information accuracy raises additional questions in order to understand the information. However, quantitative data from interviewees suggests a higher level of awareness through accurate management accounting information, although this difference is not significant. This research finds a positive impact of accuracy on risk emphasis (proposition 2b) which overall leads to a positive impact of accuracy on interpretation (proposition 2f). Concerning the impact of accuracy on communication, this research proposes that accurate management accounting information contributes to interactive use and helps to focus discussions on the meaning of information. Accurate information seems to minimize discussions about the measurement method (proposition 3e).

Finally, this research suggests that timeliness, flexibility, and accessibility promote communications about strategic issues (proposition 3h). Accessibility has also a positive relationship with interpretation as it is associated with an emphasis on chances (proposition 2a). For the hitherto unexplored relationship between media richness and observation this study does not find any evidence. The missing evidence from the interviews combined with a lack of theoretical relationships from an organizational learning perspective suggests that media richness has no impact on observation.

*(2) Verification of previous findings in strategic sensemaking context*: This research confirms tentative theoretical relationships between 'scope', 'integration', 'formalization' and strategic sensemaking processes.

Firstly, the information quality dimension scope has not been investigated explicitly in the strategic sensemaking context yet. Most research has focused on the impact of 'scope' on decision-making and did not distinguish between operational and strategic decisions. This research finds that broad scope information contributes to observation in strategic sensemaking both through focused search and scanning (proposition 1g and 1h). Furthermore, broad scope information helps in the interpretation of strategic issues by increasing awareness (proposition 2d) and by both emphasizing chances and risks (proposition 2a and 2b). Broad scope information also serves as a basis to communicate about strategic issues (proposition 3h).

Secondly, this research confirms the previously identified positive relationship between 'integration' and observation. It shows that integrated management accounting systems contribute to innovation and organizational learning by emphasizing chances (proposition 2a) and by promoting communications about strategic issues between different functions (proposition 3f).

Thirdly, the impact of formalized management accounting systems on strategic sensemaking has been investigated. In line with organizational literature, this research finds a positive impact of formalization on focused search and a negative impact on scanning (proposition 1g and 1h). Since managers use management accounting systems mainly for focused search it seems that a balanced level of formalization is most suited for observation in strategic sensemaking (proposition 1f). Contrary to extant literature, this study does not find evidence for a suppression of chances by formalized management accounting systems (proposition 2c). Instead, it shows that formalization emphasizes both chances and risks (proposition 2a and 2b), which seems to be related to the awareness increasing effect of formalized processes (proposition 2d). This research shows that formalized management accounting systems can ensure sufficient information flows that also increase the likelihood of identifying dysfunctional behavior (proposition 2e). A balanced level of formalization encourages communication of strategic issues by providing regular opportunities for discussions (proposition 3g).

Overall, the results on the impact of management accounting system dimensions on the strategic sensemaking processes observation, interpretation, and communication can be combined in the following proposition:

> *PROPOSITION 4: The information quality dimensions scope, timeliness, format, and accuracy, and the system quality dimensions integration, flexibility, accessibility, formalization, and media richness contribute positively to the use of management accounting systems for strategic sensemaking. Overly high levels of formalization have a negative impact on the observation and communication of strategic issues.*

A shortcoming of this research is that the small sample size does not allow to simultaneously analyze the impact of multiple management accounting system dimensions on strategic sensemaking and to assess the strengths of the identified relationships. Furthermore, this research shows that the analytical separation of the strategic sensemaking process in observation, interpretation and communication is not sufficient to fully explain the role of management accounting systems. Findings suggest that managers are more likely to observe strategic issues through informal sources than through management accounting systems (proposition 1a). Middle managers use management accounting systems to search for additional information that helps them to substantiate potential strategic issues gleaned from these informal sources (proposition 1b). However, the systems-structural perspective of information processing with its focus on information acquisition is not sufficient to explain the impact of management accounting systems on strategic sensemaking (proposition 3a). The interactive use of management accounting information by upper level managers is especially important as it facilitates interactions during the preparation of information and focuses attention on strategic uncertainties (proposition 3b). This suggests a relationship between the use of management accounting information by upper level managers and the preparation of management accounting information by middle managers that cannot be easily explained through interdependencies of observation, interpretation and communication. The chosen exploratory approach of this research allows investigating these relationships in more detail. The next section proposes a model that draws differently on the systems-structural perspective and the interpretive perspective in order to explain the role of management accounting systems in strategic sensemaking.

## 2. Roles of Management Accounting Systems in Strategic Sensemaking

The interviews suggest that management accounting systems have different roles in individual managers' strategic sensemaking. During the analysis of the interviews the author found that managers described different ways of using management accounting systems for strategic sensemaking. The interviews provide evidence that management accounting systems can help middle managers to explain performance deviations and to prepare countermeasures. Management accounting systems seem to facilitate communication with peers and other managers. This contributes to an improved understanding of issues and a reconciliation of measures to deal with these issues. Interviews with upper level managers suggest a different way of using management accounting systems. In these cases management accounting systems provide an information basis that helps to verify gut feelings and to look for developments that could become potential issues. Some interview partners report that management accounting information serves as a basis to challenge middle managers and can become a starting point for discussions about business developments.

To better understand the different roles of management accounting systems in strategic sensemaking this research proposes to distinguish three different ways of using management accounting systems or information: adaptation, preparation, and utilization. Adaptation is the alignment of management accounting systems with strategic uncertainties (section E2.1). Preparation includes the processes predominantly performed by middle management to prepare management accounting information (section E2.2). Utilization is the use of management accounting information, mainly by upper management levels (section E2.3). The interviews suggest that management accounting system dimensions contribute to these different ways of using management accounting systems or information in strategic sensemaking (section E2.4)

Extant literature has so far focused on disaggregating the strategic sensemaking process in observation, interpretation and action, and analyzing the interdependencies at the individual and organizational level.[674] This separation considers the systems-structural perspective of information processing at the observation step and utilizes the interpretive perspective to explain interpretation and action processes. Results for this perspective on strategic sensemaking have been presented in the previous section. It is also possible to relate the different perspectives on information processing to the proposed differentiation along adaptation, preparation and utilization. The preparation of management accounting information describes processes to acquire and distribute data, which can be explained with help of the systems-structural perspective of information processing.[675] But the preparation of management accounting information also requires middle managers to interpret data and to share their interpretations with other managers. A theoretical foundation for these processes can be found in the interpretive perspective of information processing.[676] This perspective is also required to explain the utilization of management accounting information by upper level managers as it involves the development of a shared interpretation of management accounting information. Furthermore, the strategic sensemaking processes observation, interpretation and

---

[674] See for example Thomas et al. (1997), p. 302 and Corner et al. (1994), p. 296.
[675] See B2.5.2.1 Systems-Structural Perspective of Information Processing, pp. 5.
[676] See B2.5.2.2 Interpretive Perspective of Information Processing, pp. 5.

communication are universal cognitive processes that occur during the adaptation of management accounting systems, and the preparation as well as the utilization of management accounting information. Therefore, the literature review on the impact of management accounting systems on strategic sensemaking provides also the theoretical foundation for the following results on the roles of management accounting systems in strategic sensemaking.[677] Especially section E2.4 will relate management accounting system dimensions to adaptation, preparation and utilization.[678]

## 2.1 Adaptation

The adaptation of management accounting systems involves the adjustment of key performance indicators and reports, or even replacement of reports, so that they reflect current strategic uncertainties. In order to analyze the impact of adaptation on strategic sensemaking, the author conducted a median split of all cases along the questionnaire variable "scanning system effectiveness" and computed the percentage of positive and negative statements about adaptation in both groups. 60% of all positive statements about adaptation were from managers with more effective management accounting systems, while managers with less effective management accounting systems made 89% of all negative statements about adaptation. These consistent results suggest that the regular adaptation of management accounting systems helps managers to focus on strategic uncertainties and contributes to their effective use for strategic sensemaking.

Statements from interview partners suggest that management accounting systems can provide directions when they are used to communicate goals and targets to the organization. Manager F2 refers to a yearly "kick-off" meeting where managers use management accounting information to communicate targets and to point-out specific threats for the next period: "We regularly communicate where we are heading, why we are heading in that direction and what we need to achieve to get there. This includes qualitative and quantitative goals. In addition we have a yearly kick-off meeting to discuss lessons learned from last year and threats for the current year to support or prevent certain developments." Interviewee A3 describes how management accounting systems not aligned with the goals of the company can undermine goal attainment: "Our company decided that a certain topic was particularly important. Everybody agreed but there was one colleague who ignored all this. He sold the usual stuff and

[677] See Chapter C Management Accounting Systems and Strategic Sensemaking, pp. 5.
[678] See E2.4 Relationship with Management Accounting System Dimensions, pp. 5.

reached his sales margins. He was the hero. That's it." At a later point this manager says: "Payments for a particular business fully determine my personal interest on certain topics." Manager F2 also refers to the attention-focusing effect of management accounting information that is used for evaluative purposes: "Quite egoistically you focus first on management accounting information that is related to your personal success and your variable payment. These are primarily financial items and so you focus on key performance indicators or reports that show the company's performance in this respect." This suggests that management accounting information that is used for evaluations especially requires a regular adaptation to ensure that it focuses on current strategic uncertainties.

Time and attention of managers is limited, and therefore it seems necessary to abolish unused reports or performance indicators, in order to free up sufficient capacity for analyses and interpretations of business developments. Manager E4 mentions that the reduction of performance indicators enabled company E to better understand and explain business developments: "At that time we had so many performance indicators that nobody knew anymore what got measured how, and how everything was related. That was crazy. But we removed many indicators. Now we have only a few key performance indicators that we can drill down into to explain the development of all business areas." Without a focus on a few specific performance measures, management accounting systems are unable to provide directions, as manager B4 describes: "There are so many different definitions. The variety of indicators does not help. We have controllers that want additional performance indicators that are inconsistent with the existing indicators. The quality department also has different indicators. The number of performance indicators is inflationary. [...] We have too many indicators so that the orientation in this area of our business requires an extreme amount of time. You have to validate and check up on everything. That is way too much work. I need management accounting information that relieves me of work and does not create additional demands."

Several managers mention that unused reports should be abolished without any prior announcement being made, because otherwise unnecessary discussions about the importance of these reports would evolve. These managers simply stopped certain reports and waited for a reaction from the report recipients, which often never happened. Interview partner B5 provides the following example: "We look for reports that are not used anymore and after three or four months we just stop them and wait for complaints. Announcements concerning the discontinuation of reports did not work at all.

There was always somebody who needed that report. Now we just remove reports." In several cases, adaptation of management accounting systems occurs annually, subsequent to the strategic planning process, as described by manager E6: "Every year we adapt the performance indicators after the planning process. We look for performance indicators that need to be changed, verify their definitions and make sure that adaptations also get applied to past performance data, so that we have a basis for future comparisons." The CFO of company F (F1) discusses possible simplifications of reports every year with the business units: "Every year we have, in our finance board, a special agenda item where we discuss possible simplifications of our reports with the countries and business units." While most management accounting systems seem to be adapted annually, it is possible to adapt computerized reports more frequently. Company B has a staff function that designs and adapts on-line reports. The head of this function (B5) is able to monitor access frequency of on-line reports. In case of declining usage he proactively approaches functional managers in order to discuss reasons and to adapt the report if necessary. He also informs managers of available reports that could be useful to them: "We have statistics that shows us what our top reports are. This helps us to get a good understanding about frequently used reports and allows us to analyze reasons for their high usage; maybe it is because of the report structure, maybe because of an interesting topic. Sometimes we also identify that certain managers do not use some reports that should be useful to them. In this case we proactively approach the manager and make sure that important information gets considered."

Overall this leads to the following proposition:

> *PROPOSITION 5a: A regular adaptation of management accounting systems contributes to the focusing of attention on areas with identified strategic uncertainties.*

Some interview partners report discussions during the adaptation of management accounting systems. Manager B2 stresses the importance of discussions how to translate the strategy into measures on the Balanced Scorecard: "There are a lot of discussions, and these discussions are very valuable. We discuss how to translate the strategy into the Balanced Scorecard. Of course there is also a lot of discussion about targets." It seems that these discussions help to align managers and also help to improve their understanding about limitations of reports and measurements. Interview partner C7 mentions the role of discussions in improving understanding of the measurements: "I would also put a lot of emphasis on communication with the organization and the methodology behind measurements so that people understand. It is also important for people in the regions, so that they could recommend the key performance indicators for their region, because I am not the one who knows what is important for the market in France, for example." Furthermore, discussions during the adaptation of management accounting systems can contribute to the alignment of managers about measurements, as suggested by manager E6: "Sometimes discussions repeat every year. This is especially the case when targets are missed. But we reach alignment relatively fast and make suggestions for how to adapt measurements or to remove performance measures because they do not add value." Questionnaire results provide further support for the relationship between adaptation and understanding of management accounting information. Adaptation as part of the flexibility dimension of management accounting systems, and user know-how about management accounting information as part of the format dimension, are highly correlated ($r = .75$ between flexibility and format).

This leads to the following proposition:

> *PROPOSITION 5b: Discussions during the adaptation of management accounting systems help to align managers and increase their knowledge about the meaning of management accounting information.*

## 2.2 Preparation

The interviews suggest that primarily middle managers prepare reports or plans and develop interpretations of strategic issues and other unexpected developments. They perform data analyses to understand root causes for developments and annotate reports in order to communicate issues to top management. Informal sources (e.g. personal networks, fairs) are especially important for the identification of new strategic issues. In order to understand the implications of these issues and to make them communicable to top management, managers use management accounting systems to analyze their potential impact on the company.[679]

In order to assess the contribution of preparation to strategic sensemaking, the author conducted a median split of all cases along the questionnaire variable "scanning system effectiveness" and computed the percentage of positive and negative statements about preparation in both groups. 78% of all positive statements about preparation

[679] See E1.1 Observation, pp. 5.

were from managers with more effective management accounting systems, while managers with less effective management accounting systems made 64% of all negative statements about preparation. These consistent results suggest that the preparation of management accounting information contributes positively to strategic sensemaking.

It seems that integrated management accounting systems are particularly useful in helping managers to develop interpretations and facilitate the bottom-up development of strategic options. Integrated management accounting systems can help managers to understand how their area of responsibility relates to other functional areas, as described by manager F4: "Everybody from all areas of my center works with performance measures. Every department has their own measures, but also measures that show how they impact others." Manager B3 mentions how reports from other functional areas help him to anticipate future developments: "We have cross-functional reports and see what is happening on the marketing or sales side. That allows us to anticipate future developments and to prepare ourselves." The information systems department of company B uses strategic Balanced Scorecard measures to signal strategic priorities. Furthermore, managers are required to quantify the impact of new projects on these measures. Interviewee B2 states that the company will not pursue a project if it has no impact on any performance indicator in the Balanced Scorecard: "If someone wants to initiate a new project to implement our strategy, we ask him about the impact of this initiative on our performance indicators. We have a baseline and therefore the person has to commit himself to an incremental improvement." Because of resource constraints, the department uses this approach to filter the most promising projects in order to deal with identified strategic uncertainties. In addition, integrated management accounting systems can provide directions to managers regarding how their functional area relates to the company as a whole. Manager B2 refers to the communication of strategy as the main use of their Balanced Scorecard: "The main use [of our Balanced Scorecard] is that we communicate our strategy and strategic priorities to the next management level. We also use these measures to agree targets. This makes our direction very clear, so that managers know what is expected from them."

Furthermore, the interviews suggest that management accounting information with emphasis on dependencies between functional areas can especially serve as communication platforms. This supports the discussion and coordination of strategic issues that affect more than one functional area. Manager F1 refers to the planning process of the business units: "There is strong information sharing within the units, because all functional areas have to contribute to the plan". He further adds: "Therefore, we meet with a very interdisciplinary team to review the planning." Different functional perspectives help managers to develop multiple interpretations of strategic issues that can increase the awareness of top managers. A formalized process, with defined meetings, forces managers to prepare management accounting information that serves as a discussion basis or that is useful to support their arguments concerning business developments. Manager F4 argues: "Most benefits arise from the preparation of reports. I like standardized reports, because they require and force managers to ask themselves certain important questions." Interview partner B4 describes the usefulness of regular reports for the preparation of meetings that create alignment: "Controlling prepares monthly reports with highlights and lowlights of our performance, and we have to provide reasons for our performance. ... This serves as the basis for a meeting to discuss details, draw conclusions and reach alignment about the findings. This coordination in meetings is very important to me."

Overall, these findings can be summarized in the following propositions:

> *PROPOSITION 6a: Integrated and formalized management accounting systems can facilitate interactions between functional areas that help to discuss strategic issues during the preparation of management accounting information.*

> *PROPOSITION 6b: Integrated management accounting systems can provide directions and help managers to prepare interpretations of strategic issues.*

However, the interviews suggest that management accounting information does not always contribute to constructive discussions and thereby helps in strategic sensemaking. Some managers report mainly discussions about data issues or the measurement methodology of performance indicators instead of discussions about the underlying reasons for trends or deviations from plans. Manager B4 complains: "Today we spend a lot of time discussing the correctness of reports, which wastes a lot of resources. It is necessary to focus more on issues, what we can learn from them, and decisions we need to take."

Managers who report constructive discussions about management accounting information also mention discussions about measurements during the adaptation of management accounting systems. Manager E6 refers to extensive prior discussions about measurements that help the company to focus on underlying issues: "We have discussed definitions of performance measures for a long time, so that they do not come up anymore. Discussions focus now on underlying reasons for deviations and the preparation of countermeasures to get us back on track." He adds that they currently adapt performance indicators for another area of the business in order to improve cross-functional discussions about issues: "We currently adapt their performance measures and standardize them. The learning process of how to use these measures in discussions has just begun."

This suggests that discussions during adaptation can have a positive impact on strategic sensemaking during the preparation of management accounting information. Otherwise, it seems that especially in the case of negative deviations, this leads to debates about measurements as a kind of defensive behavior. This behavior can delay the detection of potential strategic issues. A co-occurrence analysis of interview statements provides further support for the finding that the adaptation of management accounting systems has an impact on the preparation of management accounting information. Table 23 below shows the percentage of statements related to preparation of management accounting information that co-occur with statements related to adaptation of management accounting systems. Overall, 75% of all statements that describe a positive impact of information preparation on strategic sensemaking co-occur with statements related to a positive adaptation of management accounting systems.

| **Statements related to preparation of management accounting information ...** | | **N** | **Percentage of statements co-occurring with statements related to ...** *Adaptation* *Positive* | *Negative* | **Comment** |
|---|---|---|---|---|---|
| Preparation | Positive | 185 | **75%** | 17% | Some positive impact of adaptation on preparation |
| | Negative | 61 | 46% | 43% | |

*Table 23: Impact of adaptation on preparation of MAS information*

This leads to the following propositions:

> *PROPOSITION 6c: Discussions about the measurement of management accounting information during the adaptation of management accounting systems help to reduce debates about data issues or measurement methodologies during the preparation of management accounting information.*

> *PROPOSITION 6d: A regular adaptation of management accounting systems contributes positively to strategic sensemaking during the preparation of management accounting information.*

It seems important that upper level managers provide feedback concerning the reports, analyses and known strategic issues to managers who are involved in preparing management accounting information. Otherwise, analyses and interpretations of strategic issues seem to deteriorate because middle managers perceive reports without feedback as unimportant to top management and spend less time on their preparation. Manager F4 argues: "Feedback is important for regular reporting. Reports without feedback work two or three times. You can forget these reports as soon as managers notice that there are no consequences and nobody takes what they report seriously." Insufficient feedback frustrates managers involved in the preparation of the information, as suggested by interviewee B4: "I feel detached from developments in the company and think that I am only the data provider so that others can show off with my numbers. This leads to frustration." Interviewee C7 adds that it is also the responsibility of middle management to ask for feedback: "There is a lot of reporting for the sake of reporting. You probably need to do some housekeeping and really clear up a lot of it, and really clarify why am I reporting, because I think it is also a weakness of middle management, to be honest. They need to ask themselves whether what their people are working on is actually a value-add or not." A co-occurrence analysis shows that 46% of all negative statements concerning the use of management accounting systems for preparation co-occur with statements related to missing feedback. This leads to the following proposition:

> *PROPOSITION 6e: Missing feedback on prepared management accounting information leads to a deterioration of future analyses and interpretations of strategic issues.*

Interviews suggest that the preparation of management accounting information can support strategic sensemaking, especially at middle management levels. Manager A2 asks managers to regularly prepare forecasts, even if a rapidly changing environment makes the forecasts inaccurate most of the time. He thinks that the process of preparing the forecast yields greater benefits than the end product itself. According to interviewee A2, the preparation of forecasts requires managers to think about the future, which in turn helps them to learn about changes in the environment. Manager B3 suggests that the preparation of management accounting information creates most value: "The value is created during preparation. The process to reach the final plan is important, because you learn about the levers that allow you to influence things." Interviewee C1 sees the main benefit for the organization in the preparation of information:

"The organization does not benefit directly from the report, but from its preparation, because they have to analyze the numbers." This leads to the final proposition:

> *PROPOSITION 6f: The preparation of management accounting information contributes to strategic sensemaking of middle managers.*

## 2.3 Utilization

Utilization is the use of management accounting information, mainly by upper management levels. Management accounting systems provide an information basis that helps these managers to stay informed about developments in their companies. Managers who report more effective management accounting systems for strategic sensemaking made 77% of all positive statements about utilization, while managers with less effective management accounting systems made 56% of all negative statements about utilization. These consistent results suggest that management accounting systems can provide management accounting information that helps managers in strategic sensemaking.

Interviews suggest that upper level managers compare management accounting information with other, often informal, information sources and sometimes use them to substantiate gut feelings. Manager A1 states that they use management accounting information to analyze potential issues indicated by top managers: "Top management has a gut feeling and then we try to verify these feelings through focused analyses of management accounting information." Interviewee G1 refers to the comparison of information from informal sources with management accounting information: "Managers such as our CEO also receive important undisclosed information through personal networks. In review meetings we also use this information and compare it with our internal information sources." The CFO from company F (F1) emphasizes the value of reports as a basis for discussions about issues: "Management reports are very valuable for me, because they provide me with a starting point to discuss certain issues. Just reading the reports would be insufficient. I draw information from the reports that help me to ask specific questions and to identify potential issues." He adds that they have sufficient opportunities to discuss issues: "We have financial reviews every few months, quarterly forecast reviews, business planning, budget and strategic reviews. I think that we have a diverse set of meetings that provides sufficient opportunities to discuss issues." However, a higher reporting frequency does not necessarily provide more information, as interviewee C7 indicates: "I think at the moment there seems to be a lot of reporting overkill. For me reporting on a quarterly basis is almost enough. I have regional interfaces on a quarterly basis, and our cycles in the regions are on a quarterly basis, so really there is not a lot of change month by month. For example I am reporting now for November, but actually it is the same as the October figures, because nothing has really changed."

The managing director from company C (C1) underlines the contribution of management reports to comprehensive discussions: "It is important that we have a report as a basis for our discussions. Without a report the regions would present and discuss isolated problems and you would not be able to get a complete understanding of the situation." In addition, reports are required to document the fact basis for decisions, especially when options have been prepared bottom-up, as top manager F2 describes: "Transparency is important. You have to document your recommendation as a fact basis for decision-making. So we have a transparent bottom-up development of recommendations as a basis for our decisions."

Several managers report that top managers use management accounting information to challenge middle managers and probe for potential issues. Reviews of business plans in particular provide opportunities to do so. Interviewee F1 describes how he and the CEO of company F use reviews to challenge business units and to identify potential issues: "The CEO and I ask the business units to present current market developments, the status of product development, and strategic objectives of their unit, in order to challenge the operational planning and to check whether the suggested improvement measures are suitable. These discussions help us to learn from the people at the front line about business developments. We also learn about signals that could indicate a certain direction." Manager G1 describes a similar use of management accounting systems to challenge the planning: "We use all these bodies and our management accounting systems to challenge and stabilize the planning in an iterative process." Management accounting information allows central functions to question decisions and investments, as described by manager B4: "Controlling uses the key performance measures to look into investment decisions and question whether they were necessary and timed correctly."

Overall, these findings suggest the following propositions:

> *PROPOSITION 7a: Management accounting information provides top managers in particular with a fact basis to identify and discuss strategic issues.*

*PROPOSITION 7b: Management accounting information enables top managers to challenge middle managers and probe for potential issues.*

*PROPOSITION 7c: The utilization of management accounting information contributes to strategic sensemaking, especially at upper management levels.*

Interviews suggest that shortcomings during the preparation of management accounting information can have a negative impact on their utilization. It seems that insufficient analyses and superficial interpretations make management accounting information less useful to top management. Manager C1 describes how insufficient analyses raise questions that could have been answered before: "We have many people that spend days or weeks ensuring that certain numbers are available, but they do not analyze the numbers. Then you have a report that raises questions that could have been answered already during the preparation of the report. ... I need comments that explain why certain deviations occur, what I can do about negative deviations or how I can sustain positive developments." Manager E6 mentions the necessity of spending more time on analyses: "My experience is that we focus too much time on fire-fighting and not enough time on analyses." He wants to increase the use of management accounting information for strategic sensemaking by focusing on improvement levers: "This is something I want to emphasize in the future. We should focus more on crosschecks and good data analyses to show top management improvement levers." Interviewee C5 adds that the organization did not focus enough on improvement measures: "We addressed the right issues, but were too imprecise in the definition of improvement measures and making sure they get implemented. We were a bit careless about the associated risks." Manager C4 adds that inconsistent management accounting information contributes to unnecessary discussions that eventually can slow down decision-making: "We make decisions too slowly. Maybe we are slow because our discussions focus too early on details and are based on imprecise data." This suggests the following proposition:

*PROPOSITION 7d: Insufficient analyses and superficial interpretations during the preparation of management accounting information can reduce the use of management accounting information for strategic sensemaking by upper level managers.*

In addition to the negative impact of insufficient analyses on utilization, the interviews suggest that an insufficient reconciliation of reports during preparation can lead to emotional conflict and information-hiding when managers are confronted with management accounting information in meetings. Manager B4 expresses his dissatisfaction because of missing reconciliations: "Often these reports create conflict. As a first reaction these reports get questioned, and than you have to go back and verify the information. A significant improvement would be a reconciliation of the findings prior to the meeting." It seems necessary to inform managers of severe deviations in advance, so that they have the opportunity to identify underlying drivers and to prepare countermeasures that can be discussed in a meeting with top management. Interviewee B5 describes how his department reconciles analyses and thereby prevents conflict: "In the beginning we presented our analyses without prior notice and that created a lot of conflict. ... Now we distribute our reports to all affected managers one week in advance so that they have time to correct our analyses in case of mistakes, or prepare for discussions with top management." This suggests:

> *PROPOSITION 7e: The reconciliation of analyses and interpretations during the preparation of management accounting information helps to reduce conflict and information-hiding during the utilization of management accounting information.*

A co-occurrence analysis of interview statements provides further support that an effective preparation of management accounting information contributes to the utilization of information for strategic sensemaking. Table 24 below shows the percentage of statements related to the utilization of management accounting information that co-occur with statements related to the preparation of management accounting systems. All statements that describe a positive impact of information utilization on strategic sensemaking co-occur with statements related to a positive preparation of management accounting information. In addition, there is some support for a positive relationship between management accounting system adaptation and the utilization of management accounting information for strategic sensemaking. This is not surprising as the previous chapter suggests a positive relationship between management accounting system adaptation and the preparation of management accounting information.

Overall this leads to the following proposition:

> *PROPOSITION 7f: An effective preparation of management accounting information contributes to strategic sensemaking during its utilization by upper level managers.*

| Statements related to utilization of management accounting information ... | | N | Percentage of statements co-occurring with statements related to ... | | | | Comment |
|---|---|---|---|---|---|---|---|
| | | | *Adaptation* | | *Preparation* | | |
| | | | *Positive* | *Negative* | *Positive* | *Negative* | |
| Utilization | Positive | 117 | **69%** | 18% | **100%** | 55% | Consistent positive impact of adaptation on utilization; some positive impact of preparation |
| | Negative | 56 | 41% | **46%** | 100% | 91% | |

*Table 24: Impact of adaptation and preparation on utilization of MAS information*

## 2.4 Relationship with Management Accounting System Dimensions

The previous sections show that the adaptation of management accounting systems, the preparation of management accounting information, and its utilization contribute in different ways to strategic sensemaking of individual managers. Management accounting systems can have different roles, and interview statements suggest that management accounting system dimensions contribute to these roles. Furthermore, section E1.4 shows that management accounting system dimensions contribute to strategic sensemaking through their impact on observation, interpretation and communication. Therefore, the author conducted several analyses to explore the relationship between management accounting system dimensions and the different roles of management accounting systems in strategic sensemaking.

First, a co-occurrence analysis of interview statements that refer both to management accounting system dimensions and adaptation, preparation or utilization in the same paragraph indicates which dimensions are particularly associated with the three ways of using management accounting systems or information. Table 25 below provides the percentages of all respondents that made co-occurring statements. A high frequency of occurrence suggests an association between management accounting system dimensions and the ways of using the system. Table 25 shows that all management accounting system dimensions except for the format of management accounting information have some association with the preparation of management accounting information. Integrated (44% of all managers) and formalized (67% of all managers) management accounting systems seem especially relevant for the preparation of management accounting information.

| Management accounting system dimensions | | N | Adaptation Positive | Adaptation Negative | Preparation Positive | Preparation Negative | Utilization Positive | Utilization Negative | Comment |
|---|---|---|---|---|---|---|---|---|---|
| | | | Percentage of respondents with statements co-occurring with ... | | | | | | |
| Scope | Broad | 27 | 4% | 0% | **19%** | 4% | 4% | 0% | Some positive impact on preparation |
| | Narrow | 27 | 0% | 0% | 0% | 4% | 0% | 4% | |
| Timeliness | High | 27 | 0% | 0% | **11%** | 0% | 0% | 0% | Consistent positive impact on preparation; some negative impact of low timeliness on utilization |
| | Low | 27 | 0% | 0% | 0% | **7%** | 4% | **11%** | |
| Format | Pos. | 27 | 4% | 0% | 4% | 0% | **15%** | 4% | Consistent positive impact on utilization; some association between negative format and adaptation |
| | Neg. | 27 | 0% | **11%** | 0% | 7% | 0% | **11%** | |
| Accuracy | High | 27 | 0% | 0% | **11%** | 0% | 0% | 0% | Consistent positive impact on preparation |
| | Low | 27 | 0% | 4% | 4% | **11%** | 0% | 7% | |
| Integration | High | 27 | 11% | 0% | **44%** | 7% | 4% | 0% | Consistent strong positive impact on preparation |
| | Low | 27 | 0% | 4% | 4% | **19%** | 0% | **19%** | |
| Flexibility | High | 27 | **41%** | 0% | **11%** | 0% | 4% | 4% | Consistent strong positive impact on adaptation and some impact on preparation |
| | Low | 27 | 0% | **7%** | 4% | **7%** | 0% | 0% | |
| Accessibility | High | 27 | 4% | 0% | **11%** | 0% | 4% | 0% | Some positive impact on preparation |
| | Low | 27 | 0% | 0% | 4% | 0% | 4% | 0% | |
| Formalization | High | 27 | 0% | 0% | **67%** | 7% | **30%** | 11% | Strong positive impact on preparation; consistent positive impact on utilization |
| | Low | 27 | 0% | 4% | 11% | 7% | 4% | **22%** | |
| Media richness | High | 27 | 4% | 0% | **30%** | 0% | **33%** | 7% | Strong positive impact on preparation and utilization |
| | Low | 27 | 0% | 0% | 0% | 0% | 4% | 4% | |

Note: Sample size is n=27 as 3 interviews were conducted with 2 interview partners each.

*Table 25: Relationships between MAS dimensions and different ways of using MAS in sensemaking*

Concerning the utilization of management accounting information, Table 25 suggests that formalization, media richness and format have a positive impact on the utilization of management accounting information. Finally, the flexibility dimension of management accounting systems has the highest association with adaptation.

Because of the small sample size of this study it is not possible to analyze structural models in order to understand the simultaneous impact of several dimensions on cognitive processes in strategic sensemaking.[680] Instead it is necessary to rely on simple statistical methods such as correlation analysis. However, the correlation analysis of management accounting system dimensions in isolation from each other runs the risk of showing unrealistic configurations. Therefore, the author performed an agglomerative hierarchical cluster analysis on the nine management accounting system dimen-

[680] See Ittner and Larcker (2001), p. 400.

sions to group the cases. In order to create tight clusters of similar cases, the complete linkage method was chosen. Dissimilarity between clusters was measured by Euclidian distances of management accounting system dimensions.

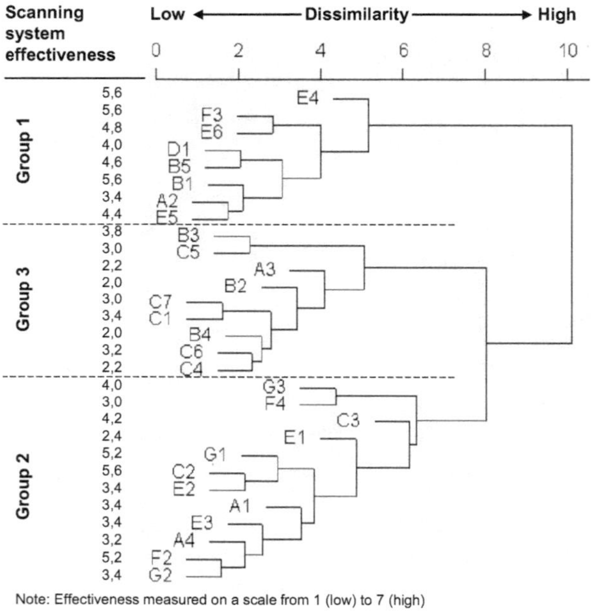


*Figure 10:Cluster dendrogram of interview cases*

Figure 10 above shows the result of the cluster analysis and suggests grouping the cases in three clusters. Group 1, with the more effective management accounting systems for strategic sensemaking, consists equally of cases from companies with short- and long-term horizons concerning strategic issues. Group 3, with the least effective management accounting systems for strategic sensemaking, contains only cases of managers from the information and communication technology industry. The environment for companies in this industry is changing quickly, and it seems that this makes it more difficult to implement effective management accounting systems. Group 2, with a mixed evaluation concerning the effectiveness of management accounting systems for strategic sensemaking, includes cases from both industries. These groupings do not suggest a systematic difference between management accounting systems in the two researched industries. Therefore, it is not necessary to conduct the analyses separately for each industry.

Table 26 below shows the average scores for management accounting system dimensions, the information acquisition modes 'focused search' and 'scanning', 'interactive use' and 'scanning system effectiveness' of all three groups. Furthermore, t-tests of the variables between all groups indicate significant differences.

| | | **Average score on a 7-point Likert scale in ...** | | | **Significance of t-test between ...** | | |
|---|---|---|---|---|---|---|---|
| **Category** | **Dimension** | **Group 1** | **Group 2** | **Group 3** | **Group 1-2** | **Group 2-3** | **Group 1-3** |
| Information quality | Scope | 4.8 | 4.4 | 3.4 | .203 | .012 | .004 |
| | Timeliness | 5.8 | 4.9 | 3.5 | .002 | < .001 | < .001 |
| | Format | 6.0 | 4.8 | 3.5 | .003 | .004 | < .001 |
| | Accuracy | 6.1 | 4.9 | 3.6 | .001 | .001 | < .001 |
| System quality | Integration | 5.6 | 4.5 | 2.5 | .005 | < .001 | < .001 |
| | Flexibility | 5.8 | 4.8 | 3.9 | .001 | .003 | < .001 |
| | Accessibility | 6.3 | 4.5 | 3.1 | < .001 | .003 | < .001 |
| | Formalization | 3.9 | 3.7 | 2.3 | .365 | .006 | .006 |
| | Media richness | 6.4 | 6.0 | 4.7 | .100 | .003 | .003 |
| Sensemaking | Scanning | 4.4 | 3.6 | 3.1 | .062 | .108 | .001 |
| | Focused search | 5.2 | 4.6 | 4.1 | .097 | .153 | .016 |
| | Interactive use | 6.1 | 5.7 | 4.4 | .078 | .006 | .003 |
| | Effectiveness | 4.8 | 3.9 | 2.8 | .026 | .005 | < .001 |

*Table 26: Differences between Management accounting system dimensions in cluster groups*

The significant differences between most management accounting system dimensions are not surprising, because the dimensions were used as variables for the clustering. However, these results show that all nine dimensions are important to distinguish the clusters. We validated our cluster solution through significance tests on variables not used for the cluster analysis.[681] Highly significant Kruskal-Wallis tests on scanning system effectiveness ($p = .0008$) and interactive use ($p = .004$) provide evidence for the external validity. Furthermore, Kruskal-Wallis tests on scanning ($p = .03$) and focused search ($p = .09$) are also significant. It seems that all management accounting system dimensions contribute, through their impact on adaptation, preparation and utilization, to the effective use of management accounting systems for strategic sensemaking.

[681] See also Aldenderfer and Blashfield (1984).

Finally, Table 27 below shows that the majority of positive statements about adaptation, preparation and utilization come from managers in groups 1 and 2. Furthermore, managers from group 3 make the majority of negative statements. This provides further evidence that management accounting system dimensions are related to the different roles of management accounting systems during adaptation, preparation and utilization.

| Statements referring to ... | | N | Percentage of statements from interview partners in ... *Group 1* | *Group 2* | *Group 3* | Comment |
|---|---|---|---|---|---|---|
| Adaptation | Positive | 42 | **40%** | **35%** | 25% | Positive statements mainly in group 1 and 2; negative statements mainly in group 3 |
| | Negative | 10 | 11% | 22% | **67%** | |
| Preparation | Positive | 185 | **37%** | **43%** | 20% | Positive statements mainly in group 1 and 2; negative statements mainly in group 3 |
| | Negative | 61 | 20% | 14% | **66%** | |
| Utilization | Positive | 117 | **34%** | **48%** | 18% | Positive statements mainly in group 1 and 2; negative statements mainly in group 3 |
| | Negative | 56 | 20% | 24% | **56%** | |

*Table 27: Distribution of statements about different ways of using MAS in cluster groups*

The following paragraphs present propositions for how management accounting system dimensions contribute to strategic sensemaking during (1) adaptation, (2) preparation and (3) utilization.

*(1) Adaptation*: Flexible management accounting systems are adapted regularly, so that they focus on current strategic uncertainties. This relationship is not surprising, because adaptation was measured as part of the flexibility dimension. Flexible management accounting systems can provide managers with information about current strategic uncertainties. According to SIMONS a management accounting system must collect and generate information that relates to the effects of strategic uncertainties on the strategy of the business in order to be used interactively.[682] A high correlation between flexibility and interactive use (r = .54) supports this statement. It seems that flexible management accounting systems create the precondition for an effective preparation and utilization of management accounting information. The correlation between flexible management accounting systems and scanning system effectiveness (r = .58) highlights the contribution of management accounting system adaptation to strategic sensemaking. This leads to the following proposition:

[682] Simons (1995), p. 109.

*PROPOSITION 8a: Flexible management accounting systems provide information that helps managers to focus on strategic uncertainties.*

*(2) Preparation*: Interview statements suggest that integrated and formalized management accounting systems in particular contribute to strategic sensemaking during the preparation of management accounting information.[683] Integrated management accounting systems can provide directions for the interpretation of strategic issues and can encourage information sharing between functions. A high correlation between integration and scanning system effectiveness (r = .70) provides further support for the impact of integration on strategic sensemaking. Furthermore, it seems that accurate and broad scope management accounting information helps managers to analyze implications of strategic issues. Information scope has the highest association with scanning system effectiveness (r = .78). This suggests the following proposition:

*PROPOSITION 8b: Broad scope and accurate management accounting information from integrated and formalized management accounting systems facilitates interactions between managers and provides an information basis for the analysis of strategic issues.*

*(3) Utilization*: Interviews suggest that effective management accounting systems can provide an information basis that allows upper level managers to challenge middle managers and discuss strategic issues. Report delivery through channels of high media richness helps managers to resolve equivocality associated with strategic issues (r = .41 between media richness and scanning system effectiveness) and provides an opportunity for top management to give feedback to managers who prepared the information. A management accounting information format that includes qualitative remarks seems to be key to initiating discussions and supporting the identification of issues. The high association between format and scanning system effectiveness (r = .62) supports this. Formalized reports help top managers to get a comprehensive overview, so that potential issues are not overlooked (r = .42 between formalization and scanning system effectiveness). This leads to the following proposition:

*PROPOSITION 8c: Formalized management accounting systems that include channels of high media richness to present semi-coded information provide top managers with an information basis to discuss strategic issues.*

---

[683] See E2.2 Preparation, pp. 5 and Table 25, p. 5.

## 3. Summary of Propositions

This study provides evidence that the main role of management accounting systems in strategic sensemaking is not the provision of information that indicates new strategic issues. Managers are more likely to observe strategic issues through informal sources than through management accounting systems (proposition 1a). However, it seems that managers would not decide on a response strategy based on information solely from informal sources. They use management accounting systems to search for additional information that helps them to substantiate potential strategic issues from informal sources (proposition 1b). The main role of management accounting systems in strategic sensemaking is to help in the interpretation and communication of strategic issues. Especially the interactive use of management accounting information contributes to strategic sensemaking by facilitating interactions between managers and by focusing attention on strategic uncertainties (proposition 1d and 3b). This suggests that the systems-structural perspective of information processing, with its focus on information acquisition and distribution, is not sufficient to explain the role of management accounting systems in strategic sensemaking (proposition 3a). Therefore, the interpretive perspective of information processing, with its emphasis on the construction of meaning through interactions between managers, is additionally required (proposition 3c).

This research proposes a model that draws on the systems-structural and interpretive perspective of information processing. The model distinguishes three different ways of using management accounting systems or information: adaptation, preparation and utilization. The adaptation of management accounting systems focuses attention on strategic uncertainties and increases alignment between managers. During the preparation of management accounting information, integrated and formalized management accounting systems help middle managers to develop interpretations of strategic issues. This information serves as a fact basis that enables top managers to challenge middle managers, and helps them to identify and discuss strategic issues. Effective management accounting systems focus organizational attention and facilitate information flows that contribute to strategic sensemaking.

Table 28 below summarizes the roles of management accounting systems in strategic sensemaking during adaptation, preparation and utilization. It shows that feed forward and feedback loops create interdependencies between the adaptation of management accounting systems and the preparation and utilization of its management accounting information. Shortcomings in one of the ways of using management accounting systems or information can impact the others.

| | **Adaptation** of management accounting systems | **Preparation** of management accounting information | **Utilization** of management accounting information |
|---|---|---|---|
| **Roles of management accounting systems** | • Focus attention on strategic uncertainties (Proposition 5a)<br>• Align managers and increase knowledge about meaning of management accounting information (Proposition 5b) | • Facilitate interactions between managers to discuss strategic issues (Proposition 6a)<br>• Provide directions that help managers to prepare interpretations of strategic issues (Proposition 6b)<br>• Contribute to strategic sensemaking of middle managers (Proposition 6f) | • Provide fact basis that helps top managers to identify and discuss strategic issues (Proposition 7a)<br>• Enable top managers to challenge middle managers and probe for potential issues (Proposition 7b)<br>• Contribute to strategic sensemaking of upper level managers (Proposition 7c) |
| **Interdependencies** | • Discussions about measurements can reduce debates about data issues and measurement methodologies during preparation (Proposition 6c)<br>• Contributes positively to strategic sensemaking during preparation (Proposition 6d) | • Insufficient analyses and superficial interpretations can reduce the use of management accounting information for strategic sensemaking by upper level managers. (Proposition 7d)<br>• Reconciliation of analyses and interpretations can reduce conflict and information-hiding during utilization (Proposition 7e)<br>• Contributes positively to strategic sensemaking during utilization (Proposition 7f) | • Missing feedback to middle managers can lead to deterioration of analyses and interpretations (Proposition 6e) |

*Table 28: Roles of management accounting systems in strategic sensemaking*

This research proposes that management accounting system dimensions contribute to the use of management accounting systems for strategic sensemaking (proposition 4).[684] The impact of management accounting system dimensions on use also shapes the role of management accounting systems during adaptation, preparation and utilization. Table 29 below summarizes the impact of management accounting system dimensions on the role of management accounting systems in strategic sensemaking.

---

[684] Table 22, p. 5 provides an overview of the proposed relationships between management accounting system dimensions and observation, interpretation and communication processes of individual managers.

| | Management accounting system dimensions | Impact on role of management accounting systems | Impact on strategic sensemaking through ... | | | | | |
|---|---|---|---|---|---|---|---|---|
| | | | | | Emphasis on ... | | | |
| | | | **Focused search** | **Scanning** | **Chances** | **Risks** | **Increased awareness** | **Interactive use** |
| Information Quality | Scope | • Provides information basis for analysis of issues (8b) | + (1g) | + (1h) | + (2a) | + (2b) | + (2d) | + (3i) |
| Information Quality | Timeliness | • Not explicitly mentioned by interview partners | + (1g) | + (1h) | | + (2b) | + (2d) | + (3g, 3i) |
| Information Quality | Format | • Semi-coded and simple information initiates discussions about strategic issues (3d, 8c) | + (1g) | | | + (2b) | + (2d) | + (3d, 3i) |
| Information Quality | Accuracy | • Provides information basis for analysis of issues (8b)<br>• Helps focusing discussions on meaning of information (3e) | + (1g) | | | + (2b) | | + (3e, 3i) |
| System Quality | Integration | • Provides directions and helps managers to prepare interpretations of strategic issues (6b)<br>• Facilitates interactions between functional areas (3f, 6a, 8b) | + (1g) | + (1h) | + (2a) | | | + (3f, 3i) |
| System Quality | Flexibility | • Adaptation helps focusing on strategic uncertainties (5a, 8a) | + (1g) | + (1h) | | + (2b) | | + (3i) |
| System Quality | Accessibility | • Not explicitly mentioned by interview partners | + (1g) | + (1h) | + (2a) | | | + (3i) |
| System Quality | Formalization | • Facilitates interactions between functional areas (6a, 8b)<br>• Provides top managers with information basis to discuss issues (8c)<br>• Encourages discussions (3g) | + (1g) | High: – (1h) | + (2a, 2c) | + (2b) | + (2d) | ± (3g, 3i) |
| System Quality | Media richness | • Provides opportunities to discuss issues (3g, 8c) | | | + (2a) | | | + (3g, 3i) |

Note: Corresponding propositions in parenthesis
Legend: + (positive); – (negative); ± (balanced)

*Table 29: Impact of MAS dimensions on role and use of management accounting systems*

# F Implications and Outlook

## 1. Theoretical Implications

Survival in a competitive environment requires top and middle managers to make sense of strategic issues. Information from the internal and external environment helps managers to relate the firm's strengths and weaknesses to specific opportunities and threats embedded in these issues. Because management accounting systems provide such information, the objective of this research was to explore their role in strategic sensemaking.

Based on cognitive theories, this research defines strategic sensemaking as a learning process with observation, interpretation, and communication as the relevant process steps at the individual level. A literature review on the impact of management accounting systems on observation, interpretation and communication of strategic issues provided tentative, theoretical relationships between management accounting systems and strategic sensemaking of individual managers. Results from information systems research helped to develop a comprehensive set of information quality and system quality dimensions. Information quality dimensions correspond to management accounting information characteristics and system quality dimensions reflect the processes required to produce the output measured by information quality. The empirical approach of this research was based on an exploratory multiple-case study design, because it allowed considering the impact of different kinds of management accounting systems and other information sources on complex strategic sensemaking activities in their natural setting. Data was collected through interviews and questionnaires from 30 top and middle managers in seven large listed companies from the information and communications technology sector, the automotive and the aeronautics/space industry. The following will summarize findings along the two research questions and will discuss their theoretical implications.

*1st Research question: How do managers use management accounting systems for strategic sensemaking?*

This research suggests that effective management accounting systems focus organizational attention on strategic uncertainties and facilitate information flows that contribute to strategic sensemaking. Managers do not primarily use management accounting systems to look for information that indicates strategic issues for the first time, as they are more likely to observe strategic issues through informal sources. Instead, they use management accounting systems to search for additional information that helps them to make sense of these issues. Especially the interactive use of management accounting systems contributes to strategic sensemaking by focusing attention on strategic uncertainties and by facilitating interactions between managers that help to resolve equivocality of strategic issues. This finding is similar to BISBE AND OTLEY's assumption that the interactive use of management accounting systems provides direction and integration to translate innovation into performance.[685] Directions supposedly signal preferences for search, while integration supports the debate about different interpretations of strategic issues. It is also in line with ABERNETHY AND BROWNELL's speculation that the interactive use of management accounting systems can serve as integrative liaison devises, that enable the interchange of information by breaking down barriers inhibiting information flows and thereby would contribute positively to performance during strategic change.[686] This suggests that the interactive use of management accounting systems not only helps to moderate the impact of innovation on performance and to improve performance during strategic change, but also helps to make sense of strategic issues.

It seems that the interactive use of management accounting systems is important to several areas of strategic management, but previous research only speculates about mechanisms how it improves performance. To better understand these mechanisms and the role of management accounting systems in strategic sensemaking, this research proposes to distinguish three different ways of using management accounting systems or information: adaptation, preparation, and utilization. (1) *Adaptation* is the alignment of management accounting systems with strategic uncertainties, (2) *preparation* includes the processes predominantly performed by middle management to prepare management accounting information, and (3) *utilization* is the use of management accounting information, mainly by upper management levels. The following will describe how these different ways of using management accounting systems and information contribute to strategic sensemaking and how they relate to their interactive use.

---

[685] Bisbe and Otley (2004), p. 727.

[686] Abernethy and Brownell (1999), p. 192 and p. 198.

*(1) Adaptation of management accounting systems*: This research proposes that a regular adaptation of management accounting systems contributes to the focusing of attention on strategic uncertainties. Furthermore, discussions during the adaptation of management accounting systems increase alignment between managers and contribute to their knowledge about the meaning and measurement of management accounting information. This can help to reduce debates about data issues and measurement methodologies during the preparation of management accounting information so that later discussions can focus on the meaning of management accounting information. These findings add a new aspect to VAIVIO's suggestion that discussions during the introduction of non-financial measures are helpful to uncover relevant local knowledge.[687] It seems that these discussions do not only have an immediate benefit because of new knowledge about local business processes, but that they are also helpful to improve understanding of management accounting information that represents these processes. This allows managers to better use management accounting information for interpretation and communication of strategic issues.

Therefore, discussions during a regular adaptation of management accounting systems contribute to two conditions for interactive use as suggested by SIMONS: Firstly, they ensure that management accounting systems collect and generate information that relates to the effects of strategic uncertainties on the strategy of the business. Secondly, these discussions ensure that management accounting information becomes simpler to understand.[688] Simple management accounting information on strategic uncertainties of the company provides the basis for discussions of strategic issues. Overall, the adaptation of management accounting systems lays the foundation for the interactive use of management accounting information and thereby contributes positively to strategic sensemaking.

*(2) Preparation of management accounting information*: Findings from this research suggest that management accounting systems can provide directions that help particularly middle managers to prepare interpretations of strategic issues and can facilitate interactions to discuss these interpretations. Comprehensive analyses and interpretations of strategic issues by middle managers are important, because they make different perspectives or strategic options available to top managers. Otherwise, manage-

---

[687] Vaivio (2004), p. 63.
[688] Simons (1995), pp. 108-109.

ment accounting information becomes of less use in strategic sensemaking of upper level managers. Furthermore, a reconciliation of analyses and interpretations during the preparation of management accounting information can reduce conflict and information-hiding when upper level managers use the information. The observed role of management accounting systems during the preparation of management accounting information supports BISBE AND OTLEY's assumption that the interactive use of management accounting systems provides directions and a forum for organizational members to engage in face-to-face dialogue and debate that helps to translate innovation into performance.[689] In addition, this research offers explanations as to how management accounting systems can fulfill this role.

Firstly, the formalization of management accounting systems through guidelines for analyses, the presence of forms or templates and pre-defined channels for the communication of strategic issues requires managers to think about the future, or about consequences of strategic issues for their business, and enforces discussions of these interpretations. According to SIMONS management accounting systems that require the re-forecasting of future states based on revised current information fulfill one condition for their interactive use.[690] This suggests that a certain level of formalization for management accounting systems contributes to their interactive use. In addition, interviews indicate that management accounting systems with a high level of formalization increase the managers' awareness of latent developments. This interpretation is similar to that of KAPLAN AND BEINHOCKER, who suggest that the goal of the strategic planning process is not to make strategy, but to build prepared minds that are capable of making sound strategic decisions.[691]

Secondly, integrated management accounting systems provide directions that help managers to develop interpretations of strategic issues. They can help middle managers to understand how their functional area relates to the company as a whole and how goals, strategy and operations are connected. Integrated management accounting systems include information from different functional areas, which facilitates interactions between managers to discuss overarching issues. These findings provide a possible explanation for the link CHENHALL found between integrative strategic performance

---

[689] Bisbe and Otley (2004), p. 727.
[690] Simons (1995), p. 108.
[691] Kaplan and Beinhocker (2003), p. 71.

measurement systems and organizational learning.[692] It could be that the integration aspect of the researched strategic performance measurement systems contributed to an interactive use of management accounting information that guided organizational learning, as suggested by SIMONS.[693] In a similar manner, VAIVIO observed how the non-financial measurements of a Balanced Scorecard stimulated horizontal debate. The Balanced Scorecard provides critical performance indicators along the company's value chain,[694] which is a characteristic of integrated management accounting systems. It seems that these integrated non-financial measures stimulated their interactive use.

Overall, the management accounting system dimensions 'integration' and 'formalization' in particular foster an interactive use of management accounting information. This contributes to strategic sensemaking of middle managers during the preparation of management accounting information.

*(3) Utilization of management accounting information*: Findings from this research suggest that management accounting systems can facilitate an information flow that provides upper level managers in particular with a fact basis to interpret and discuss strategic issues. Management accounting information that is discussed in face-to-face meetings enables top managers to challenge middle managers and probe for potential issues. Especially important is that top managers provide feedback to middle managers involved in the preparation of management accounting information. This research suggests that management accounting information that is not discussed in meetings, or where no feedback is provided, can become ineffective. Missing feedback can lead to a deterioration of analyses and interpretations when middle managers do not see the benefit of their work. As a consequence, insufficient interpretations provide fewer perspectives on strategic issues and therefore limit the possibility of resolving equivocality through the discussion of different interpretations. It is also a waste of resources, since the preparation of management accounting information adds significantly to the workload of middle management.[695] These findings supplement MALINA AND SELTO's proposition that reporting without feedback is a direct cause of conflict or tension.[696] This research shows that ineffective communication has negative consequences for the

---

[692] Chenhall (2005), p. 415.
[693] Simons (1994), p. 184.
[694] Vaivio (2004), p. 53.
[695] See also Tuomela (2005), p. 314.
[696] Malina and Selto (2001), p. 70.

preparation of management accounting information and therefore limits their usefulness in strategic sensemaking both at middle and upper management levels.

Overall, the interactive use of management accounting information by upper level managers allows management accounting systems to become a communication platform for strategic sensemaking, which helps managers to develop a shared interpretation of strategic issues.

Previous research did not investigate interdependencies between different ways of using management accounting systems or information and how this contributes to their interactive use. This research proposes that the adaptation of management accounting systems creates preconditions for the interactive use of management accounting information. Furthermore, the preparation and utilization of management accounting information are interlinked through feed forward and feedback channels. The use of management accounting systems for the interpretation of strategic issues by middle managers provides top management with management accounting information that helps to discuss these issues. Thereby, management accounting information becomes an important and recurring agenda addressed by the top management.[697] Previous research summarizes all these mechanisms and interdependencies through the concept of interactive use. Therefore, future research should focus on adaptation, preparation and utilization as specific ways of using management accounting systems or information. This could further improve understanding how the interactive use of management accounting systems contributes to strategic management.

*2nd Research question: How do management accounting system dimensions shape the role and use of management accounting systems in strategic sensemaking?*

This research proposes that information quality dimensions (scope, timeliness, format, and accuracy) and system quality dimensions (integration, flexibility, accessibility, formalization, and media richness) contribute positively to the use of management accounting systems for strategic sensemaking. These dimensions shape the different roles of management accounting systems in strategic sensemaking.

Firstly, flexible management accounting systems provide information that helps managers to focus on strategic uncertainties. Flexible management accounting systems are adapted regularly and do not prescribe the use of management accounting information.

---

697 Simons (1995), p. 97.

This helps managers to use management accounting information for strategic sense-making.

Secondly, broad scope and accurate management accounting information from integrated and formalized management accounting systems facilitates interactions between managers and provides an information basis for the analysis of strategic issues. Contrary to assumptions from FERRIS AND HASKINS and DENT,[698] inaccurate management accounting information does not contribute to observation through scanning and does not increase awareness during issue interpretation. Instead, accurate management accounting information contributes to interactive use and helps to focus discussions on the meaning of information by minimizing discussions about the measurement method.

Thirdly, formalized management accounting systems that include channels of high media richness to present semi-coded information provide top managers with an information basis to discuss strategic issues. This research provides empirical evidence for SIMONS' assertion that management accounting information in a semi-coded format increases awareness and initiates discussions about strategic.[699]

Previous research on the relationship between management accounting systems and strategic sensemaking or decision-making has mostly neglected the importance of management accounting system quality dimensions. MOLLOY AND SCHWENK conclude in their work on the effects of information technology on strategic decision-making, that information quality is the single most critical factor.[700] However, this research shows that in addition to information quality dimensions, especially the system quality dimensions 'integration', 'formalization' and 'flexibility' contribute positively to the use of management accounting systems in strategic sensemaking. Therefore, future research should not neglect the impact of management accounting system quality dimensions on the use of management accounting systems in strategic decision-making.

Another implication of this research is related to the relationship between quality dimensions and the interactive use of management accounting systems. Management accounting researchers seem to imply that the interactive use of management accounting

---

[698] See Ferris and Haskins (1988), p. 3 and Dent (1990), p. 19.
[699] Simons (1995), pp. 193-194.
[700] Molloy and Schwenk (1995), p. 302. They refer to the appropriateness of data through the attributes quality, accuracy and timeliness.

systems is a voluntary choice of managers. For example BISBE AND OTLEY emphasize the importance of a proper (interactive) use of management accounting systems to convert innovation successfully into improved performance.[701] However, this research shows that the interactive use of management accounting systems is not necessarily an intended choice of managers. Management accounting information quality and especially system quality dimensions are associated with an interactive use of management accounting systems. This study suggests that management accounting system dimensions encourage interactive use, but it is also possible that the observed systems were adapted in such a way as to support their intended interactive use. Since this research did not include longitudinal case studies, it is not possible to resolve the direction of causality.

Finally, VANDENBOSCH asks whether it is possible to encourage a certain information use, and which particular attributes of information or technology foster the different ways of using information.[702] This research indicates that in particular the system quality dimensions 'integration', 'flexibility', 'formalization', and the information quality dimension 'format' encourage and support the interactive use. These findings provide a preliminary and partial answer to VANDENBOSCH's question and encourage further research. Such research would contribute even further to the managerial implications presented in the next section.

## 2. Managerial Implications

This study provides implications both for top and middle managers who use management accounting systems, and for managers who are responsible for designing such systems. It suggests that management accounting systems can significantly support the observation, interpretation and communication of strategic issues and strategic changes if they are designed in the right way. Three design principles for management accounting systems have emerged:

*(1) Utilization of management accounting systems as communication platforms*: Managers need to discuss management accounting information in management meetings and not only during alignment loops prior to the meeting. For example, the managers

[701] Bisbe and Otley (2004), p. 730.
[702] Vandenbosch (1999), p. 89.

in company E regularly use their management accounting system to discuss reasons for deviations in their key performance indicators, and to develop measures to resolve negative deviations. Every month, all managers are required to comment on their key performance indicators and these comments are visible (including name and telephone number of the responsible manager) to the top management. In addition, a larger meeting is held every quarter, where the management accounting system is used to discuss severe negative deviations of key performance indicators from targets. Every responsible manager is asked to present his countermeasures in person, which provides top management with an opportunity to discuss things that have gone wrong or underlying strategic issues. Results suggest that the content of a management accounting system is only subject to discussion when it provides relevant information related to daily business. Company B failed several times with the introduction of a Balanced Scorecard, because managers were unable to link the information provided to their daily work. They still used their own reports and indicators for discussions and ignored the Balanced Scorecard. Only the IT department has introduced key performance indicators that focus also on operational details, which provides them with a fact basis to discuss and monitor strategic projects.

*(2) Regular adaptation of management accounting systems*: Management accounting systems can only focus attention on strategic uncertainties when they are regularly adapted to changes in the environment. This also requires regular feedback from top management to middle managers involved in the preparation of management accounting information. Company C had, in the past, a multitude of reports with a very high reporting frequency. Upper management did not discuss the suitability of these reports and did not provide feedback to middle managers involved in preparing them. As a result a vicious circle started, where interpretations of issues by middle managers deteriorated due to lack of feedback, and then upper management stopped using the reports, because these poor-quality interpretations were of little use to them. Middle management noticed the reduced usage and put even less effort into the preparation. Finally, frustration on all levels emerged. Middle managers complained that they were "reporting for the sake of reporting" and knew neither the recipient of some reports, nor their purpose. As part of a restructuring of the management accounting systems, reports were replaced and the content realigned with current strategic uncertainties. Upper management now provides regular feedback to increase the quality of reports, in order to make them more useful for decision-making. This research suggests that managers who participate in regular discussions about the adaptation of management

accounting systems have a higher knowledge about the meaning of management accounting information and know the limitations of their measurement. Discussions about adaptations can help to reduce unproductive debates about measurement details later. This allows managers to focus on root causes and countermeasures for observed deviations, instead of questioning the validity of the information.

*(3) Facilitation of interactions between managers*: Management accounting systems contribute to strategic sensemaking when they facilitate interactions between functions and hierarchies. These interactions provide different perspectives and help to integrate information from different areas of the company, in order to get a better understanding of issues. Integrated management accounting systems that provide non-financial information at the interface between different functional areas can create opportunities for discussion. Managers need to resolve ambiguity associated with different perspectives created by integrated information in order to coordinate their actions. Company B uses a simple product/channel matrix as a daily management accounting report to increase interactions between product and channel managers. This research shows that qualitative information especially contributes to different perspectives and fosters discussions between managers. However, the preparation of qualitative information is more difficult, as it is not readily available from transaction systems. It requires a certain level of formalization in order to ensure a minimum information flow.

If designed in the right way, management accounting systems do not only contribute to strategic sensemaking at the top management level. Processes associated with the preparation of information seem to particularly contribute to the strategic sensemaking of middle managers. This does not require fully automated management accounting systems. More important are management accounting systems that provide an accurate information basis about the most important areas of the business and help managers to analyze and discuss potential issues.

## 3. Limitations and Outlook

As with all exploratory research, this research is subject to some limitations and provides directions for further research.

First, results of this study are based on a small sample of 30 top and middle managers in seven large corporations. The purpose of the chosen exploratory case-study design was to achieve analytical, rather than statistical, generalization. The study included informants from two different industries: the information/communication technology industry and the aerospace/automotive industry. Results do not show significant differences concerning the role of management accounting systems in strategic sensemaking between these two industries. While the composition of specific management accounting systems differs among companies, or even between different functional areas of the same company, the overall role of management accounting systems seems to remain the same: facilitating information flows that contribute to an effective interpretation of strategic issues. In order to increase the statistical generalizability of this research's findings, it seems advisable to conduct further survey-based empirical research. Such research would allow path analysis and causal modeling in order to simultaneously analyze the impact of management accounting system dimensions on the different roles of management accounting systems in strategic sensemaking. It would also improve understanding of the relative importance of each information quality and system quality dimension and provide further insights on their relationships with information acquisition, interactive use, scanning system effectiveness and finally performance. For this research it was necessary to adapt several measurement instruments in the questionnaire. High Cronbach alphas of all measurement instruments except for scanning and one sub-dimension of flexibility suggest sufficient reliability.[703] However, it seems worthwhile to further improve and validate the psychometric properties of the measurement instruments.

Second, this research did not explicitly consider environmental context factors. In order to develop better recommendations for practitioners it is important to understand how different context factors influence the relationship between management accounting system dimensions, the different ways of using management accounting systems and information, and performance. As MOORES AND YUEN suggest, it seems fruitful to conduct further research on configurations of management accounting systems.[704] An improved understanding of different configurations of effective management accounting systems and context factors that distinguish between these configurations would help to develop more suitable recommendations for an effective management accounting system design. It could also help to understand how management accounting systems evolve over time and whether their role in strategic sensemaking changes.

---

[703] See Table 15, p. 5.

[704] Moores and Yuen (2001), p. 352.

Third, this research is based on a broad definition of management accounting systems. Management accounting systems were defined as all formal systems that prepare and provide information to mangers from the internal and external environment. Therefore, the findings cannot be easily transferred to specific management accounting systems. However, the suggested management accounting system dimensions seem to be applicable to all systems, and it would be valuable to understand their importance for specific systems. Furthermore, analyses of interdependencies between different management accounting systems for planning and control could provide interesting insights that could further help to understand the role of management accounting systems in strategic sensemaking.

Fourth, the level of analysis of this research is the individual manager. As a first step the restriction to the individual manager was necessary to understand how management accounting systems can have an impact on cognitive processes during strategic sensemaking. However, researchers like HAMBRICK AND MASON suggest that top management teams have a significant impact on strategic sensemaking.[705] Top management teams usually make strategic decisions, and therefore it is important to understand whether management accounting systems contribute differently to sensemaking in teams.

Finally, this research is not based on longitudinal case studies. Longitudinal research could help to identify the direction of causality between management accounting system dimensions and interactive use. It could also further our understanding of how effective management accounting systems for strategic sensemaking evolve over time. Notwithstanding these limitations this research contributes to the understanding of management accounting systems in the important context of strategic sensemaking.

---

[705] See Hambrick and Mason (1984).

# Appendix

The following questionnaire has been adapted. It includes only measurement instruments used for this research and provides the original items in square brackets.

## Fragebogen

**Zum Thema "Einfluss von Controllingsystemen auf die strategische Früherkennung"**

EUROPEAN BUSINESS SCHOOL

Lehrstuhl für Controlling
Prof. Dr. Utz Schäffer
z.Hd. Marcus Heidmann
Schloß Reichartshausen
65375 Oestrich-Winkel

Fax: 089 – 2423 3383
E-Mail: Marcus.Heidmann@ebs.de
Mobil: 0175 – 318 3382

Ich möchte mich auf diesem Wege nochmals für Ihr Interesse an meinem Forschungsvorhaben zur strategischen Früherkennung danken.

Vor **Beginn** unseres Interviews möchte ich Sie bitten, den folgenden Fragebogen auszufüllen.
**Zur Beantwortung benötigen Sie ca. 15-20 Minuten.**

**Weitere Erläuterungen zum Fragebogen**

- Unter dem Begriff **Früherkennung** verstehen wir die Beobachtung, Interpretation und Reaktion auf **strategisch relevante Veränderungen** im Marktumfeld.
- Als **Controllingsysteme** bezeichnen wir alle **formalen Systeme**, die Ihnen Informationen über das Unternehmen und sein Umfeld zur Verfügung stellen. Controllingsysteme umfassen z.B. regelmäßig erstellte Berichte, Marktreports, Abweichungsanalysen, Planungen, Prognosen, Kennzahlen, die Balanced Scorecard sowie computerbasierte Informationssysteme.
- **Controllinginformationen** sind alle in den Controllingsystemen enthaltenen Informationen. Es kann sich hierbei sowohl um **interne und externe**, um **quantitative und qualitative** als auch um **finanzielle und nicht-finanzielle** Informationen handeln.
- Der Fragebogen dient rein **wissenschaftlichen Zwecken**. Alle Angaben werden **streng vertraulich** behandelt und anonym ausgewertet.
- *Im Fragebogen werden verschiedene Sachverhalte durch **ähnliche Fragestellungen** erfasst. Wir bitten Sie hierfür um Verständnis, da dies aus statistischen Gründen erforderlich ist. Die **Vollständigkeit Ihrer Antworten** ist von **großer Bedeutung**. Bitte beantworten Sie alle Fragen, auch wenn Sie bei einigen Fragen nur eine ungefähre Antwort geben können.*
- Wir möchten Sie nun bitten, zu folgenden vier Bereichen Angaben zu machen:
  - **Qualität der Controllinginformationen**
  - **Qualität der Controllingsysteme**
  - **Umgang mit Controllinginformationen**
  - **Erfolg der Früherkennung**

**Vielen Dank für Ihre Zeit und Ihre Unterstützung!**

**I. Bitte machen Sie nun Angaben zur Qualität der Controllinginformationen.**

| **Sind die folgenden Informationen in Ihren Controllingsystemen in ausreichendem Umfang für die Früherkennung vorhanden?** | Trifft nicht zu 1 | 2 | 3 | 4 | 5 | Trifft voll zu 6 |
|---|---|---|---|---|---|---|
| Note: Scope measured by items 1-6 | | | | | | |
| 1. Informationen bezüglich allgemeiner Faktoren außerhalb Ihres Unternehmens, wie z.B. wirtschaftliche Rahmenbedingungen, Bevölkerungswachstum, technologische Entwicklungen. [Information on broad factors external to your organization, such as economic conditions, population growth, technological developments, etc.] | ☐ | ☐ | ☐ | ☐ | ☐ | ☐ |
| 2. Nicht-finanzielle Informationen, wie z.B. Kundenpräferenzen, Mitarbeitermeinungen, Arbeitgeber-Arbeitnehmer-Beziehungen, Haltungen von Regierung/regulatorischen Behörden und Verbraucherverbänden, Verhalten von Wettbewerbern. [Noneconomic information, such as customer preferences, employee attitudes, labor relations, attitudes of government and consumer bodies, competitive threats, etc.] | ☐ | ☐ | ☐ | ☐ | ☐ | ☐ |
| 3. Nicht-finanzielle Informationen aus dem Marktumfeld, wie z.B. Marktanteile, Marktgröße, Marktwachstum. (Wenn eine finanzielle Interpretation von Absatzinformationen Ihren Bedürfnissen am meisten entgegenkommt, kreuzen Sie bitte die Skala am linken Ende an.) [Nonfinancial information that relates to the following areas: market information such as market size, growth share, etc. (If you find that a financial interpretation of production and marketing information is most useful for your needs, please mark the lower end of the scale.)] | ☐ | ☐ | ☐ | ☐ | ☐ | ☐ |
| 4. Nicht-finanzielle Informationen in Bezug auf die Produkterstellung/Dienstleistungserbringung, wie z.B. Effizienz, Leistungsangaben, Krankheitsstand. [Nonfinancial information that relates to the following areas: production information such as output rates, scrap levels, machine efficiency, employee absenteeism, etc.] | ☐ | ☐ | ☐ | ☐ | ☐ | ☐ |
| 5. Informationen, die sich auf mögliche zukünftige Ereignisse beziehen, wie z.B. Szenarien, Planungen, Trends. (Falls Ihnen nur historische Informationen zur Verfügung stehen, kreuzen Sie bitte die Skala am linken Ende an.) [Information which relates to possible future events (if historical information is most suitable for your needs, mark the lower end of the scale).] | ☐ | ☐ | ☐ | ☐ | ☐ | ☐ |
| 6. Eintrittswahrscheinlichkeiten von zukünftigen Ereignissen. [Quantification of the likelihood of future events occurring (e.g., probability estimates).] | ☐ | ☐ | ☐ | ☐ | ☐ | ☐ |

| **Wie kann man die für die Früherkennung relevanten Controllinginformationen am besten charakterisieren?** | Trifft nicht zu 1 | 2 | 3 | 4 | 5 | Trifft voll zu 6 |
|---|---|---|---|---|---|---|
| Note: Timeliness measured by items 1-6 | | | | | | |
| 1. Angeforderte Informationen werden unverzüglich bereitgestellt. [Requested information arrives immediately upon request] | □ | □ | □ | □ | □ | □ |
| 2. Controllinginformationen erhalte ich häufig und regelmäßig. [Reports are provided frequently on a systematic, regular basis: e.g., daily reports, weekly reports (for less frequent reporting, mark lower end of scale).] | □ | □ | □ | □ | □ | □ |
| 3. Controllinginformationen stehen automatisch nach Ende der Bearbeitung bzw. nach deren Eingabe in das Informationssystem zur Verfügung. [Information supplied to you automatically upon its receipt into information systems or as soon as processing is completed.] | □ | □ | □ | □ | □ | □ |
| 4. Relevante Controllinginformationen über aufgetretene Ereignisse werden unverzüglich berichtet. [There is no delay between an event occurring and relevant information being reported to you] | □ | □ | □ | □ | □ | □ |
| 5. Die Informationen in den Controllingsystemen sind immer auf dem neuesten Stand. [The information from ... is always up to date] | □ | □ | □ | □ | □ | □ |
| 6. Die wichtigsten Controllinginformationen werden in Echtzeit bereitgestellt. | □ | □ | □ | □ | □ | □ |

| **Inwieweit stimmen Sie folgenden Aussagen über Controllinginformationen zu?** | Trifft nicht zu 1 | 2 | 3 | 4 | 5 | Trifft voll zu 6 |
|---|---|---|---|---|---|---|
| Note: Format measure includes user know-how (items 1-3) and semi-coding (items 4-5); Accuracy measured by items 6-9 | | | | | | |
| 1. Ich weiß, wie die Controllinginformationen erstellt werden. | □ | □ | □ | □ | □ | □ |
| 2. Der Aussagegehalt der Controllinginformationen ist mir klar. | □ | □ | □ | □ | □ | □ |
| 3. Ich könnte Controllinginformationen ohne weiteres einem Dritten erklären. | □ | □ | □ | □ | □ | □ |
| 4. Die Controllinginformationen enthalten in ausreichendem Maße qualitative Angaben, wie z.B. Erläuterungen, Begründungen, Aussagen und erklärende Texte. | □ | □ | □ | □ | □ | □ |
| 5. Quantitative Controllinginformationen werden übersichtlich, z.B. durch Tabellen oder Grafiken, dargestellt. | □ | □ | □ | □ | □ | □ |
| 6. Die Controllingsysteme produzieren korrekte Informationen. [... produces correct information.] | □ | □ | □ | □ | □ | □ |
| 7. Es sind wenige Fehler in den Informationen, die ich von den Controllingsystemen erhalte. [There are few errors in the information I obtain from ....] | □ | □ | □ | □ | □ | □ |
| 8. Die Informationen in den Controllingsystemen sind genau. [The information provided by ... is accurate.] | □ | □ | □ | □ | □ | □ |
| 9. Die Informationen aus verschiedenen Controllingsystemen sind konsistent. | □ | □ | □ | □ | □ | □ |

**II. Bitte machen Sie nun Angaben zur Qualität der Controllingsysteme.**

| **Wie würden Sie den Integrationsgrad Ihrer Controllingsysteme beschreiben?** | Trifft nicht zu 1 | 2 | 3 | 4 | 5 | Trifft voll zu 6 |
|---|---|---|---|---|---|---|
| Note: Integration measure includes source integration (items 1-3) and strategic/operational linkages (items 4-6) | | | | | | |
| 1. Die Controllingsysteme integrieren sehr effektiv Informationen aus verschiedenen Unternehmensbereichen. [... effectively integrates data from different areas of the company] | ☐ | ☐ | ☐ | ☐ | ☐ | ☐ |
| 2. Die Controllingsysteme bündeln Informationen aus verschiedenen Teilen des Unternehmens. [... pulls together information that used to come from different places in the company] | ☐ | ☐ | ☐ | ☐ | ☐ | ☐ |
| 3. Die Controllingsysteme kombinieren sehr effektiv Informationen aus verschiedenen Unternehmensbereichen. [... Effectively combines data from different areas of the company] | ☐ | ☐ | ☐ | ☐ | ☐ | ☐ |
| 4. Die Controllingsysteme schaffen eine klare und sich gegenseitig verstärkende Verbindung zwischen der kurzfristigen Leistung meiner Einheit und der langfristigen Strategie des Geschäftsbereiches. [It provides consistent and mutually reinforcing links between current operating performance of your work group and long term strategies of the business unit.] | ☐ | ☐ | ☐ | ☐ | ☐ | ☐ |
| 5. Die Controllingsysteme verbinden alle Aktivitäten meines Geschäftsbereiches mit der Erreichung von Unternehmenszielen. [It links together all business unit activities to the achievement of goals and objectives of the organization.] | ☐ | ☐ | ☐ | ☐ | ☐ | ☐ |
| 6. Die Controllingsysteme stellen die Auswirkung von Aktivitäten meines Geschäftsbereiches auf andere Unternehmensbereiche dar. [It shows how activities of this business unit affect activities of other units within the organization.] | ☐ | ☐ | ☐ | ☐ | ☐ | ☐ |

| **Wie kann man die Anpassungsfähigkeit und Flexibilität Ihrer Controllingsysteme am besten charakterisieren?** | Trifft nicht zu 1 | 2 | 3 | 4 | 5 | Trifft voll zu 6 |
|---|---|---|---|---|---|---|
| Flexibility measure includes adaptation (items 1-4) and analytic capability (items 5-6) | | | | | | |
| 1. Die Controllingsysteme werden von Zeit zu Zeit an neue Anforderungen angepasst. | ☐ | ☐ | ☐ | ☐ | ☐ | ☐ |
| 2. Die Controllingsysteme wurden einmal entwickelt und sind seitdem nicht mehr verändert worden. (reversed-coded item) | ☐ | ☐ | ☐ | ☐ | ☐ | ☐ |
| 3. Bei organisatorischen Änderungen, z.B. neue Strategie, Organisationsstruktur, neue Technologien, werden die Controllingsysteme angepasst. | ☐ | ☐ | ☐ | ☐ | ☐ | ☐ |
| 4. Bei wesentlichen Änderungen des Marktumfeldes werden die Controllingsysteme auf ihre Zweckmäßigkeit überprüft. | ☐ | ☐ | ☐ | ☐ | ☐ | ☐ |
| 5. Die computergestützten Controllingsysteme besitzen nützliche Analysefunktionen in Hinblick auf die Unternehmensperformance. [Usefulness of ESS for analyzing company performance] | ☐ | ☐ | ☐ | ☐ | ☐ | ☐ |
| 6. Die computergestützten Controllingsysteme unterstützen mich bei der Entwicklung neuer Methoden zur Analyse von Informationen. [Usefulness of ESS for developing new ways to analyze data] | ☐ | ☐ | ☐ | ☐ | ☐ | ☐ |

| **Welche Rolle spielen die Controllingsysteme bei Ihrer Leistungsbewertung?** | Trifft nicht zu 1 | 2 | 3 | 4 | 5 | Trifft voll zu 6 |
|---|---|---|---|---|---|---|
| Note: Flexibility measure also includes "long-run use of target" (items 1-4) | | | | | | |
| 1. Bei der Bewertung meiner Leistung werden Zielvorgaben flexibel gehandhabt. [Targets are used with flexibility in my evaluation.] | ☐ | ☐ | ☐ | ☐ | ☐ | ☐ |
| 2. Mein Vorgesetzter erwartet grundsätzlich, dass ich in Einklang mit meinen vorgegebenen Zielen handele, hat aber auch ein offenes Ohr für die Ursachen von negativen Abweichungen. [My superior expects me to operate in line with my targets, but allows me to explain reasons for any unfavourable variance.] | ☐ | ☐ | ☐ | ☐ | ☐ | ☐ |
| 3. Meinem Vorgesetzten ist die Erreichung von kurzfristigen Ergebnisverbesserungen wichtiger als die Steigerung der langfristigen Erfolgswirksamkeit. (reverse coded) [My superior is more concerned with actions which produce good short-term results than with long-run effectiveness.] | ☐ | ☐ | ☐ | ☐ | ☐ | ☐ |
| 4. Mein Vorgesetzter glaubt, dass zur Bewertung meiner Leistung neben Angaben zur Zielerreichung auch andere Arten von Informationen benötigt werden. [My superior believes that target-related information must be supplemented with other types of information to assess my performance.] | ☐ | ☐ | ☐ | ☐ | ☐ | ☐ |

| **Wie schätzen Sie den Formalisierungsgrad in Ihrem Unternehmen ein?** | Trifft nicht zu 1 | 2 | 3 | 4 | 5 | Trifft voll zu 6 |
|---|---|---|---|---|---|---|
| Note: Formalization measured by items 1-3 | | | | | | |
| 1. Für die Analyse von Controllinginformationen haben wir Formulare und Vorlagen für fast alle Aspekte. [Within the strategic/long-term planning we have forms and on-screen templates for everything.] | ☐ | ☐ | ☐ | ☐ | ☐ | ☐ |
| 2. Es gibt klare Vorschriften über Aussehen und Inhalte von Abweichungsanalysen. [Within the framework of strategic/long-term planning we use extensive rules about content, size and outer Form of planning documents.] | ☐ | ☐ | ☐ | ☐ | ☐ | ☐ |
| 3. Für die Kommunikation von Unregelmäßigkeiten und Abweichungen in den Controllinginformationen gibt es klar definierte Kanäle und Vorgehensweisen. [Within the framework of strategic/long-term planning we follow largely standardized planning procedures.] | ☐ | ☐ | ☐ | ☐ | ☐ | ☐ |

| **Wie häufig nutzen Sie die folgenden Kanäle zur Kommunikation von Informationen über mögliche Veränderungen im Unternehmensumfeld?** | Niemals 1 | 2 | 3 | 4 | 5 | Sehr häufig 6 |
|---|---|---|---|---|---|---|
| Note: Media richness measured by items 1-2 | | | | | | |
| 1. Gruppenmeetings, z.B. mit Mitarbeitern, Vorgesetzten oder anderen Kollegen. | ☐ | ☐ | ☐ | ☐ | ☐ | ☐ |
| 2. Direkter persönlicher Kontakt, z.B. Einzelgespräche oder Telefonanrufe. | ☐ | ☐ | ☐ | ☐ | ☐ | ☐ |
| 3. Schriftlicher und persönlicher Kontakt, z.B. E-Mail oder Memos. | ☐ | ☐ | ☐ | ☐ | ☐ | ☐ |
| 4. Schriftlicher und unpersönlicher Kontakt, z.B. Abweichungsbegründungen, Formulare, Datenbankeinträge, Mailinglisten. | ☐ | ☐ | ☐ | ☐ | ☐ | ☐ |

| **Inwieweit treffen die folgenden Aussagen für die Früherkennung zu?** | Trifft nicht zu 1 | 2 | 3 | 4 | 5 | Trifft voll zu 6 |
|---|---|---|---|---|---|---|
| Note: Accessibility measured by items 1-3<br>Interactive use measured by items 4-7 | | | | | | |
| 1. Die Controllingsysteme ermöglichen mir einen problemlosen Zugang zu den Informationen. [... allows information to be readily accessible to me] | □ | □ | □ | □ | □ | □ |
| 2. Die Controllingsysteme machen Informationen sehr leicht zugänglich. [... makes information very accessible] | □ | □ | □ | □ | □ | □ |
| 3. Die Controllingsysteme machen den Zugriff auf Controllinginformationen leicht. [... makes information easy to access] | □ | □ | □ | □ | □ | □ |
| 4. Einige Controllinginformationen diskutiere ich mit Kollegen, weil sie für den Geschäftsbereich entscheidende Aspekte betreffen. | □ | □ | □ | □ | □ | □ |
| 5. Einige Controllinginformationen dienen als Grundlage für Diskussionen über Veränderungen in der Umwelt und den damit verbundenen Chancen und Risiken. | □ | □ | □ | □ | □ | □ |
| 6. Einige Controllinginformationen veranlassen mich und meine Mitarbeiter, die grundlegenden Annahmen unseres Geschäfts zu hinterfragen und Maßnahmen zu diskutieren. | □ | □ | □ | □ | □ | □ |
| 7. Auf einige Controllinginformationen richten meine Kollegen und ich sehr oft und regelmäßig unsere Aufmerksamkeit. | □ | □ | □ | □ | □ | □ |

**III. Bitte machen Sie nun Angaben zu Ihrem Umgang mit Controllinginformationen**

| **Wie nutzen Sie die Controllingsysteme, um Veränderungen in Ihrem Marktumfeld zu erkennen?** | Trifft nicht zu 1 | 2 | 3 | 4 | 5 | Trifft voll zu 6 |
|---|---|---|---|---|---|---|
| Note: Focused search measured by items 1-5, scanning measured by items 6-9 | | | | | | |
| 1. Ich nutze die Controllingsysteme, um Antworten auf spezifische Fragen zu erhalten. [I use the ESS to find answers to specific questions] | □ | □ | □ | □ | □ | □ |
| 2. Ich konzentriere mich regelmäßig auf spezielle Controllinginformationen. [I regularly focus on specific information in the ESS] | □ | □ | □ | □ | □ | □ |
| 3. Zur Nutzung der Controllingsysteme folge ich einem festen Ablauf. [I have a set routine for using the ESS] | □ | □ | □ | □ | □ | □ |
| 4. Ich nutze die Controllingsysteme, um Zahlen einzusehen, die ich benötige. [I use the ESS to look up numbers I need] | □ | □ | □ | □ | □ | □ |
| 5. Ich sehe mir immer die gleichen Controllinginformationen an. [I review a consistent set of reports in the ESS] | □ | □ | □ | □ | □ | □ |
| 6. Ich nutze die Controllingsysteme, um nach Neuigkeiten zu suchen. [I use the ESS to see what's new] | □ | □ | □ | □ | □ | □ |
| 7. Ich durchstöbere die Controllingsysteme ohne bestimmte Absichten. [I randomly browse through information contained in the ESS] | □ | □ | □ | □ | □ | □ |
| 8. Im Allgemeinen sehe ich mir jedes Mal andere Controllinginformationen an. [I vary the information I look at in the ESS] | □ | □ | □ | □ | □ | □ |
| 9. Ich betrachte ein weites Spektrum an Informationen in unseren Controllingsystemen. [My scanning of the ESS is wide-ranging] | □ | □ | □ | □ | □ | □ |

| **Inwieweit stimmen Sie folgenden Aussagen zu?** | Trifft nicht zu 1 | 2 | 3 | 4 | 5 | Trifft voll zu 6 |
|---|---|---|---|---|---|---|
| Note: Dysfunctional behavior measured by items 1-5 | | | | | | |
| 1. Ich neige dazu, bestimmte, auf meine Arbeit bezogene Aktivitäten zu ignorieren, weil sie von meinem Vorgesetzten nicht überwacht werden. [I tend to ignore certain job-related activities simply because they are not monitored by the division.] | □ | □ | □ | □ | □ | □ |
| 2. Ich habe Informationen so angepasst, dass meine Leistung besser im Einklang mit übergeordneten Zielen steht. [I have adjusted marketing data to make my performance more in line with division goals.] | □ | □ | □ | □ | □ | □ |
| 3. Bei der Präsentation von Informationen gegenüber Vorgesetzten betone ich vor allem Informationen, die mich gut aussehen lassen. [When presenting data to upper management, I try to emphasize data which reflect favorably upon me.] | □ | □ | □ | □ | □ | □ |
| 4. Bei der Präsentation von Informationen gegenüber Vorgesetzten versuche ich nicht der Überbringer schlechter Nachrichten zu sein. [When presenting data to upper management, I try to avoid being the bearer of bad news.] | □ | □ | □ | □ | □ | □ |
| 5. Selbst wenn meine Produktivität nicht erwartungsgemäß ist, versuche ich sie als erwartungsgemäß darzustellen. [Even if my productivity is inconsistent, I still try to make it appear consistent.] | □ | □ | □ | □ | □ | □ |

**IV. Bitte machen Sie nun Angaben zum Erfolg der Früherkennung.**

| **Sind die Ihnen zur Verfügung stehenden Controllingsysteme angemessen, um Ihnen ...** | Nicht angemessen 1 | 2 | 3 | 4 | 5 | Sehr angemessen 6 |
|---|---|---|---|---|---|---|
| Note: Scanning system effectiveness measured by items 1-5 | | | | | | |
| 1. ... relevante Probleme und Chancen bewusst zu machen? | □ | □ | □ | □ | □ | □ |
| 2. ... Stärken und Schwächen zu verdeutlichen? | □ | □ | □ | □ | □ | □ |
| 3. ... die Rahmenbedingungen des Marktumfelds bewusst zu machen? | □ | □ | □ | □ | □ | □ |
| 4. ... eine schnelle Anpassung an neue Produkttrends zu erleichtern? | □ | □ | □ | □ | □ | □ |
| 5. ... eine frühzeitige Identifikation von wechselnden Kundenbedürfnissen zu ermöglichen? | □ | □ | □ | □ | □ | □ |

| Wie beurteilen Sie Ihre Erkenntnisse über Zulieferer/Partner, Kunden und andere Märkte? | Trifft nicht zu 1 | 2 | 3 | 4 | 5 | Trifft voll zu 6 |
|---|---|---|---|---|---|---|
| Note: Information Acquisition Scope measured by items 1-13 | | | | | | |
| 1. Wir sind über technische und technologische Entwicklungen in unserer Branche stets auf dem Laufenden. [We are well aware of technological and technical developments within our industry.] | ☐ | ☐ | ☐ | ☐ | ☐ | ☐ |
| 2. Wir sammeln Informationen aus allen Branchen, die eine ähnliche Technologie wie wir einsetzen. [Our information gathering efforts cover all industries that employ the sort of technology that we use.] | ☐ | ☐ | ☐ | ☐ | ☐ | ☐ |
| 3. Wir beobachten besonders stark technologisch verwandte Branchen (technologisch verwandt sind z.B. Telekommunikation und die Computerindustrie) [A careful watch is kept on industries that are technologically related to ours (e.g., telecom and computer industries are technologically related).] | ☐ | ☐ | ☐ | ☐ | ☐ | ☐ |
| 4. Wir suchen nur selten nach Informationen über Möglichkeiten wie wir unsere bestehende Produktionstechnologie für neue Produktbereiche einsetzen können. (Reverse coded) [We acquire little information on opportunities to employ our existing production facilities in new product domains.] | ☐ | ☐ | ☐ | ☐ | ☐ | ☐ |
| 5. Wir beobachten sehr intensiv Unternehmen, die nicht in unserem Produktbereich tätig sind, aber über ähnliche Fähigkeiten und Wissen wie wir verfügen. [We closely monitor companies not active in our product area, but having skills and know-how comparable to ours.] | ☐ | ☐ | ☐ | ☐ | ☐ | ☐ |
| 6. Unser Unternehmen überwacht genau die Fortschritte in der Produkt- und Prozesstechnologie unserer Zulieferer/Partner. [In our company, there is close surveillance of advancements in product and process technologies in supplier industries.] | ☐ | ☐ | ☐ | ☐ | ☐ | ☐ |
| 7. Wir beobachten sehr genau Marketingstrategien anderer Unternehmen, die unsere Kunden adressieren. [Marketing strategies of companies targeting our customers are closely followed by us.] | ☐ | ☐ | ☐ | ☐ | ☐ | ☐ |
| 8. Wir behalten die Veränderungen der Produktpräferenzen unserer Kunden stets im Auge. [We have a finger on the pulse as far as changes in the product preferences of our customers are concerned.] | ☐ | ☐ | ☐ | ☐ | ☐ | ☐ |
| 9. Uns sind Entwicklungen in Branchen, die mit ganz anderen Produkten ein ähnliches Kundenbedürfnis wie wir erfüllen, sehr gut bekannt (z.B. erfüllen Bahn- und Luftverkehr beide das Kundenbedürfnis nach Mobilität). [Developments in industries that fulfill the same customer need as we do albeit with a completely different product are well known to us (e.g., air and train transport both fulfill customer need for mobility).] | ☐ | ☐ | ☐ | ☐ | ☐ | ☐ |
| 10. Wir beobachten sehr genau die Aktivitäten von Unternehmen mit komplementären Produkten (komplementäre Produkte sind z.B. Kameras und Filmrollen, da sie vom Kunden gemeinsam genutzt werden). [We keep close track of activities of companies that offer complementary products (e.g., cameras and film rolls are complementary products as they are used together by customers).] | ☐ | ☐ | ☐ | ☐ | ☐ | ☐ |
| 11. Wir sind über alle wichtigen Chancen in den von uns bedienten geographischen Regionen informiert. [We are knowledgeable about all important opportunities in the geographic regions in which we operate.] | ☐ | ☐ | ☐ | ☐ | ☐ | ☐ |
| 12. Wir sind gut über Preis- und Qualitätsaspekte von Produkten in benachbarten geographischen Regionen informiert. [We are well informed about the price and quality aspects of products in neighboring geographic regions.] | ☐ | ☐ | ☐ | ☐ | ☐ | ☐ |
| 13. Wir beobachten sehr genau die Aktivitäten von Unternehmen in unserer Branche, die derzeit in anderen geographischen Märkten tätig sind. [We closely follow the activities of companies in our industrial sector but operating outside our geographic area.] | ☐ | ☐ | ☐ | ☐ | ☐ | ☐ |

## References

**ABERNETHY, M.A./BROWNELL, P. (1999)**: The Role of Budgets in Organizations Facing Strategic Change: An Exploratory Study, in: Accounting, Organizations & Society 24 (3): pp. 189-204.

**AGUILAR, F.J. (1967)**: Scanning the Business Environment, New York, Macmillan.

**AKGÜN, A.E./LYNN, G.S./BYRNE, J.C. (2003)**: Organizational Learning: A Socio-Cognitive Framework, in: Human Relations 56 (7): pp. 839-868.

**ALDENDERFER, M.S./BLASHFIELD, R.K. (1984)**: Cluster Analysis, Newbury Park, CA, Sage.

**ALDRICH, H.E./AUSTER, E.R. (1986)**: Even Dwarfs Started Small, in: STAW, B.M./CUMMINGS, L.L., Eds., Research in organizational behavior, Greenwich, CT, JAI Press, Inc.: pp. 165-198.

**ALLISON, P.D. (2001)**: Missing Data, Thousand Oaks, Sage.

**ANSARI, S./EUSKE, K.J. (1987)**: Rational, Rationalizing, and Reifying Uses of Accounting Data in Organizations, in: Accounting, Organizations & Society 12 (6): pp. 549-568.

**ANSOFF, H.I. (1975)**: Managing Strategic Surprise by Response to Weak Signals, in: California Management Review 18 (2): pp. 21-38.

**ANSOFF, H.I. (1980)**: Strategic Issue Management, in: Strategic Management Journal 1 (2): pp. 131-148.

**ANSOFF, H.I. (1990)**: Implanting Strategic Management (2nd ed.), New York, Prentice Hall.

**ANTHONY, R.N. (1965)**: Plannning and Control Systems: A Framework for Analysis, Boston, MA, Graduate School of Business Administration, Harvard University.

**ANTHONY, R.N./GOVINDARAJAN, V. (2000)**: Management Control Systems (10th ed.), McGraw-Hill.

**ARGYRIS, C. (1976)**: Single-Loop and Double-Loop Models in Research on Decision Making, in: Administrative Science Quarterly 21 (3): pp. 363-377.

**ARGYRIS, C. (1990)**: Overcoming Organizational Defenses: Facilitating Organizational Learning, Boston, Allyn and Bacon.

**ARGYRIS, C. (1992)**: On Organizational Learning, Cambridge, Blackwell Publishers.

**ARGYRIS, C./SCHÖN, D. (1978)**: Organizational Learning: A Theory of Action Perspective, Reading, MA, Addison-Wesley.

**ASHMOS, D.P./DUCHON, D./MCDANIEL, R.R. (1998)**: Participation in Strategic Decision Making: The Role of Organizational Predisposition and Issue Interpretation, in: Decision Sciences 29 (1): pp. 25-51.

**ATKINSON, A.A. et al. (2001)**: Management Accounting (3rd ed.), Upper Saddle River, NJ, Prentice Hall.

**BAINES, A./LANGFIELD-SMITH, K. (2003)**: Antecedents to Management Accounting Change: A Structural Equation Approach, in: Accounting, Organizations & Society 28 (7/8): pp. 675-698.

**BAPUJI, H./CROSSAN, M. (2004)**: From Questions to Answers: Reviewing Organizational Learning Research, in: Management Learning 35 (4): pp. 397-417.

**BATESON, G. (1972)**: Steps to an Ecology of Mind, San Francisco, CA, Chandler.

**BAUM, J.R./WALLY, S. (2003)**: Strategic Decision Speed and Firm Performance, in: Strategic Management Journal 24 (11): pp. 1107-1129.

**BECKER, M.C. (2004)**: Organizational Routines: A Review of the Literature, in: Industrial & Corporate Change 13 (4): pp. 643-677.

**BELL, S.J./WHITWELL, G.J./LUKAS, B.A. (2002)**: Schools of Thought in Organizational Learning, in: Journal of the Academy of Marketing Science 30 (1): pp. 70-86.

**BIRNBERG, J.G./SHIELDS, J.F. (1989)**: Three Decades of Behavioral Accounting Research: A Search for Order, in: Behavioral Research in Accounting 1: pp. 23-74.

**BISBE, J./OTLEY, D.T. (2004)**: The Effects of the Interactive Use of Management Control Systems on Product Innovation, in: Accounting, Organizations and Society 29 (8): pp. 709-737.

**BOGNER, W.C./BARR, P.S. (2000)**: Making Sense in Hypercompetitive Environments: A Cognitive Explanation for the Persistence of High Velocity Competition, in: Organization Science: A Journal of the Institute of Management Sciences 11 (2): pp. 212-226.

**BOISOT, M./CANALS, A. (2004)**: Data, Information and Knowledge: Have we got it right?, in: Journal of Evolutionary Economics 14 (1): pp. 43-67.

**BONTIS, N./CROSSAN, M.M./HULLAND, J. (2002)**: Managing an Organizational Learning System by Aligning Stocks and Flows of Knowledge, in: Journal of Management Studies 39 (4): pp. 437-469.

**BOUWENS, J./ABERNETHY, M.A. (2000)**: The Consequences of Customization on Management Accounting System Design, in: Accounting, Organizations and Society 25 (3): pp. 221-241.

**BRIERS, M./HIRST, M.K. (1990)**: The Role of Budgetary Information in Performance Evaluation, in: Accounting, Organizations & Society 15 (4): pp. 373-398.

**BRUINING, H./BONNET, M./WRIGHT, M. (2004)**: Management Control Systems and Strategy Change in Buyouts, in: Management Accounting Research 15 (2): pp. 155-177.

**BRUNS, W./MCKINNON, S. (1993)**: Information and Managers: A Field Study, in: Journal of Management Accounting Research (5): pp. 84-108.

**BÜCHEL, B./RAUB, S. (2001)**: Media Choice and Organizational Learning, in: DIERKES, M. et al., Eds., Organizational Learning and Knowledge, New York, Oxford University Press: pp. 518-534.

**BURCHELL, S. et al. (1980)**: The Role of Accounting in Organizations and Society, in: Accounting, Organizations & Society 5 (1): pp. 5-27.

**BURNES, B. (2004)**: Kurt Lewin and the Planned Approach to Change: A Re-appraisal, in: Journal of Management Studies 41 (6): pp. 977-1002.

**Carlson, J.R./Zmud, R.W. (1994)**: Channel Expansion Theory: A Dynamic View of Media and Information Richness Perceptions, in: Academy of Management Proceedings: pp. 280-284.

**Carlson, J.R./Zmud, R.W. (1999)**: Channel Expansion Theory and the Experiential Nature of Media Richness Perceptions, in: Academy of Management Journal 42 (2): pp. 153-170.

**Chakravarthy, B.S. (1982)**: Adaptation: A Promising Metaphor for Strategic Management, in: Academy of Management Review 7 (1): pp. 35-44.

**Chattopadhyay, P./Glick, W.H./Huber, G.P. (2001)**: Organizational Actions in Response to Threats and Opportunities, in: Academy of Management Journal 44 (5): pp. 937-955.

**Chenhall, R.H. (2003)**: Management Control Systems Design within its Organizational Context: Findings from Contingency-based Research and Directions for the Future, in: Accounting, Organizations and Society 28 (2/3): pp. 127-168.

**Chenhall, R.H. (2005)**: Integrative Strategic Performance Measurement Systems, Strategic Alignment of Manufacturing, Learning and Strategic Outcomes: An Exploratory Study, in: Accounting, Organizations & Society 30 (5): pp. 395-422.

**Chenhall, R.H./Morris, D. (1986)**: The Impact of Structure, Environment, and Interdependence on the Perceived Usefulness of Management Accounting Systems, in: The Accounting Review 61 (1): pp. 16-35.

**Chetty, S. (1996)**: The Case Study Method for Research in Small- and Medium-sized Firms, in: International Small Business Journal 15 (1): pp. 73-85.

**Chia, Y.M. (1995)**: Decentralization, Management Accounting System (MAS) Information Characteristics and Their Interaction Effects on Managerial Performance, in: Journal of Business Finance & Accounting 22 (6): pp. 811-830.

**Chong, V.K. (1996)**: Management Accounting Systems, Task Uncertainty and Managerial Performance: A Research Note, in: Accounting, Organizations & Society 21 (5): pp. 415-421.

**Choo, C.W. (1998)**: The Knowing Organization: How Organizations Use Information to Construct Meaning, New York, Oxford University Press.

**Coates, J./Davis, T./Stacey, R. (1995)**: Performance Measurement Systems, Incentive Reward Schemes and Short-Termism in Multinational Companies: A Note, in: Management Accounting Research 6 (2): pp. 125-135.

**Cohen, M.D. (1991)**: Individual Learning and Organizational Routine: Emerging Connections, in: Organization science 2 (1): pp. 135-139.

**Corner, P.D./Kinicke, A.J./Keats, B.W. (1994)**: Integrating Organizational and Individual Information Processing Perspectives on Choice, in: Organization Science 5 (3): pp. 294-308.

**Cronbach, L.J. (1951)**: Coefficient Alpha and the Internal Structure of Tests, in: Psychometrika 16 (3): pp. 297-334.

**Crossan, M.M./Berdrow, I. (2003)**: Organizational Learning and Strategic Renewal, in: Strategic Management Journal 24 (11): pp. 1087-1105.

**Crossan, M.M./Lane, H.W./White, R.E. (1999)**: An Organizational Learning Framework: From Intuition to Institution, in: Academy of Management Review 24 (3): pp. 522-537.

**Crossan, M.M. et al. (1995)**: Organizational Learning: Dimensions for a Theory, in: International Journal of Organizational Analysis 3 (4): pp. 337-360.

**Cyert, R.M./March, J.G. (1963)**: A Behavioral Theory of the Firm, Englewood Cliffs, NJ, Prentice Hall.

**Daft, R.L./Huber, G.P. (1987)**: How Organizations Learn: A Communication Framework, in: Bacharach, S.B./DiTomaso, N., Eds., Research in the Sociology of Organizations. A Research Annual, Greenwich, Conn., JAI Press, 5: pp. 1-36.

**Daft, R.L./Lengel, R.H. (1984)**: Information Richness: A New Approach to Managerial Behavior and Organization Design, in: Research in Organizational Behavior 6: pp. 191-233.

**Daft, R.L./Lengel, R.H. (1986)**: Organizational Information Requirements, Media Richness and Structural Design, in: Management Science 32 (5): pp. 554-571.

**DAFT, R.L./SORMUNEN, J./PARKS, D. (1988)**: Chief Executive Scanning, Environmental Characteristics, and Company Performance: An Empirical Study, in: Strategic Management Journal 9 (2): pp. 123-139.

**DAFT, R.L./WEICK, K.E. (1984)**: Toward a Model of Organizations as Interpretation Systems, in: Academy of Management Review 9 (2): pp. 284-295.

**DAS, T.K./TENG, B.S. (1999)**: Cognitive Biases and Strategic Decision Processes: An Integrative Perspective, in: Journal of Management Studies 36 (6): pp. 757-778.

**DAVENPORT, T.H. (1993)**: Process Innovation, Boston, MA, Harvard Business School Press.

**DAVIS, G.B. (1974)**: Management Information Systems: Conceptual Foundations, Structure and Development, New York, McGraw-Hill.

**DAY, G.S. (1994)**: Continuous Learning about Markets, in: California Management Review 36 (4): pp. 9-31.

**DAY, G.S. (2002)**: Managing the Market Learning Process, in: The Journal of Business & Industrial Marketing 17 (4): pp. 240-252.

**DE VAUS, D.A. (2001)**: Research Design in Social Research, London, Thousand Oaks, New Delhi, Sage Publications.

**DELONE, W.H./MCLEAN, E.R. (1992)**: Information Systems Success: The Quest for the Dependent Variable, in: Information Systems Research 3 (1): pp. 60-95.

**DELONE, W.H./MCLEAN, E.R. (2003)**: The DeLone and McLean Model of Information Systems Success: A Ten-Year Update, in: Journal of Management Information Systems 19 (4): pp. 9-30.

**DENT, J.F. (1990)**: Strategy, Organization and Control: Some Possibilities for Accounting Research, in: Accounting, Organizations & Society 15 (1/2): pp. 3-45.

**DENT, J.F. (1991)**: Accounting and Organizational Cultures: A Field Study of the Emergence of a New Organizational Reality, in: Accounting, Organizations & Society 16 (8): pp. 705-732.

**DODGSON, M. (1993)**: Organizational Learning: A Review of Some Literatures, in: Organization Studies 14 (3): pp. 375-394.

**DUBÉ, L./PARÉ, G. (2003)**: Rigor in Information Systems Positivist Case Research: Current Practices, Trends, and Recommendations, in: MIS Quarterly 27 (4): pp. 597-535.

**DURAND, R. (2003)**: Predicting a Firm's Forecasting Ability: the Roles of Organizational Illusion of Control and Organizational Attention, in: Strategic Management Journal 24 (9): pp. 821-838.

**DUTTON, J.E. (1987)**: Categorizing Strategic Issues: Links to Organizational Action, in: Academy of Management Review 12 (1): pp. 76-90.

**DUTTON, J.E. (1993)**: Interpretations on Automatic: A Different View of Strategic Issue Diagnosis, in: Journal of Management Studies 30 (3): pp. 339-357.

**DUTTON, J.E./DUNCAN, R.B. (1987)**: The Creation of Momentum for Change Through the Process of Strategic Issue Diagnosis, in: Strategic Management Journal 8 (3): pp. 279-295.

**DUTTON, J.E./FAHEY, L./NARAYANAN, V.K. (1983)**: Toward Understanding Strategic Issue Diagnosis, in: Strategic Management Journal 4 (4): pp. 307-323.

**DUTTON, J.E./JACKSON, S.E. (1987)**: Categorizing Strategic Issues: Links to Organizational Action, in: Academy of Management Review 12 (1): pp. 76-90.

**DUTTON, J.E./OTTENSMEYER, E. (1987)**: Strategic Issue Management Systems: Forms, Functions, and Contexts, in: Academy of Management Review 12 (2): pp. 355-365.

**DUTTON, J.E./WALTON, E.J./ABRAHAMSON, E. (1989)**: Important Dimensions of Strategic Issues: Separating the Wheat from the Chaff, in: Journal of Management Studies 26 (4): pp. 380-396.

**EASTERBY-SMITH, M. (1997)**: Disciplines of Organizational Learning: Contributions and Critiques, in: Human Relations 50 (9): pp. 1085-1113.

**EASTERBY-SMITH, M./CROSSAN, M./NICOLINI, D. (2000)**: Organizational Learning: Debates Past, Present and Future, in: Journal of Management Studies 37 (6): pp. 783-796.

**EDENIUS, M./HASSELBLADH, H. (2002)**: The Balanced Scorecard as an Intellectual Technology, in: Organization 9 (2): pp. 249-274.

**EGELHOFF, W.G. (1991)**: Information-processing Theory and the Multinational Enterprise, in: Journal of International Business Studies 22 (3): pp. 341-368.

**EISENHARDT, K.M. (1989)**: Building Theories from Case Study Research, in: Academy of Management Review 14 (4): pp. 532-550.

**EISENHARDT, K.M. (1989)**: Making Fast Strategic Decisions in High-Velocity Environments, in: Academy of Management Journal 32 (3): pp. 543-576.

**EISENHARDT, K.M. (1991)**: Better Stories and Better Constructs: The Case for Rigor and Comparative Logic, in: Academy of Management Review 16 (3): pp. 620-627.

**EISENHARDT, K.M./BOURGEOIS, L.J. (1988)**: Politics of Strategic Decision Making in High-Velocity Environments: Toward A Midrange Theory, in: Academy of Management Journal 31 (4): pp. 737-770.

**ELLIS, S./SHPIELBERG, N. (2003)**: Organizational Learning Mechanisms and Managers' Perceived Uncertainty, in: Human Relations 56 (10): pp. 1233-1254.

**ELSBACH, K.D./BARR, P.S./HARGADON, A.B. (2005)**: Identifying Situated Cognition in Organizations, in: Organization Science 16 (4): pp. 422-433.

**FELDMAN, M./MARCH, J.G. (1981)**: Information in Organizations as Signal and Symbol, in: Administrative Science Quarterly 26 (2): pp. 171-186.

**FERRIS, K./HASKINS, M.E. (1988)**: Perspectives on Accounting Systems and Human Behavior, in: Accounting, Auditing & Accountability Journal 1 (2): pp. 3-18.

**FIOL, C.M. (1994)**: Consensus, Diversity, and Learning in Organizations, in: Organization Science 5 (3): pp. 403-420.

**FIOL, M.C./LYLES, M.A. (1985)**: Organizational Learning, in: Academy of Management Review 10 (4): pp. 803-813.

**Floyd, S.W./Wooldridge, B. (1997)**: Middle Management's Strategic Influence and Organizational Performance, in: Journal of Management Studies 34 (3): pp. 465-487.

**Fornell, C./Larcker, D. (1981)**: Evaluating Structural Equation Models with Unobservable Variables and Measurement Error, in: Journal of Marketing Research 18 (1): pp. 39-50.

**Fredrickson, J.W. (1986)**: The Strategic Decision Process and Organizational Structure, in: Academy of Management Review 11 (2): pp. 280-297.

**Fulk, J. (1993)**: Social Construction of Communication Technology, in: Academy of Management Journal 36 (5): pp. 921-950.

**Fulk, J./Boyd, B. (1991)**: Emerging Theories of Communication in Organizations, in: Journal of Management 17 (2): pp. 407-446.

**Galbraith, J.R. (1974)**: Organization Design: An Information Processing View, in: Interfaces 4 (3): pp. 28-36.

**Galbraith, J.R. (1977)**: Organizational Design, Reading, MA, Addison-Wesley.

**Gambino, R. (1993)**: Review: Economic Challenges in Higher Education, in: Annals of the American Academy of Political and Social Science 525: pp. 190-191.

**Garg, V.K./Walters, B.A./Priem, R.L. (2003)**: Chief Executive Scanning Emphases, Environmental Dynamism, and Manufacturing Firm Performance, in: Strategic Management Journal 24 (8): pp. 725-744.

**Gibbins, M./Jamal, K. (1993)**: Problem-centred Research and Knowledge-based Theory in the Professional Accounting Setting, in: Accounting, Organizations & Society 18 (5): pp. 451-466.

**Gill, G.T. (1995)**: High-tech Hidebound: Case Studies of Information Technologies that Inhibited Organizational Learning, in: Accounting, Management & Information Technology 5 (1): pp. 41-60.

**Gioia, D.A./Thomas, J.B. (1996)**: Sensemaking during Strategic Change in Academia, in: Administrative Science Quarterly 41 (3): pp. 370-403.

**Glaser, B./Strauss, A. (1967)**: The Discovery of Grounded Theory: Strategies for Qualitative Research, Chicago, Aldine.

**Goleman, D. (1985)**: Vital Lies, Simple Truths: The Psychology of Self-Deception, New York, Simon and Schuster.

**Gordon, L.A. (1984)**: Management Accounting Systems, Perceived Environmental Uncertainty and Organization Structure: An Empirical Investigation, in: Accounting, Organizations and Society 9 (1): pp. 33-47.

**Goulding, C. (2001)**: Grounded Theory: A Magical Formula or a Potential Nightmare, in: The Marketing Review 2 (1): pp. 21-33.

**Gul, F.A./Chia, Y.M. (1994)**: The Effects of Management Accounting Systems, Perceived Environmental Uncertainty and Decentralization on Managerial Performance: A Test of Three-way Interaction, in: Accounting, Organizations and Society 19 (4/5): pp. 413-426.

**Hambrick, D.C./Mason, P.A. (1984)**: Upper Echelons: The Organization as a Reflection of Its Top Managers, in: Academy of Management Review 9 (2): pp. 193-206.

**Heath, R.L. (1994)**: The Management of Corporate Communication, Hillsdale, NJ, Erlbaum.

**Hedberg, B. (1981)**: How Organizations Learn and Unlearn, in: Nystrom, P.C./Starbuck, W.H., Eds., Handbook of Organizational Design, London, Oxford University Press: pp. 3-27.

**Hedberg, B./Jönsson, S. (1978)**: Designing Semi-confusing Information Systems for Organizations in Changing Environments, in: Accounting, Organizations & Society 3 (1): pp. 47-64.

**Helson, H. (1964)**: Adaptation-Level Theory, New York, Harper & Row.

**Henri, J.-F. (2006)**: Management Control Systems and Strategy: A Resource-based Perspective, in: Accounting, Organizations & Society 31 (6): pp. 529-558.

**Hirschhorn, L. (1988)**: The Workplace Within, Cambridge, MA, MIT Press.

**HIRST, M.K./BAXTER, J.A. (1993)**: A Capital Budgeting Case Study: An Analysis of a Choice Process and Roles of Information, in: Behavioral Research in Accounting 5: pp. 187-210.

**HODGKINSON, G.P. et al. (1999)**: Breaking the Frame: An Analysis of Strategic Cognition and Decision Making under Uncertainty, in: Strategic Management Journal 20 (10): pp. 977-985.

**HOGARTH, R.M. (1993)**: Accounting for Decisions and Decisions for Accounting, in: Accounting, Organizations & Society 18 (5): pp. 407-424.

**HOGARTH, R.M./MAKRIDAKIS, S. (1981)**: Forecasting and Planning: An Evaluation, in: Management Science 27 (2): pp. 115-138.

**HOLMQVIST, M. (2004)**: Experiential Learning Processes of Exploitation and Exploration Within and Between Organizations: An Empirical Study of Product Development, in: Organization Science 15 (1): pp. 70-81.

**HOPWOOD, A.G. (1972)**: An Empirical Study of the Role of Accounting Data in Performance Evaluation, in: Journal of Accounting Research Supplement: pp. 156-182.

**HOPWOOD, A.G. (1989)**: Behavioral Accounting in Retrospect and Prospect, in: Behavioral Research in Accounting 1: pp. 1-22.

**HORNGREN, C.T./SUNDEM, G.L./STRATTON, W.O. (2002)**: Introduction to Management Accounting (12th ed.), Upper Saddle River, NJ, Prentice Hall.

**HOSKISSON, R.E./HITT, M.A./HILL, C.W.L. (1991)**: Managerial Risk Taking in Diversified Firms: An Evolutionary Perspective, in: Organization Science: A Journal of the Institute of Management Sciences 2 (3): pp. 296-314.

**HUBER, G.P. (1990)**: A Theory of the Effects of Advanced Information Technologies on Organizational Design, Intelligence, and Decision Making, in: Academy of Management Review 15 (1): pp. 47-71.

**HUBER, G.P. (1991)**: Organizational Learning: The Contributing Processes and the Literatures, in: Organization science 2 (1): pp. 88-115.

**Huber, G.P./Daft, R.L. (1987)**: The Information Environments of Organizations, in: Jablin, F. et al., Eds., Handbook of Organizational Communication, Newbury Park, California, Sage: pp. 130-164.

**Huff, A.S./Huff, J.O./Barr, P.S. (2000)**: When Firms Change Direction, New York, Oxford University Press.

**Isabella, L.A. (1990)**: Evolving Interpretations as a Change Unfolds: How Managers Construe Key Organizational Events, in: Academy of Management Journal 33 (1): pp. 7-41.

**Ittner, C.D./Larcker, D.F. (1997)**: Quality Strategy, Strategic Control Systems, and Organizational Performance, in: Accounting, Organizations & Society 22 (3-4): pp. 293-314.

**Ittner, C.D./Larcker, D.F. (2001)**: Assessing Empirical research in managerial accounting: a value-based management perspective, in: Journal of Accounting & Economics 32 (1-3): pp. 349-410.

**Ittner, C.D./Larcker, D.F./Randall, T. (2003)**: Performance Implications of Strategic Performance Measurement in Financial Services Firms, in: Accounting, Organizations & Society 28 (7/8): pp. 715-741.

**Jaworski, B.J./Young, S.M. (1992)**: Dysfunctional Behavior and Management Control: An Empirical Study of Marketing Managers, in: Accounting, Organizations and Society 17 (1): pp. 17-35.

**Kahnemann, D./Tversky, A. (1979)**: Prospect Theory: an Analysis of Decision under Risk, in: Econometrica 47 (2): pp. 263-291.

**Kaplan, R.S./Norton, D.P. (1996)**: The Balanced Scorecard: Translating Strategy into Action, Boston, MA, Harvard Business School Press.

**Kaplan, R.S./Norton, D.P. (1996)**: Using the Balanced Scorecard as a Strategic Management System, in: Harvard Business Review January-February 1996: pp. 75-85.

**KAPLAN, R.S./NORTON, D.P. (2001)**: Building a Strategy-focused Organization, in: HORVÁTH, P., Ed., Strategien erfolgreich umsetzen, Stuttgart, Schäffer-Poeschel Verlag: pp. 1-13.

**KAPLAN, S./BEINHOCKER, E.D. (2003)**: The Real Value of Strategic Planning, in: MIT Sloan Management Review Winter 2003: pp. 71-76.

**KELLER, R.T. (1994)**: Technology-information Processing Fit and the Performance of R&D Project Groups: A Test of Contingency Theory, in: Academy of Management Journal 37 (1): pp. 167-179.

**KHALIL, O.E.M. (2005)**: EIS Information: Use and Quality Determinants, in: Information Resources Management Journal 18 (2): pp. 68-93.

**KIESLER, S./SPROULL, L. (1982)**: Managerial Response to Changing Environments: Perspectives on Problem Sensing from Social Cognition, in: Administrative Science Quarterly 27 (4): pp. 548-570.

**KIM, D.H. (1993)**: The Link between Individual and Organizational Learning, in: Sloan Management Review 35 (1): pp. 37-50.

**KIM, D.H. (2001)**: Organizing for Learning: Strategies for Knowledge Creation and Enduring Change, Waltham, Pegasus.

**KONRAD, L. (1991)**: Strategische Früherkennung - Eine kritische Analyse des "weak signals"-Konzeptes, Bochum, Universitätsverlag Dr. N. Brockmeyer.

**KUVAAS, B. (2002)**: An Exploration of Two Competing Perspectives on Informational Contexts in Top Management Strategic Issue Interpretation, in: Journal of Management Studies 39 (7): pp. 977-1001.

**LAL, M./DUNK, A.S./SMITH, G.D. (1996)**: The Propensity of Managers to Create Budgetary Slack: A Cross-national Re-examination Using Random Sampling, in: The International Journal of Accounting 31 (4): pp. 483-496.

**LANGFIELD-SMITH, K. (1997)**: Management Control Systems and Strategy: A Critical Review, in: Accounting, Organizations & Society 22 (2): pp. 207-232.

**LANT, T.K./MEZIAS, S.J. (1992)**: An Organizational Learning Model of Convergence and Reorientation, in: Organization Science 3 (1): pp. 47-71.

**LAVERTY, K.J. (1996)**: Economic 'Short-termism': The Debate, the Unresolved Issues, and the Implications for Management Practice and Research, in: Academy of Management Review 21 (3): pp. 825-860.

**LAVERTY, K.J. (2004)**: Managerial Myopia or Systemic Short-termism?: The Importance of Managerial Systems in Valuing the Long Term, in: Management Decision 42 (8): pp. 949-962.

**LEE, T.W. (1999)**: Using Qualitative Methods in Organizational Research, Thousand Oaks, Sage Publications, Inc.

**LEIDNER, D.E./ELAM, J.J. (1995)**: The Impact of Executive Information Systems on Organizational Design, Intelligence, and Decision Making, in: Organization Science: A Journal of the Institute of Management Sciences 6 (6): pp. 645-664.

**LEVITT, B./MARCH, J.G. (1988)**: Organizational Learning, in: Annual Review of Sociology 14: pp. 319-340.

**LEWIN, K. (1946)**: Action Research and Minority Problems, in: LEWIN, G.W., Ed., Resolving Social Conflict, London, Harper & Row.

**LEWIN, K. (1947)**: Group Decisions and Social Change, in: NEWCOMB, T.M./HARTLEY, E.L., Eds., Readings in Social Psychology, New York, Henry Holt.

**MAIER, N.R.F. (1945)**: Reasoning in Humans: III. The Mechanisms of Equivalent Stimuli and of Reasoning, in: Journal of Experimental Psychology 35: pp. 349-360.

**MAITLIS, S. (2005)**: The Social Processes of Organizational Sensemaking, in: Academy of Management Journal 48 (1): pp. 21-49.

**MALHORTA, N. (1993)**: Marketing Research: An Applied Orientation, Englewood Cliffs, NJ.

**MALINA, M.A./SELTO, F.H. (2001)**: Communicating and Controlling Strategy: An Empirical Study of the Effectiveness of the Balanced Scorecard, in: Management Accounting Research 13 (1): pp. 47-90.

**MARCH, J.G. (1991)**: Exploration and Exploitation in Organizational Learning, in: Organization science 2 (1): pp. 71-87.

**MARCH, J.G./OLSEN, J.P. (1975)**: The Uncertainty of the Past: Organizational Learning under Ambiguity, in: European Journal of Political Research 3: pp. 147-171.

**MARCH, J.G./SIMON, H.A. (1958)**: Organizations, New York, Wiley.

**MARGINSON, D. (2002)**: Management Control Systems and Their Effects on Strategy Formation at Middle-management Levels: Evidence from a U.K. Organization, in: Strategic Management Journal 23 (11): pp. 1019-1031.

**MARKUS, M.L. (1994)**: Electronic Mail as the Medium of Managerial Choice, in: Organization Science: A Journal of the Institute of Management Sciences 5 (4): pp. 502-527.

**MCCUTCHEON, D.M./MEREDITH, J.R. (1993)**: Conducting Case Study Research in Operations Management, in: Journal of Operations Management 11: pp. 239-256.

**MCFADDEN, D. (1999)**: Rationality for Economists?, in: Journal of Risk and Uncertainty 19 (1-3): pp. 73-105.

**MCKINSEY (2005)**: The McKinsey Global Survey of Business Executives, in: McKinsey Quarterly (1): pp. 58-65.

**MENON, A. et al. (1999)**: Antecedents and Consequences of Marketing Strategy Making: A Model and a Test, in: Journal of Marketing 63 (2): pp. 18-40.

**MENON, A./VARADARAJAN, P.R. (1992)**: A Model of Marketing Knowledge Use Within Firms, in: Journal of Marketing 56 (4): pp. 53-71.

**MERCHANT, K.A. (1990)**: The Effects of Financial Controls on Data Manipulation and Management Myopia, in: Accounting, Organizations and Society 15 (4): pp. 297-313.

**MIA, L. (1993)**: The Role of MAS Information in Organizations: An Empirical Study, in: British Accounting Review 25: pp. 269-285.

**MIA, L./CHENHALL, R.H. (1994)**: The Usefulness of Management Accounting Systems, Functional Differentiation and Managerial Effectiveness, in: Accounting, Organizations & Society 19 (1): pp. 1-13.

**MILES, M.B./HUBERMAN, A.M. (1984)**: Qualitative Paper Analysis: A Source Book of New Methods, Beverly Hills, Sage.

**MILLER, C.C./CARDINAL, L.B. (1994)**: Strategic Planning and Firm Performance: A Synthesis of More Than Two Decades of Research, in: Academy of Management Journal 37 (6): pp. 1649-1665.

**MILLER, D. (1993)**: The Architecture of Simplicity, in: Academy of Management Review 18 (1): pp. 116-138.

**MILLER, D. (1994)**: What Happens after Success: The Perils of Excellence, in: Journal of Management Studies 31 (3): pp. 325-358.

**MILLIKEN, F.J. (1990)**: Perceiving and Interpreting Environmental Change: An Examination of College Administrators' Interpretation of Changing Demographics, in: Academy of Management Journal 33 (1): pp. 42-63.

**MINER, A.S./MEZIAS, S.J. (1996)**: Ugly Duckling No More: Pasts and Futures of Organizational Learning Research, in: Organization Science 7 (1): pp. 88-99.

**MINTZBERG, H./AHLSTRAND, B./LAMPEL, J. (1998)**: Strategy Safari: A Guided Tour Through the Wilds of Strategic Management, New York, Free Press.

**MOLLOY, S./SCHWENK, C.R. (1995)**: The Effects of Information Technology on Strategic Decision Making, in: Journal of Management Studies 32 (3): pp. 283-311.

**MOORES, K./YUEN, S. (2001)**: Management Accounting Systems and Organizational Configuration: A Life-cycle Perspective, in: Accounting, Organizations and Society 26 (4-5): pp. 351-389.

**NELSON, R.R./TODD, P.A./WIXOM, B.H. (2005)**: Antecedents of Information and System Quality: An Empirical Examination Within the Context of Data Warehousing, in: Journal of Management Information Systems.

**NOHRIA, N./GULATI, R. (1996)**: Is Slack Good or Bad for Innovation?, in: Academy of Management Journal 39 (5): pp. 1245-1264.

**NORMAN, D.A. (1982)**: Learning and Memory, San Francisco, W. H. Freeman.

**NUNNALLY, J. (1978)**: Psychometric Theory (2nd ed.), New York.

**OCASIO, W. (1995)**: The Enactment of Economic Diversity: A Reconciliation of Theories of Failure-induced Change and Threat-rigidity, in: CUMMINGS, L.L./STAW, B., Eds., Research in Organizational Behavior, Greenwich, CT, JAI Press, 17: pp. 287-331.

**OCASIO, W. (1997)**: Towards an Attention-based View of the Firm, in: Strategic Management Journal 18, Summer Special Issue: pp. 187-206.

**OSBORN, C.S. (1998)**: Systems for Sustainable Organizations: Emergent Strategies, Interactive Controls and Semi-formal Information, in: Journal of Management Studies 35 (4): pp. 481-509.

**OTLEY, D./FAKIOLAS, A. (2000)**: Reliance on Accounting Performance Measures: Dead End or New Beginning?, in: Accounting, Organizations & Society 25 (4/5): pp. 497-510.

**OTLEY, D.T./BERRY, A.J. (1994)**: Case Study Research in Management Accounting and Control, in: Management Accounting Research 5 (1): pp. 45-65.

**OUCHI, W.G. (1979)**: A Conceptual Framework for the Design of Organizational Control Mechanisms, in: Management Science 25 (9): pp. 833-848.

**PAPADAKIS, V.M./LIOUKAS, S./CHAMBERS, D. (1998)**: Strategic Decision-Making Processes: The Role of Management and Context, in: Strategic Management Journal 19 (2): pp. 115-147.

**PAWLOWSKY, P. (2001)**: The Treatment of Organizational Learning in Management Science, in: DIERKES, M. et al., Eds., Handbook of Organizational Learning and Knowledge, Oxford, Oxford University Press: pp. 61-88.

**PETERSON, R. (1994)**: A Meta-Analysis of Cronbach's Alpha, in: Journal of Consumer Research 21 (2): pp. 381-391.

**PIAGET, J. (1954)**: The Construction of Reality in the Child, New York, Basic Books.

**RAI, A./LANG, S.S./WELKER, R.B. (2002)**: Assessing the Validity of IS Success Models: An Empirical Test and Theoretical Analysis, in: Information Systems Research 13 (1): pp. 50-69.

**ROBEY, D./BOUDREAU, M.C./ROSE, G.M. (2000)**: Information Technology and Organizational Learning: A Review and Assessment of Research, in: Accounting Management and Information Technologies 10 (2): pp. 125-155.

**ROSCH, E. (1978)**: Principles of Categorization, in: ROSCH, E./LLOYD, B.B., Eds., Cognition and Categorization, Hillsdale, NJ, Erlbaum: pp. 27-48.

**SANDT, J. (2004)**: Management mit Kennzahlen und Kennzahlensystemen, Wiesbaden, Deutscher Universitäts-Verlag.

**SCHÄFFER, U. (2001)**: Kontrolle als Lernprozess, Wiesbaden, Gabler Edition Wissenschaft.

**SCHIEMENZ, B. (1993)**: Production and Information, in: STOWELL, F.A., Ed., Systems Science - Adressing Global Issues, New York and London: pp. 519-524.

**SCHNEIDER, S.C./ANGELMAR, R. (1993)**: Cognition in Organizational Analysis: Who's Minding the Store?, in: Organization Studies 14 (3): pp. 347-374.

**SCHNEIDER, S.C./DE MEYER, A. (1991)**: Interpreting and Responding to Strategic Issues: The Impact of National Culture, in: Strategic Management Journal 12 (4): pp. 307-320.

**SCHREYÖGG, G./STEINMANN, H. (1987)**: Strategic Control: A New Perspective, in: Academy of Management Review 12 (1): pp. 91-103.

**SCHULZ, M. (2001)**: The Uncertain Relevance of Newness: Organizational Learning and Knowledge Flows, in: Academy of Management Journal 44 (4): pp. 661-681.

**SCHWENK, C.R. (1988)**: The Cognitive Perspective on Strategic Decision Making, in: Journal of Management Studies 25 (1): pp. 41-55.

**SENGE, P.M. (1990)**: The Fifth Discipline: The Art and Practice of the Learning Organization, New York, Doubleday.

**SHANK, M.E. et al. (1988)**: Predictors of Top Management Team Environmental Perception Accuracy: A Model and Propositions, in: Academy of Management Proceedings: pp. 37-41.

**SHANNON, C.E./WEAVER, W. (1949)**: The Mathematical Theory of Communication, Urbana, IL, University of Illinois Press.

**SHIELDS, M.D. (1997)**: Research in Management Accounting by North Americans in the 1990s, in: Journal of Management Accounting Research 9: pp. 3-61.

**SHIFFRIN, R.M./SCHNEIDER, M.W. (1977)**: Controlled and Automatic Human Information Processing. II. Perceptual Learning, Automatic Attending and a General Theory, in: Psychological Review 84 (2): pp. 127-190.

**SIDHU, J.S./VOLBERDA, H.W./COMMANDEUR, H.R. (2004)**: Exploring Exploration Orientation and its Determinants: Some Empirical Evidence, in: Journal of Management Studies 41 (6): pp. 913-932.

**SIMON, H.A. (1955)**: A Behavioral Model of Rational Choice, in: Quarterly Journal of Economics 69: pp. 99-118.

**SIMON, H.A. (1991)**: Bounded Rationality and Organizational Learning, in: Organization Science 2 (1): pp. 125-134.

**SIMONS, R. (1987a)**: Accounting Control Systems and Business Strategy: An Empirical Analysis, in: Accounting, Organizations & Society 12 (4): pp. 357-374.

**SIMONS, R. (1987b)**: Planning, Control, and Uncertainty: A Process View, in: BRUNS, W.J./KAPLAN, R.S., Eds., Accounting & Management: Field Study Perspectives, Boston, MA, Harvard Business School Press: pp. 339-362.

**SIMONS, R. (1990)**: The Role of Management Control Systems in Creating Competitive Advantage: New Perspectives; The Enactment of Management Control Systems, in: Accounting, Organizations & Society 15 (1/2): pp. 127-143.

**SIMONS, R. (1991)**: Strategic Orientation and Top Management Attention to Control Systems, in: Strategic Management Journal 12 (1): pp. 49-62.

**SIMONS, R. (1994)**: How New Top Managers Use Control Systems as Levers of Strategic Renewal, in: Strategic Management Journal 15 (3): pp. 169-189.

**SIMONS, R. (1995)**: Levers of Control, Boston, MA, Harvard Business School Press.

**SMITH, K.G. et al. (1994)**: Top Management Team Demography and Process: The Role of Social Integration and Communication, in: Administrative Science Quarterly 39: pp. 412-438.

**SMITH, P. (1993)**: Outcome-related Performance Indicators and Organizational Control in the Public Sector, in: British Journal of Management 4 (3): pp. 135-151.

**SNELL, S.A. (1992)**: Control Theory in Strategic Human Resource Management: The Mediating Effect of Administrative Information, in: Academy of Management Journal 35 (2): pp. 292-327.

**STARBUCK, W.H./MILLIKEN, F.J. (1988)**: Executives' Perceptual Filters: What they Notice and How they Make Sense, in: HAMBRICK, D.C., Ed., The Executive Effect: Concepts and Methods for Studying Top Managers, Greenwich, Connecticut, JAI Press: pp. 35-66.

**STAW, B.M./SANDELANDS, L.E./DUTTON, J.E. (1981)**: Threat-Rigidity Effects in Organizational Behavior: A Multilevel Analysis, in: Administrative Science Quarterly 26 (4): pp. 501-524.

**STRAUB, D./KARAHANNA, E. (1998)**: Knowledge Worker Communications and Recipient Availability: Toward a Task Closure Explanation of Media Choice, in: Organization Science 9 (2): pp. 160-175.

**STRONG, D.M./LEE, Y.W./WANG, R.Y. (1997)**: Data Quality in Context, in: Communications of the ACM 40 (5): pp. 103-110.

**SUTCLIFFE, K.M. (1994)**: What Executives Notice: Accurate Perceptions in Top Management Teams, in: Academy of Management Journal 37 (5): pp. 1360-1378.

**SUTCLIFFE, K.M. (2001)**: Organizational Environments and Organizational Information Processing, in: JABLIN, F./PUTNAM, L., Eds., The New Handbook of Organizational Communication: Advances in Theory, Research, and Methods, Thousand Oaks, California, Sage Pub.: pp. 197-230.

**TEMPLETON, G.F. et al. (2004)**: Methodological and Thematic Prescriptions for Defining and Measuring the Organizational Learning Concept, in: Information Systems Frontier 6 (3): pp. 263-276.

**THOMAS, D.A./GIOIA, D.A./KETCHEN JR., D.J. (1997)**: Strategic Sensemaking: Learning through Scanning, Interpretation, Action and Performance, in: WALSH, J.P./HUFF, A.S., Eds., Advances in Strategic Management, Greenwich, CT., JAI Press: pp. 299-329.

**THOMAS, J.B./CLARK, S.M./GIOIA, D.A. (1993)**: Strategic Sensemaking and Organizational Performance: Linkages Among Scanning, Interpretation, Action, and Outcomes, in: Academy of Management Journal 36 (2): pp. 239-270.

**THOMAS, J.B./MCDANIEL, R.R. (1990)**: Interpreting Strategic Issues: Effects of Strategy and the Information-Processing Structure of Top-Management Teams, in: Academy of Management Journal 33 (2): pp. 286-306.

**THOMAS, J.B./SHANKSTER, L.J./MATHIEU, J.E. (1994)**: Antecedents to Organizational Issue Interpretation: The Roles of Single-level, Cross-level, and Content Cues, in: Academy of Management Journal 37 (5): pp. 1252-1284.

**TUCHMAN, G. (1973)**: Making News by Doing Work: Routinizing the Unexpected, in: American Journal of Sociology 79: pp. 110-131.

**TUOMELA, T.-S. (2005)**: The Interplay of Different Levers of Control: A Case Study of Introducing a New Performance Measurement System, in: Management Accounting Research 16 (3): pp. 293-320.

**TUSHMAN, M.L./NADLER, D.A. (1978)**: Information Processing as an Integrating Concept in Organizational Design, in: Academy of Management Review 3 (3): pp. 613-624.

**TVERSKY, A./KAHNEMANN, D. (1974)**: Judgment Under Uncertainty: Heuristics and Biases, in: Science 185: pp. 1124-1131.

**VAIVIO, J. (1999)**: Exploring a 'Non-financial' Management Accounting Change, in: Management Accounting Research 10 (4): pp. 409-437.

**VAIVIO, J. (2004)**: Mobilizing Local Knowledge with 'Provocative' Non-financial Measures, in: European Accounting Review 13 (1): pp. 39-71.

**VAN DE VEN, A.H./POOLE, M.S. (1995)**: Explaining Development and Change in Organizations, in: Academy of Management Review 20 (3): pp. 510-540.

**Van der Stede, W.A. (2000)**: The Relationship Between Two Consequences of Budgetary Controls: Budgetary Slack Creation and Managerial Short-term Orientation, in: Accounting, Organizations and Society 25: pp. 609-622.

**Vandenbosch, B. (1999)**: An Empirical Analysis of the Association between the Use of Executive Support Systems and Perceived Organizational Competitiveness, in: Accounting, Organizations and Society 24 (1): pp. 77-92.

**Vandenbosch, B./Higgins, C.A. (1995)**: Executive Support Systems and Learning: a Model and Empirical Test, in: Journal of Management Information Systems 12 (2): pp. 99-130.

**Vandenbosch, B./Higgins, C.A. (1996)**: Information Acquisition and Mental Models: An Investigation into the Relationship Between Behavior and Learning, in: Information Systems Research 7 (2): pp. 198-214.

**Vandenbosch, B./Huff, S.L. (1997)**: Searching and Scanning: How Executives Obtain Information from Executive Information Systems, in: MIS Quarterly 21 (1): pp. 81-107.

**Verona, G. (1999)**: A Resource-Based View of Product Development, in: The Academy of Management Review 24 (1): pp. 132-142.

**Vickery, S.K. et al. (2004)**: The Performance Implications of Media Richness in a Business-to-Business Service Environment: Direct Versus Indirect Effects, in: Management Science 50 (8): pp. 1106-1119.

**Wang, R.Y./Strong, D.M. (1996)**: Beyond Accuracy: What Data Quality Means to Data Consumers, in: Journal of Management Information Systems 12 (4): pp. 5-33.

**Weber, J./Grothe, M./Schäffer, U. (2000)**: ZP-Stichwort: Mentale Modelle, in: Zeitschrift für Planung 11: pp. 239-244.

**Weick, K.E. (1979)**: The Social Psychology of Organizing (2nd ed.), Reading, MA, Addison-Wesley.

**Weick, K.E. (1988)**: Enacted Sensemaking in Crisis Situations, in: Journal of Management Studies 25 (4): pp. 305-317.

**WEICK, K.E. (1995)**: Sensemaking in Organizations, Thousand Oaks, CA, Sage Publications.

**WEICK, K.E./ASHFORD, S.J. (2001)**: Learning in Organizations, in: JABLIN, F./PUTNAM, L., Eds., The New Handbook of Organizational Communication: Advances in Theory, Research, and Methods, Thousand Oaks, California, Sage Pub.: pp. 705-731.

**WEICK, K.E./SUTCLIFFE, K.M./OBSTFELD, D. (2005)**: Organizing and the Process of Sensemaking, in: Organization Science 16 (4): pp. 409-421.

**WHITFIELD, J.M./LAMONT, B.T./SAMBAMURTHY, V. (1996)**: The Effects of Organization Design on Media Richness in Multinational Enterprises, in: Management Communication Quarterly 10 (2): pp. 209-226.

**WILLIAMS, C./MITCHELL, W. (2004)**: Focusing Firm Evolution: The Impact of Information Infrastructure on Market Entry by U.S. Telecommunications Companies, 1984-1998, in: Management Science 50 (11): pp. 1561-1575.

**YASAI-ARDEKANI, M./HAUG, R.S. (1997)**: Contextual Determinants of Strategic Planning Processes, in: Journal of Management Studies 34 (5): pp. 729-767.

**YASAI-ARDEKANI, M./NYSTROM, P.C. (1996)**: Designs for Environmental Scanning Systems: Tests of a Contingency Theory, in: Management Science 42 (2): pp. 187-204.

**YIN, R.K. (2003)**: Case Study Research: Design and Methods (3rd ed.), Thousand Oaks, Sage Publications.

**ZOLLO, M./WINTER, S.G. (2002)**: Deliberate Learning and the Evolution of Dynamic Capabilities, in: Organization Science: A Journal of the Institute of Management Sciences 13 (3): pp. 339-351.

FSC
www.fsc.org
MIX
Papier | Fördert
gute Waldnutzung
FSC® C083411

Kolibri 360 GmbH
Ferdinand-Jühlke-Straße 7
99095 Erfurt, Deutschland
produktsicherheit@kolibri360.de

FSC
www.fsc.org
MIX
Papier | Fördert
gute Waldnutzung
FSC® C083411

Kolibri 360 GmbH
Ferdinand-Jühlke-Straße 7
99095 Erfurt, Deutschland
produktsicherheit@kolibri360.de